Economics for Hospitality Management

Series in Tourism and Hospitality Management

Series Editors:
Professor Roy C. Wood
The Scottish Hotel School, University of Strathclyde, UK

Stephen J. Page
Massey University, New Zealand

Series Consultant:
Professor C. L. Jenkins
The Scottish Hotel School, University of Strathclyde, Uk

Textbooks in this series:

Economics for Hospitality Management

Peter Cullen

Leeds Metropolitan University

INTERNATIONAL THOMSON BUSINESS PRESS

I(T)P An International Thomson Publishing Company

London • Bonn • Boston • Johannesburg • Madrid • Melbourne • Mexico City • New York • Paris
Singapore • Tokyo • Toronto • Albany, NY • Belmont, CA • Cincinnati, OH • Detroit, MI

Economics for Hospitality Management

Copyright © 1997 Peter Cullen

The Thomson Learning logo is a registered trademark used herein under license

British Library Cataloguing-in-Publication Data
A catalogue record for this book is available from the British Library

First edition 1997
Reprinted 1999
Reprinted 2000

Printed in the UK by The Alden Group, Oxford

ISBN 1-86152-179-0

Thomson Learning
Berkshire House
High Holborn
London WC1V 7AA
UK

http://www.thomsonlearning.co.uk

330.024647

Contents

List of tables

List of figures

Series editors' foreword

The International Thomson Business Press Series in Tourism and Hospitality Management is dedicated to the publication of high quality textbooks and other volumes that will be of benefit to those engaged in tourism, hotel and hospitality education, especially at degree and postgraduate level. The *Series* is based on core textbooks in key areas of the curriculum and is complimented by highly focused and shorter texts on particular themes and issues. All the authors in the series are experts in their own fields, actively engaged in teaching, research and consultancy in tourism and hospitality. Each book comprises an authoritative blend of subject-relevant theoretical considerations and practical applications. Furthermore, a unique quality of the series is that it is student oriented, offering accessible texts that take account of the realities of administration, management and operations in tourism and hospitality contexts, being constructively critical without losing sight of the overall goal of providing clear accounts of essential concepts, issues and techniques.

The series is committed to quality, accessibility, relevance and originality in its approach. Quality is ensured as a result of a vigorous refereeing process, unusual in the publication of textbooks. Accessibility is achieved through the use of innovative textual design techniques, and the use of discussion points, case studies and exercises within books, all geared to encouraging a comprehensive understanding of the material contained therein. Relevance and originality together result from the experience of authors as key authorities in their fields.

The tourism and hospitality industries are diverse and dynamic industries and it is the intention of the editors to reflect this diversity and dynamism by publishing quality texts that enhance topical subject without losing sight of enduring themes. The Series Editors and Consultant are grateful to Steven Reed of International Thomson Business Press for his commitment, experience and support of this philosophy.

Series Editors
Dr Stephen J. Page
Massey University – Albany
Auckland, New Zealand

Professor Roy C. Wood
The Scottish Hotel School
University of Strathclyde, UK

Series Consultant
Professor C. L. Jenkins
The Scottish Hotel School
University of Strathclyde, UK

Acknowledgement

I would like to thank Steven Reed and the editorial and production staff at International Thomson Business Press for their patience with the long delays that various events have caused in delivering this work. I am also grateful to John Margerison for helping me clarify the discussion of finance in Chapter 1. Finally, I am deeply grateful to Roy Wood who has indirectly, but in no small way, influenced the direction of this book through his support and intellectual converse in areas of mutual concern.

Introduction

The theme of this book is managing economic change in the hospitality industry. Major social, economic and technological changes during the last twenty years have had a major impact on the hospitality industry. The industry is now one of the major employers in the UK. It has also changed as large hotel companies have grown to dominate the market and transform hotels, fast food has been firmly established in the UK and pubs have changed their social and economic role.

These changes are the outcome of economic forces operating on the industry. They have occurred whether people in the industry wished them to or not, even though specific business leaders are needed to carry them through. New technology and management skills have also changed the industry and brought new opportunities and challenges. A generation ago, the hospitality manager saw himself (or occasionally, at that time, herself) as a hotel or catering professional first. The inspired entrepreneur and the skilled specialist still operate successfully in many areas of the industry, but the role and position of the hospitality manager have changed and increased in importance. The new hospitality manager has a wider view of the hospitality industry in a complex, service-oriented society. Now one must say *he or she* has affinity with leisure or retailing managers and uses similar skills and knowledge in dealing with the interaction between work, leisure and social activity (Gilbert and Guerrier, 1997).

This book shows you how to use economics to analyse and manage these developments in the hospitality industry and related activities in tourism, leisure and recreation. As you work through this book, you will understand, learn and apply basic concepts and techniques so that you can:

- Explain economic trends and their implications for your firm or organization.
- Manage the impact of economic fluctuations on your firm or organization.
- Improve your firm's position in the hospitality market.
- Improve the production and delivery of hospitality services.

We analyse the rapid changes in industry structure, ownership and products that have occurred since the 1980s. We concentrate on the real issues of change using relevant data and avoid the detailed description using masses of data that will rapidly go out of date. Much of our information comes from accessible, industry-centred material such as the weekly magazine *Caterer & Hotelkeeper* and the valuable (though expensive) market reports published by *Key Note* and other organizations. As a regular reader of *Caterer & Hotelkeeper* and similar publications, you will get a good feel for the changes that are taking place. Reading this book should help you to see them as the natural outcome of the economic forces continuing to operate on the industry.

This book does not assume any previous knowledge of economics. It also assumes only a basic level of mathematical knowledge, such as the rules of arithmetic, graphs and elementary algebra, such as most hospitality students will have acquired through GCSE or other numeracy studies at school or further education college.

This book is self-contained so that it should not be necessary to use alternative texts. Sections in each chapter on further reading refer to specific textbooks. These are not required reading, but examples of *some* of the better texts available to allow you broaden and deepen your understanding and application of economics. The further reading lists are not exhaustive and there are other, numerous college texts on the market, which can be used by referencing the appropriate sections from them (using the index is often a better guide to content than chapter headings). However you are advised to skip the more complex analyses of consumer behaviour, of the firm and of macreoconomic activity in these books, at least initially, as they may not justify the extra time and effort spent on them. The further reading sections may also refer you to accessible journal articles that should be readily understandable.

A full bibliography is included, and all the source books used throughout the text are listed there. Some of them may be too complex or mathematical, so do not expect to be able to read them all.

TO ECONOMICS AND BUSINESS TUTORS

This book is specifically written for students of hospitality management and related studies. The material has been selected to show hospitality managers how they can use economic analysis when dealing with change in their organization and industry, using material that can be covered in a one-semester course, but which can serve for extended study. Consequently, the material differs from standard first-year texts in the following ways:

- There is a longer-term perspective on change.
- The interaction of household structure and functioning with hospitality markets is important.
- This text is concerned with understanding the impact of fluctuation, rather than on the development of macroeconomic theory. The simplistic income–expenditure model is avoided, and an aggregate demand and

supply approach has been used as it is more accessible to the student and easier to use than more complex models.

- Care has been taken to provide a good basis of ideas that can serve for further study of the activities of firms but complex theory is avoided where it would be too abstruse or of little practical relevance. The economic perspective on the intermingling of service production and marketing is included, as it is felt to be more important than theoretical discussions of oligopoly pricing, which have therefore been avoided.
- Economic forces mean that, for many students and managers, the reality of delivering hospitality services is largely the same whether the organization is national or international. Consequently, I have not dwelt at length on the topic of internationalization, although increasing attention is being paid to it in academic studies and course development.
- Hospitality courses normally contain modules or course components in areas such as organization, finance and human resource management. This book avoids unnecessary duplication of material and provides a different perspective where overlap occurs.

There is, of course, nothing new in this book. The intellectual foundation of this book is the work of Gary Becker, Kelvin Lancaster, Oliver Williamson and other economists who, in a way that I am sure Alfred Marshall would approve of, have pushed economics into investigating many areas of human activity and have truly made economics the study of people in the everyday business of living. Others may well see their hidden hand in this work.

Basics PART 1

The approach to economics | 1

Key concepts

In this chapter we:

- explain how economics investigates problems;
- introduce the marginal principle;
- examine the economic structure of businesses;
- examine the factors an organization needs to consider in its operations.

THE DEFINITION AND MEANING OF ECONOMICS

Economics analyses the ways in which individuals, groups and organizations use resources to improve their well-being.

Well-being or welfare depends on the individual or organization concerned. An individual may measure his welfare in terms of wealth, power, friendship; an organization may do so in terms of survival and profits. These represent the goals of the person or organization. They can be highly subjective and difficult to measure, like having a good time, because they depend on the individual concerned. Or they can be objective, such as maximizing consumption, because anybody following the same rules of measurement would get the same result.

We have three basic resources or commodities we can use to improve our welfare:

1. *human capital* – our resources of energy and skill.
2. non-human capital or *wealth*: this consists of
   (a) physical assets – such as property;
   (b) financial assets – such as bank deposits and insurance policies;
   (c) cash.
3. *time*.

Getting the most out of these resources is the basic question of economics. For instance, by working in the market we trade time and energy for money to buy various goods and services. However, we also need time and energy to spend the money we earn, which is why we do not spend all our time working.

SCARCITY AND CHOICE

Our limited resources mean that we have the problem of *scarcity*, that is *we do not have enough resources to do all that we want to do.*

We should note that a resource is scarce relative to what we want to do with it. We measure this scarcity by the *opportunity cost* of the resource, or what we have to do without in order to use it. In the same way we measure the opportunity cost of doing a particular activity or buying a particular product by the activities or products we have to go without instead. For convenience, we usually express this opportunity cost in monetary terms, although we may also wish to measure the time-cost of an activity, simply because we have a limited amount of time.

A group or society deals with scarcity by rationing the *supply* or availability of a commodity between those who *demand* it or want to use it through the *market process* of buying and selling or else through some *political process*.

Individuals and organizations also decide what to do and how to use their resources. Very often the decision is based on experience, as experience can teach us the best ways of dealing with familiar situations. These become *rules of thumb* that are simple to use and achieve the required result. However, experience becomes less reliable when the underlying conditions change and so economics systematically analyses methods for dealing with new situations.

We assume that people act in their own interest, that is, they compare the relative costs and benefits of the different choices available and *choose the alternative with the greatest net benefit.*

We should note that:

- people often make decisions that imply that they compare monetary and non-monetary benefits and costs by converting them to the same monetary basis;
- people need not be selfish, but can take into account the effect of any action on others, such as family and friends, when calculating benefits and costs.

Allowing for these provisos, we can state the following principle of economic analysis:

People do more of an activity when its benefits increase relative to its costs.

They do less of the activity when the benefits decrease relative to costs.

Choices in reality

In practice, people make mistakes for two main reasons.

1. *They do not have enough information to calculate costs and benefits correctly.* Gathering information costs time and money. However, it is

difficult to determine how valuable any extra information would be, so people can easily gather too much or too little information.

2. *They process the information incorrectly.* For instance, studies have shown that people can handle only relatively small amounts of information at any one time. Selecting the appropriate information is in itself an important task.

Selecting the appropriate information is the key to economics and simplifies the process of analysis considerably. This basic concept is then extended by bringing in two further concepts:

1. marginal analysis;
2. the relationship between capital and income.

THE IMPORTANCE OF MARGINAL ANALYSIS

Economics frequently uses the concept of the marginal (or additional, or incremental) quantity. For instance:

- *marginal spending* means the extra amount spent;
- *marginal gain* means the extra benefit received, usually from the last pound spent.

Two important economic principles result from the application of marginal analysis: the principle of diminishing returns and the principle of equi-marginal returns.

The principle of diminishing returns

The extra or marginal return or benefit from spending extra resources in any area varies with the existing level of spending. One bottle of wine may be highly pleasurable, a second slightly less so, but eventually any extra bottle yields relatively little satisfaction. This illustrates the principle of diminishing (marginal) returns:

The value of extra spending on an activity eventually declines.

This is the reason why we do not spend all our money on just one product.

The principle of equi-marginal returns

This principle states that:

The marginal spending on any activity or product should give the same increase in benefit per pound spent.

For instance, spending an extra £1 on equipment in the housekeeping department should give the same return as an extra £1 spent on kitchen equipment. If spending another £1 on housekeeping gives a bigger return than spending another £1 on kitchen equipment, we should transfer spending from kitchen equipment to housekeeping. This would reduce the marginal return on spending in the housekeeping department and increase the marginal return from spending on kitchen equipment. We should continue transferring money from kitchen equipment to housekeeping until the two marginal returns are equal.

CAPITAL AND INCOME

We think of capital as a sum of money, an asset or an investment. For instance, we can say that a particular hotel is worth £1 million, meaning that it should fetch £1 million pounds if it were to be sold on the open market. But why would anyone pay £1 million pounds for a hotel? Presumably because they could use the hotel to make a profit, perhaps over a number of years, that is equivalent to at least £1 million. Profit is, of course, calculated after meeting all other expenses of staff, maintenance, materials and so on. So capital is just another way of expressing future income. We can see this by asking what the value would be if nobody ever stayed in the hotel. You might be able to put the hotel to some other use, but you would not get £1 million for it.

The time cost of money

£1 today is different from £1 next year. Why? Because you can invest £1 today and get it back next year with interest. If the rate of interest is 5% per annum, then £1 today will be worth £1.05 in one year's time. The rate of interest is the exchange rate between present and future money, just as we can quote an exchange rate for the pound against the dollar when we are going abroad. This is quite separate from the effect of inflation on the purchasing power or real value of money. Normally, but not always, the rate of interest should be greater than the rate of inflation so that by saving and investing people do become relatively richer in the future. This means that, where the rate of interest is greater than zero, a hotel company making an investment of £1,000 would need to make significantly more than £1,000 in future profits or cost savings in order to be able to make a profit on the investment, that is to recover the cost of the capital investment and the interest on the capital invested. In the hotel example above, anybody wanting to buy the hotel would have to make more than £1 million of future profit for it to be worthwhile paying £1 million for the hotel.

THE BUSINESS FIRM

We now turn to the business firm, first because we are dealing with management of hospitality firms; and secondly, because the behaviour of firms is critical to an understanding of economic activity. Our definition of a firm is:

A firm is any organization producing and supplying goods or services.

A firm may be:

- a commercial (profit-oriented) organization, or a welfare (non-profit) institution;
- privately owned or part of central or local government.

We now identify the institutional framework within which firms operate, especially their legal and financial structures as they affect their size and activities.

Business structure

There are two major classes of business firm: the unincorporated business and the company or corporation.

The unincorporated business

There is no legal distinction between the business and its owner(s), although business income and expenses are treated differently for tax purposes from the income and expenses of ordinary employment. An unincorporated business can be:

1. A *sole proprietorship,* run by a self-employed person, working for him- or herself, who may also employ others in the business. Funding is by the owner's own investment (equity investment) and by loans, usually secured on the assets of the business or on the owner's home or property. This naturally limits the size of the business to no more than a few establishments that the owner can personally manage or oversee.
2. A *partnership,* where two or more individuals own and operate the business according to a partnership agreement. Legally, each partner is liable for the actions of the other partners in regard to the business. The risks involved and the difficulties in monitoring the partners' contributions usually limits the number of partners to two or three, though family partnerships may be larger. Funding is from the investments made by the partners and loans from banks and financial institutions. Financial constraints and the need for the partners to be active in the business limit the size of the business and the number and size of the establishments in the business.

The exact number of these businesses is difficult to estimate. The number of self-employed people is about 3.5 million, but this includes company directors, who may not own any part of a business. The number of unincorporated businesses registered for VAT (Value Added Tax) is about 0.7 million, but small firms do not have to register for VAT unless their turnover (gross sales) exceeds a certain limit (£47,000 in 1996).

The company (or corporation)

This is a distinct legal entity owned by *shareholders* according to the amount of shares they have in the company. The Articles of Association and the Memorandum of Agreement regulate the amount of share capital, funding arrangement, decision-making powers and areas of operation of the company. The company is run by a board of directors on behalf of the shareholders. The board of directors is also responsible for recommending how much of the profits are retained for reinvestment (ploughed back) or distributed among the shareholders. This is usually done twice-yearly. Retained profits appear as the *reserves* in the accounts. Distributed profits is paid out as a *dividend* to the shareholders according to the size of their shareholding.

In the UK, each share has a *nominal* value (for instance £1) that corresponds to the nominal share capital in the company's accounts. Shares can be traded on the market at a price depending on people's expectations about future earnings and other factors. This price determines the value of shareholdings in the company, but does not affect the actual assets of the company. It does, however, affect the cost to the company of raising more money. Established firms may also sell more shares at a premium, with the extra money being recorded as part of the company's reserve capital.

All companies can take advantage of *limited liability*. This means that investors in the company are only liable for the debts of their company up to limit of their investment. Limited liability encourages the flow of funds required for many modern businesses by protecting those investors who are unable to take an active part in the running of the company.

It should be noted that a company may have issued shares that are only partly paid up, say, 50p for each £1 share. A shareholder must pay the other 50p (or forfeit the shares) when required by the company, or if the company becomes insolvent or goes into liquidation.

In practice, limited liability for the small business does not always mean limited liability for the major shareholders, who often have to give personal guarantees of some extra security to the banks providing much of the loan capital.

There are two types of company:

1. The *private company*. The directors may only raise money through personal contact and from those who would normally have a good understanding of that area of business. This often restricts the growth of the business. There are over half a million private companies in the UK, though a significant number are merely shell companies, formed for financial reasons, or they do not trade.
2. The *public company*. The directors may appeal to the general public to subscribe to loans and shares. In return, the company is subject to more stringent regulation, particularly in relation to the disclosure of information. In the UK, shares in a public company may be placed through financial institutions (the normal method for most UK

companies), or (for a growing number) they may be traded on the Alternative Investment Market. There are over 50,000 public companies in the UK. A small number (under 3,000) of them are Quoted Public Companies. These have a Stock Exchange *quotation* so that their shares may be traded on the Stock Exchange. This gives them a wider market for their shares and ultimately for their financing.

The value of the business

The actual value of a business depends on its ability to generate profits, and is based on the property it operates from, although intangibles, such as a sandwich delivery round, also have value. Prospective buyers take into account a business's recent profit history, market growth and the state of the economy, including the rate of interest. This value is usually greater than the alternative use value of the property the business owns, because of the specific value the existing owners have built up in their market.

For sole proprietorships and partnerships, the value of the business is often measured by the value of the property owned. However, there are some firms that have much of their value in intangible assets. For example, the value of a sandwich delivery firm is based on the goodwill established with its customers giving it a competitive edge in the market and therefore higher profits. This means, for instance, that the market value of a hotel business increases when:

- property prices generally are increasing;
- the business has a better profit record than similar businesses nearby;
- interest rates have been falling significantly;
- the general level of profitability has been increasing.

The market value of a company is the market value of the shares held in it. This depends on how investors view the firm's prospects according to the state of the economy and of the industry, prospects for market growth, previous financial history, management effectiveness and current dividend policy. The dividend is more than just a distribution of profit. It is a statement by the directors of the company about the company's long-term prospects. An increase in dividend implies a sustained increase in profits for some time to come and usually raises the share price in the market. However, if the increase in the dividend is unrealistic, the market interprets this as bad financial management. The share price may then drop. On the other hand, a cut in dividend signals a decrease in expected future profits, and shares will fall in price.

The share price does not affect the amount of money already invested in the business, but it is important because it

- indicates the relative health of the company to banks and other creditors;
- provides the asset base on which loans are made;
- affects the price at which firms can raise new money through selling shares.

THE FINANCIAL FEATURES OF BUSINESSES

The economic position of the company in the market ultimately rests on its financial position, in relation to its stages of growth and the state of the economy. This can be assessed from its accounts, chiefly its balance sheet, profit and loss account and cash flow statement.

The company's balance sheet details the company's assets and the method of funding them (called liabilities). These assets consist of:

1. *Fixed assets*: These comprise physical capital (land, buildings and vehicles) plus financial investments. However, the valuation of these items can be problematical, particularly for hotel companies, as the value of property can change significantly between booms and slumps in the economy.
2. *Current assets*: These are usually listed as the sum of stocks (of raw materials, work in progress and finished products not yet sold) plus debtors (owing money to the firm) minus creditors (to whom the firm owes money) plus cash. However, these assets may also be difficult to value as stock prices can change significantly and debtors do not always pay up.

Assets are financed from a mixture of sources (denoted as liabilities in the company accounts). They fall into two main categories: long-term capital funds and working capital.

Long-term capital funds

The firm is assured of the availability of the finance over a long period of time, provided it continues to honour any contractual obligations to the providers of the funds. These funds consist of:

1. *Equity capital* This comprises the original investment by the owners, or shareholders in companies, plus retained profits (listed as reserves in the accounts). In companies this equity capital comprises:
   (a) *Ordinary shares*: Ordinary shareholders are the ultimate risk takers. They own the assets (equity) of the business after all other investors and lenders have been paid. The number of ordinary shares may be increased to fund new investment, but in the normal course of events some of the profit earned is retained or ploughed back into the business. This increases the *equity* of the business and so the value of the ordinary shares.
   (b) *Preference shares*: These are a small percentage of the total shareholdings in most companies. Preference shareholders receive up to a certain percentage of the nominal share value as a dividend before ordinary shareholders receive any dividend. They also have priority over ordinary shareholders in any company liquidation. In return they receive a dividend which is less than the ordinary shareholders would expect and usually do not have voting rights. Companies do not use them much because of their tax disadvantage:

any dividend paid is treated as a distribution of profit, whereas interest paid on a loan is regarded as reducing profit and so reduces the company's tax bill.

2. *Debt (loan) capital* The major form of loan stock is the debenture. This is usually a fixed term loan sold in specified units of nominal value such as £1,000. The firm pays interest on the loan, normally at a fixed rate, until the maturity date, when the loan has to be repaid. The firm may then issue further loan stock to repay this debt. Failure to meet interest payments can lead to insolvency. Debentures may be secured against particular assets of the company (mortgage debentures) or against the business as a whole.

Working capital

This is the money used to finance the day-to-day operations of the business. It consists of cash, bank overdrafts, short-term loans and credit. It is used to pay for materials, wages and other expenses, such as local taxes, until the firm receives payment for the products it sells. This economic view of working capital is somewhat different from the accountant's view, which is calculated as current assets *minus* current liabilities (Davies, 1992). In practice the difference between working capital and fixed capital funding is blurred. Increases in material costs increase the amount of money that the firm requires to maintain operations and necessarily reduces the amount of funding available for fixed investment.

Financial targets

There are three essential requirements of business operation: security, profitability and liquidity.

Security

The firm's physical assets must have sufficient market value to provide security for its present and future borrowings. Commercial practice requires firms to keep a balance between the amount of debt and equity investment (= value of shares in the company), called the *gearing* ratio. If a company's funds are made up of:

25% from borrowing and	the gearing ratio is 1:3 and
75% from shareholders' funds	the company is low geared;
50% from borrowing and	the gearing ratio is 1:1 and
50% from shareholders' funds	the company is moderately geared;
75% from borrowing and	the gearing ratio is 3:1 and
25% from shareholders' funds	the company is highly geared.

A normally acceptable ratio is about 1:1, though this varies with the type of industry and the current state of the national economy and the firm itself. For instance, during the 1990–93 recession, some large firms in the hospitality and other industries were operating on very high gearing ratios. Even in relatively good times, hotel company gearing can be relatively high, because there is a relatively short credit line extended to customers. This means that less of the company's assets are tied up in credit to customers. This allows the company to operate relatively safely with higher debt ratios.

Gearing up by increasing its debt ratio has two benefits for the company:

1. It may be able to borrow the money at a rate of interest below its expected profit rate, because a loan is less risky for the lender than taking a share in the business. This increases the net return to the owners of the business.
2. The original owners retain a greater control over their business.

However, high gearing can cause problems for the company:

1. The company is highly exposed to any downturn in the economy or other factor that affects the market. It may not make sufficient profit to service (= pay interest on) its debts. If this happens it is not in a good position to increase its overdraft or other borrowing to finance its activities. It will then become insolvent.
2. The firm will find it difficult to raise new money from expansion and will face pressure from its bankers and financial institutions to sell off assets to reduce its borrowing.

Profitability

Profit is the surplus of income over cost. It can be distributed to the owners or reinvested in the business. The contribution of current production to profits is given by:

Operating profit = Turnover (sales revenue) – Cost of sales – Administration and other costs.

However, the actual profit for the firm is reduced by taxes, interest payments and any special payment from restructuring the company including redundancy costs.

There are a number of factors to consider in profit. Administration and other costs can be excessively high, particularly in a large group with several units. This can be particularly damaging during the early stages of a recession when interest rates are also high. The group may become insolvent even though individual hotels are operating at a profit, as was the case with several firms during the 1990–92 recession. A firm can improve its profitability through:

- the appropriate timing of investment over the macroeconomic cycle;
- slimming down its organization with management geared to delivering the product;
- good financial management which can reduce interest payments and taxation.

Liquidity

The firm must have sufficient *liquid assets* (cash or credit) to pay its bills as and when required. Importantly, it must have a suitable cash flow profile through the appropriate timing of investment and its returns.

The firm's liquidity changes as its *bank* and *cash balances* change. This can be seen from the *funds flow* analysis in the accounts. Importantly, the liquidity of the company increases when:

- profits go up;
- fixed assets are sold;
- shares are issued for cash;
- creditors increase (the firm makes use of trade credit more).

The liquidity of the firm decreases when:

- dividends are increased;
- taxes are paid;
- assets are bought;
- the company is reorganized;
- stocks are increased;
- debtors (people owing money) are increased.

Stocks and debtors appear to be part of the financial assets of the company, but can badly affect liquidity if they are excessively large and may not convert into actual cash. Financial evaluation uses various ratios to assess the liquidity of the organization, though the appropriate range of values may conventionally differ from industry to industry according to the modes of operation and payment practices in that particular industry.

BUSINESS PERSPECTIVES

Each organization or firm faces competition for customers and for resources. It requires a business strategy to achieve its profit or welfare goals. The strategy has to be based on an appropriate analysis of the political, economic and social factors that affect the ability of the firm to successfully supply its markets. The firm has to take account of the factors discussed in the next four paragraphs. These matters are dealt with in subsequent chapters. Chapter 2, however, provides an introduction to the working of the market. An understanding of these market principles underpins much of the subsequent analysis.

Structural change in the economy

These are the longer-term changes in the economy that affect the markets for the services provided by the firm and its competitors. Analysing these changes should identify those new products the firm could provide. The firm must evaluate its products and their role in the consumption process of households and/or individuals, or, where appropriate, in the activities of potential industrial users. In this way the firm can look for those changes that are going to affect its position in the market.

Short-term fluctuations in economic activity

These include changes in output, incomes, inflation and unemployment in the national and international economy over a relatively short period of time (up to five years). Many of these changes affect demand for the product and the costs of producing it for the market. For instance, demand for certain services follows the general ups and downs in consumer spending, whereas the number of foreign visitors is affected by changes in the value of the pound against foreign currencies.

The market position of the firm relative to actual and potential rivals

This depends on:

1. creating identifiable products with strong selling points; and
2. on the market structure, the number and size of firms, which limits its freedom of action in setting prices or in product specification.

Structure of production

The management of the firm can be judged by its *effectiveness* in providing the market with appropriate products and its *efficiency* in doing so at minimum cost. It does this by producing its products at a low enough cost and selling them at a high enough price. This depends on its bargaining position in relation to suppliers and buyers and the strength of the competition.

CASE STUDY: ORCHARD FOOD SERVICE

The following cautionary tale from *Food Service Management* shows the importance of taking account of basic economic and political factors in business planning.

Orchard Food Service was the £4m award-winning cook–chill central production unit (CPU) owned by Anglia and Oxford Regional Health Authority. The Regional Health Authority (RHA) had decided in the mid-1980s to update their catering facilities to meet the need for greater consumer responsiveness and quality at its many varied sites, some of which did not have full kitchen facilities. It chose to invest in the newer, more capital intensive methods of cook–chill production rather than using an older, more labour intensive technology.

However, the authority could not find an outside supplier that it considered reliable on price and quality. So it chose to produce in-house and built three units. One of these was to become the Orchard plant, another at Kettering which continued to thrive and a third at Reading which closed six months after opening in 1994.

Orchard opened in 1993, primarily to serve the internal hospital and healthcare market, but also to supply commercially any large scale buyer of prepared meals. However, it came up against effective competition from outside suppliers who had developed significant facilities in the early 1990s. The CPU only ever achieved a weekly output of 40,000 lb of food, well below its design capacity of 60,000 lb of food weekly. It closed in 1995 with accounting losses running at £30,000 a month.

The problems that were identified were:

- Collapse of the core market (internally within the RHA) caused by the rapid restructuring of the National Health Service with NHS Trusts and the closure of mental and psychiatric hospitals.
- Increased competition from commercial suppliers.
- The effects of the recession which exacerbated price competition.
- Annual capital charge levied by the government of £750,000.
- The Regional Health Authority had to divest itself of central services by 1996.

The business manager commented: 'We were meticulous in our initial studies, checking that the market was ready and committed and to our service. But this was a situation we could never have anticipated.'

Source: Jane Baker: Orchard's Bitter Fruit, *Food Service Management*, July 1995, pp. 14–15.

ANALYSIS

It is easy to analyse problems with hindsight, but some of the problems could have been foreseen by using a bit of economic reasoning.

Structural change: government policy and the long-term market

Government actions were consistent with its economic policy in the face of the rising cost of healthcare provision. The National Health Service (NHS) would have to look for financial savings by reducing and/or shifting part of the burden. Alternative forms of treatment would reduce hospital occupancy to more acute cases, effectively reducing the growth in demand for ancillary services.

The 'market discipline' brought in by successive Conservative governments would be extended. A possible Labour government would not have reversed the trend. Hence the health service, and particularly the NHS Trusts that were to be established, would not be captive markets.

Economic fluctuations: short-term problems

The recession was bound to aggravate the pricing problems of competing in an increasingly competitive market.

Competitors

The unit was centred on the hospitals. So it could only compete against competitors in the open market if it had a secure base from which to operate. Without a tradition in servicing the contract market, the organization faced considerable problems in entering the market and did not have compensating advantages elsewhere. Other producers, particularly those supplying, or owned by, contract caterers and serving a varied market would eventually have the edge in flexibility and would be less disadvantaged in entering the recently opened hospital market.

Production and delivery methods: cook–chill and the size of the market

Capital-intensive methods require a large steady demand over a number of years to be financially viable. There is a certain amount of inflexibility in the system and problems were being identified with the running of cook–chill systems. There is always a tendency to over-estimate the benefits and under-estimate the costs of relatively new technology.

A large amount of economic analysis is common sense, but its systematic application is an important part of that analysis. The events described do not reflect badly on the business but indicate the need to incorporate economic analysis more explicitly into planning. It is a common tale, affecting many well-meaning businesses that do not have a broad enough understanding of economic trends. Half of all investments are unsuccessful. It is tough when the investment is your whole business.

FURTHER READING

There are a large number of introductory textbooks in economics. Use of the index or chapter headings in such books will give you the appropriate material. Choose books you feel comfortable with according to the particular topic. Some examples of useful books are given below, but they should not be regarded as required reading (all chapters are written to avoid the need for other books). You may of course find books that you are more comfortable with.

Begg, D., Fischer, S. and Dornbush, R., 1994, *Economics (4th edn)*. London: McGraw-Hill, chs. 1, 7 (7.1–7.2; pp. 95–102).

Griffiths, A. and Wall, S. (eds.), 1995, *Applied Economics: An Introductory Course (6th edn.)*. London: Longman, ch. 2.

Parkin, M. and King, D., 1995, *Economics (2nd edn.)*. Wokingham: Addison-Wesley, chs. 1, 9.

Other economics texts usually have an introductory chapter that covers similar material on the meaning, scope and method of economics.

Office of National Statistics, *Social Trends*: London: HMSO. This has been published annually since 1970 and describes changes in UK society, households, consumption, work and leisure, with special articles in each issue covering various topics. It provides useful information for understanding the economic and social context of change in the hospitality industry.

2 The market

Key concepts
In this chapter we investigate the implications of market activity for the firm. We:

- show how supply and demand determine price and output in the market;
- analyse the process of change in market;
- introduce the concept of elasticity and its application;
- apply supply and demand analysis to changes in the hospitality industry;
- show how understanding market processes can help managers improve their planning.

Prerequisite: Chapter 1.

THE MARKET SYSTEM

The market system is an important characteristic of Western economies. It is *a general system of open exchange* where most goods and services can be freely bought and sold. It is also called the *price system*, because the price changes to make sellers provide the right amount that buyers wish to buy, given their preferences and resources.

A key feature of the system is that it is *impersonal*, that is, independent of who is buying and selling. For instance, the hotel should not be concerned with who you are but only whether you are prepared to pay the price for the room (as long as you do not put other people off from coming). Discrimination of any kind actually makes the market work less efficiently, although governments may impose certain restrictions, such as banning the sale of alcohol to minors, in the public interest.

There are two groups of people in the market:

1. the sellers (producers or suppliers), who *supply* the product by offering to sell it at a given price;
2. the buyers (consumers), who *demand* the product by offering to buy it at the given price.

The following analysis shows how buyers and sellers between them determine price and output.

Supply and the supply curve

The quantity supplied is the amount offered for sale. This depends on the price the producers expect to get: some low-cost producers can supply a product quite cheaply, while others need a higher price to make it worthwhile. So we define the supply of the commodity in the following way:

Supply is the relationship between price and the quantity supplied of a commodity.

We represent this relationship by the supply curve in Figure 2.1.

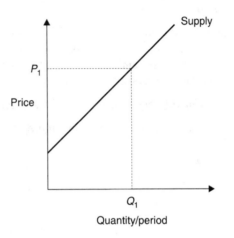

Figure 2.1 Supply of a commodity

Q_1 is the quantity supplied at price P_1 *during a given period* when goods or services are produced. However, if we are referring to a stock of an item, such as land, then Q_1 is the quantity offered for sale, without the time dimension.

P_1 is the supply price for quantity Q_1. It depends on the costs of production and is the minimum price suppliers will accept to sell quantity Q_1.

The supply curve usually slopes upward to show that suppliers need a higher price in order to sell more, particularly as the cost per unit goes up when firms try to increase output quickly.

Suppliers could operate above their supply curve and charge a higher price than they need. They would then make a surplus, called economic profit, over their normal level of profit. However, where there are several suppliers, customers can shop around for the best price for similar products. The suppliers are competing against one another and this forces them down to their supply curve so that the consumer pays the lowest price possible.

The following important points should be noted:

1. *The supply curve is independent of what buyers are prepared to buy.* For instance, more people would want to be hotel managers at £30,000 a year than at £15,000 a year, even though there may not be enough jobs for everyone at that wage.
2. *A change in the price of a product only alters the quantity offered for sale.* It does not alter the shape or position of the supply curve.
3. *The supply curve can have different shapes.* However, for simplicity, we usually draw it as a straight line, upward-sloping from left to right, unless there are special reasons for drawing it differently. *The supply curve does not normally go through the origin* – this would mean that some firms would supply a product even when the price is very low.

Demand and the demand curve

The quantity demanded is the amount buyers wish to buy, which depends on the price they have to pay. Some consumers will pay a higher price than others, depending on their desires and the amount of money they have. So we define the demand for the commodity in the following way:

Demand is the relationship between price and the quantity demanded.

We represent demand by the demand curve in Figure 2.2.

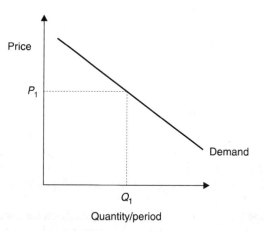

Figure 2.2 Demand for a commodity

Q_1 is the quantity demanded at price P_1. P_1 is the demand price. It is the maximum amount buyers will pay for the quantity Q_1 and depends on income and prices of substitutes and complements.

The demand curve *slopes downward* from left to right as people buy more as the price falls.

Buyers could operate below their demand curve and buy the product for less than they would be willing to pay. The lower price would give the consumer an extra *consumer surplus*. (This is not always a good thing, especially if the 'consumers' are firms getting your labour cheap). However, where there are several buyers, suppliers can sell to those who will pay the best price. The buyers compete against one another and this forces them up to their demand curve so that firms get the best price for their products.

The following important points should be noted:

1. *Demand is independent of supply.* For instance, more people would take a holiday weekend at £50 a head than at £100 a head, even if there were none available at the lower price.
2. *A change in the price of a product only alters the quantity demanded.* It does not alter the shape or position of the demand curve.
3. There are some situations where higher prices may appear to encourage greater demand. For instance, consumers may use price as a guide to the relative quality of different brands when they cannot judge the quality and reliability of a product before buying it. Such cases do not affect our analysis of the market for a type of product (say, three-star hotels), since the higher the average price the less consumers will buy of that type of product.
4. Demand curves are not usually straight lines. However, we draw the demand curve as a straight line, to keep our diagrams simple, unless it is important to show it otherwise.

Market equilibrium

Figure 2.3 merges Figures 2.1 and 2.2 to show the interaction of supply and demand. At the point (Q_0, P_0), where the two curves cross, quantity supplied equals quantity demanded. If conditions stay the same, buyers and sellers continue to trade the same amounts at the same price. (Q_0, P_0) is known as the equilibrium point. P_0 is then the *equilibrium price* and Q_0 is the *equilibrium quantity*.

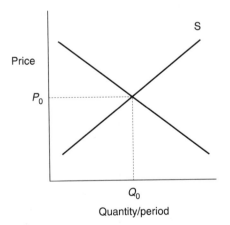

Figure 2.3 Market equilibrium

MARKET STABILITY

If buyers and sellers expect the market to be different, their plans will not coincide: either there will be too much offered for sale or too little. The market is then in disequilibrium. However, this is not a serious problem, since the markets are usually self-adjusting, so that they move fairly quickly towards equilibrium by changing price. The change in price is the signal for buyers and sellers to change their behaviour so that the right amount of the commodity is produced. A rise in price makes it more attractive for prospective sellers and less attractive for prospective buyers; and conversely for a fall in price. So we state the fundamental rule of the market:

The market price changes automatically to ensure that the amount sellers offer for sale is the same amount that buyers wish to buy at that price.

This process is shown in Figure 2.4.

When too much is produced:	⇒	there is a surplus
	⇒	sellers reduce price and cut output
	⇒	buyers buy more
	⇒	surplus is eliminated
When too little is produced:	⇒	there is a shortage
	⇒	sellers raise prices and increase output
	⇒	buyers want to buy less
	⇒	shortage is eliminated

Figure 2.4 Market adjustment

We now discuss this process working in the two situations where the market is not in equilibrium.

Price above equilibrium price: excess supply

This is shown in Figure 2.5, where suppliers have more for sale than people want to buy.

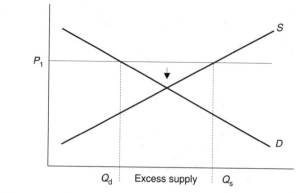

Figure 2.5 Excess supply

At the market price, P_1, quantity demanded, Q_d, is less than quantity supplied, Q_s. This is a situation of excess supply or glut, where firms see stocks rising or occupancy rates too low. Competition between firms forces them to cut prices to sell off surplus output or increase occupancy rates. Firms also cut back on the most expensive output by cutting overtime, reducing part-time labour or cutting jobs. Some less efficient firms may shut down altogether. As price falls, people buy more, moving down their demand curve. This process continues until price reaches equilibrium price (or close to it) and the surplus is eliminated.

Price below equilibrium price: excess demand

This is shown in Figure 2.6, where suppliers have less for sale than buyers want to buy.

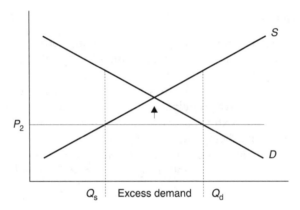

Figure 2.6 Excess demand: Price too low

At price P_2 the quantity demanded, Q_d, is greater than the quantity supplied, Q_s. This is a situation of excess demand or shortage, where firms see stocks falling or occupancy rates higher than expected. Firms try to expand output, but this is relatively difficult and expensive at short notice, as pressure may increase errors, or less skilled staff may have to be employed or overtime rates may have to be paid. So firms raise prices, expecting customers to pay those higher prices. Competition between consumers forces them to accept the higher price. As the price rises, consumers want to buy less and move up their demand curve. So the market moves towards the equilibrium position and the shortage is eliminated.

These two cases show that, when the market is out of equilibrium, market forces push it back towards equilibrium. That means that:

we can predict the effect of a change in demand or supply on price and output by comparing the equilibrium price and output before and after the change.

GOVERNMENT CONTROLS

The Government may regulate the market for various political or economic reasons. There are two types of control: quantity control (*quota* restrictions) or price controls. These controls prevent the market from moving towards equilibrium. So if the government relaxes its restrictions, price and/or output will change and the market moves towards its true equilibrium. Conversely, with a tightening of restrictions, price and output will change and the market will move away from its true equilibrium.

Quota restriction

Figure 2.7 shows the effect of a quota, given by the vertical line, Q_1.

For a quantity Q_1, buyers would be willing to pay up to price P_1. They could possibly pay less, but suppliers are usually better organized than consumers and so can extract the maximum price. This higher price is only profit if the firms have anticipated the quota, otherwise it may only partially offset the extra cost of the over-investment in plant and equipment that is not being used. In any case, businesses that own quota rights can sell them at a premium that takes into account the extra profit. If the government relaxes the quota to Q_2, the price falls and the quantity sold increases.

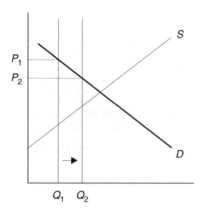

Figure 2.7 Changing a quota

Change in price controls

Maximum price control

If the government imposes a maximum price on the market below equilibrium price, there will be a shortage on the market, as in Figure 2.5. The government may be able to exercise some control by introducing some form of rationing. However, it will not be long before some type of black market emerges, in which some of the available supply is diverted to illegal trading. Black market prices are generally above the free market equilibrium price, because of the extra costs of trading, including the risk of detection and subsequent punishment. If the government relaxes its control, the legal market price rises as far as it can and the actual quantity sold also increases.

Minimum price control

The effect of a minimum price control is similar to Figure 2.4, where a surplus exists. The minimum price may not be a legal minimum, but may be an effective minimum price because the government agrees to buy up any surplus at a guaranteed price, as in the Common Agricultural Policy (CAP) of the European Union (EU). This becomes increasingly expensive for the government and even the EU has tried to reduce the rising cost of the CAP by reducing the guaranteed price. This reduces the market price, but increases the quantity sold to consumers.

A legal minimum wage would cause unemployment if there were a competitive market for labour. The argument for a minimum wage implies that some employers have significant market power in the labour market, enabling them to get their labour more cheaply than they are actually prepared to pay.

CHANGE IN THE MARKET

Unless there is some government control in the market, price and output are determined by demand and supply. Therefore, we can say:

The price of the commodity and the quantity sold do not change by themselves. Price and quantity change only when there is:

1. a change in demand; or
2. a change in supply.

CHANGES IN DEMAND

A change in demand means a change in the quantity demanded at each price.

Increase in demand

An increase in demand is an increase in the quantity demanded at any given price. This is shown in Figure 2.8. At the original price P_1, quantity demanded increases from Q_1 to Q_2 and the demand curve shifts *outwards* (rightwards or upwards). As the diagram shows, it also means that buyers will pay a higher price, P_3, for the original amount Q_1.

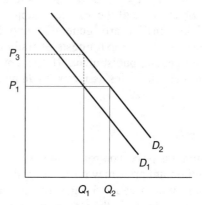

Figure 2.8 Increase in demand

Decrease in demand

A decrease in demand is a decrease in the quantity demanded at any given price. It also means that buyers will only pay a lower price for the same quantity as before. This is shown in Figure 2.9.

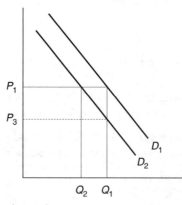

Figure 2.9 Decrease in demand

At the original price P_1, there is a fall in quantity demanded from Q_1 to Q_2. This is equivalent to shifting the demand curve *inwards* (leftwards or downwards). We can also see that consumers will now only pay the lower price, P_3, for the original amount Q_1.

Reasons for a demand change

There are four reasons why demand changes, as illustrated in Table 2.1.

Table 2.1 Reasons for a change in demand

Demand increase	Demand decrease
1. Rise in income (normal good)	Fall in income (normal good)
Fall in income (inferior good)	Rise in income (inferior good)
2. Rise in price of substitute	Fall in price of substitute
3. Fall in price of complement	Rise in price of complement
4. Quality characteristics now more valuable	Quality characteristics now less valuable

An increase in income can have a positive or negative effect on demand, depending on the type of product. Most products are *normal goods*, that is, we buy more of them as our incomes increase. However, there are some *inferior goods*, such as bread and potatoes, that we buy less of as we switch spending to more expensive products.

A *substitute* is simply an alternative product that people demand (and so buy) more of as the price of the other product rises. It does not have to be a technical substitute for a particular commodity. For instance, gas and electricity are substitutes for many purposes because a rise in the price of electricity encourages people to switch to gas.

A *complement* is a commodity that people buy less of when the price of the other product rises. For instance, a rise in the price of travel reduces the demand for hotel accommodation.

Consumers value a product according to its characteristics. If these characteristics become more important or more valuable to the consumer, the value for money factor increases and consumers want to buy more of the product. Conversely, if consumers now see the characteristics as less important or less valuable than before, demand falls. For instance, if people really take the threat of skin cancer seriously, the demand for holidays in hot, sunny resorts will fall.

It should be noted that a change in price of a product does not alter its demand curve, just its position on the curve, as in Figure 2.10. So we say that a change in price leads to a movement along the demand curve and *increases* or *decreases the quantity demanded*.

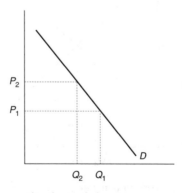

Figure 2.10 Change in quantity demanded

The effects of an increase in demand

When the demand curve shifts, the new equilibrium position in the market is given by the intersection of the new demand curve with the supply curve. We see the effect of the demand change by comparing the new equilibrium position with the old one as in Figure 2.11.

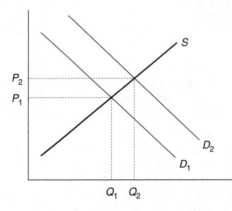

Figure 2.11 Effect of an increase in demand

The new equilibrium price and quantity are both higher. The supply curve is upward sloping, so firms need higher prices to be able to produce more. So the price rises and customers buy more.

The effects of a decrease in demand

Figure 2.12 shows the effect of a decrease in demand.

The new equilibrium price and quantity are less. Producers cut back on less efficient production so that the remaining output can be sold more cheaply.

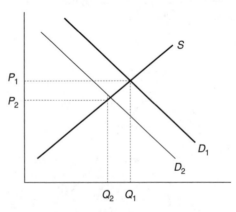

Figure 2.12 Effect of a decrease in demand

CHANGES IN SUPPLY

A change in supply occurs when there is a change in the quantity supplied at each price.

Increase in supply

An increase in supply occurs when there is an increase in the quantity supplied at any given price. This is shown in Figure 2.13.

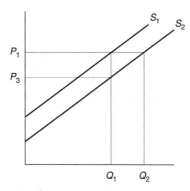

Figure 2.13 Increase in supply

At the price, P_1, suppliers increase the amount they will sell from Q_1 to Q_2. The supply curve shifts *outwards* (rightwards or downwards) and firms will accept a lower price, P_3 for the same quantity Q_1.

Decrease in supply

A decrease in supply means a fall in the quantity supplied at any given price. This is the same as saying that suppliers now require a higher price for any given quantity, as shown in Figure 2.14, where the supply curve shifts *inwards* (leftwards or upwards)

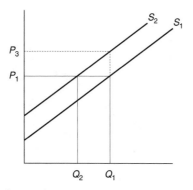

Figure 2.14 Decrease in supply

Reasons for a supply change

The three reasons for a supply change are given in Table 2.2.

Table 2.2 Reasons for a supply change

Increase in supply	Decrease in supply
1. Fall in costs of production or sale	Rise in costs of production or sale
2. Fall in taxes on production or sale	Rise in taxes on production or sale
3. Fewer business opportunities elsewhere	More business opportunities elsewhere

A fall in the cost of production can occur because of new technology, improved productivity or the fall in the cost of materials. The effect is the same: firms can reduce their price and still operate profitably. The opposite occurs for a rise in production costs.

Taxes on production or sale include excise taxes and Value Added Tax (VAT). They increase the cost of production and supply, which must be covered to enable firms to operate profitably. A cut in taxes allows firms to operate profitably at a lower price, while a rise in taxes means that firms need to charge a higher price. Although tax and cost changes have similar effects on price and output, we treat them as separate cases because they have different effects on the methods of production and delivery.

Business opportunities elsewhere do not affect the level of profitability in a particular market. However, investors will look at different investment opportunities. For instance, if returns on investment stay the same in three-star hotels but increase for budget hotels, investors will tend to switch money into budget hotels.

It should be noted that a change in the price of a product does not alter its supply curve, just its position on the curve as in Figure 2.15. So we say that a change in price leads to a movement along the supply curve and *increases* or *decreases the quantity supplied.*

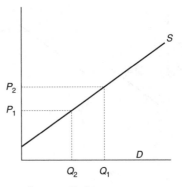

Figure 2.15 Change in quantity supplied

Effect of an increase in supply

The effect of an increase in supply is shown in Figure 2.16.

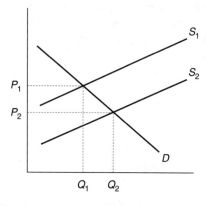

Figure 2.16 Effect of an increase in supply

The price has fallen and the quantity sold increased. This is because the fall in costs allows firms to supply the product more cheaply, which encourages people to buy more.

Effect of a decrease in supply

The effect of a decrease in supply is shown in Figure 2.17.

The price has risen and the quantity sold decreases, because a rise in costs means suppliers require a higher price and this discourages people from buying.

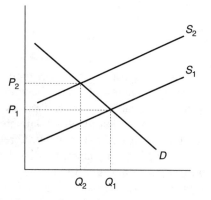

Figure 2.17 Effect of a decrease in supply

MARKET CHANGES IN PRACTICE

Identifying change in the market

Changes in the market are usually a mixture of supply and demand changes. However, during a particular period, we can determine whether change has been predominantly on the demand or supply side by looking at the direction of price and quantity changes, using Figure 2.18.

Increase in demand	$\Rightarrow$	Price goes up;	Quantity sold goes up
Decrease in demand	$\Rightarrow$	Price goes down;	Quantity sold goes down
Increase in supply	$\Rightarrow$	Price goes down;	Quantity sold goes up
Decrease in supply	$\Rightarrow$	Price goes up;	Quantity sold goes down

Figure 2.18 Comparing supply and demand changes

EXAMPLE 2.1: SEASONAL VARIATIONS IN PRICES

Seasonal factors often cause variations in the price of various products such as fresh food items and hotel accommodation. These variations are caused by a regular pattern of supply and demand changes that average out over the year. We can, however, determine whether the price changes are caused largely by supply or demand changes by looking at the variation in output as well as price.

EXAMPLE 2.2: FRESH FOOD

In this case we know from experience that most foods have a particular season during which they are plentiful. At the beginning and the end of the season, the quantity available is low and prices are high. At the height of the season, however, the quantity available is high and the price is low. Price and output move in opposite directions and so we conclude that it is mostly the supply curve that has been shifting. This makes sense as our tastes do not tend to change very much over the year, except perhaps for certain items, such as turkeys at Christmas.

EXAMPLE 2.3: HOTEL ACCOMMODATION

In this case, we know from experience that more people stay in a hotel in the summer than they do in the winter. Prices are also higher in the summer than in the winter. In this case price and quantity move in the same direction and so we conclude that it is mostly the demand curve that shifts. This makes sense because we know that the amount of hotel accommodation available does not vary much during the year, even though some hotels close for the winter.

Adjustments to changes in supply and demand

Producers and consumers need time to adjust to changes in market conditions. Producers have already invested in production equipment and training according to their expectations about the market. Any unexpected change in the market means that they have invested in the wrong amount of equipment, but they can adjust only slowly to begin with. Consumers also plan their lives according to their expectations of the future. They can make some changes fairly easily in relation to frequent, recurrent purchases. Some decisions, however, involve the purchase of capital goods, such as cars, or are an investment in a way of life, such as choice of occupation. In these cases, consumers adjust, but only over a period of time.

Key variables in the adjustment process

There are three important factors in market adjustment.

Profitability

Profit is usually expressed in so many pounds or dollars. However, profitability is expressed as a rate of return on some variable such as investment or capital employed and is expressed as a percentage. *Normal profit* or *normal profitability* is the level of profitability that a firm needs in order to get the investment funding or other critical resources it requires to stay in business. The rate of return on investment that equates with normal profit varies with the industry concerned.

Any profit greater than normal profit is called *excess* or *economic profit*. It is the possibility of earning excess profits that attracts firms into an industry or activity.

If firms are earning less than normal profit, they will not attract sufficient funding to continue in business and will eventually leave the industry.

Free entry and exit

Free entry and exit mean that firms may enter and leave an industry without any kind of penalty. A firm can compete on equal terms with other firms already in the industry. When there is free entry, firms enter an industry whenever there is the chance of excess profits. As they enter the industry, they increase competition and cause price to fall. Profitability then falls and the process continues until just normal profits are being earned.

Free exit is also necessary for the health of the industry. If profitability falls below normal profits, the industry needs to reduce the amount of competition so that prices can rise far enough for normal profits to return. Free exit allows the industry to adjust capacity downward more easily.

The short term and the long term

Markets adjust to changes continually. Some firms adjust sooner than others, depending on their assessment of how permanent changes are likely to be and also on their own particular circumstances. Economics divides the process of adjustment into time periods. The time periods most frequently used are:

1. *The short term or short run.* This occurs when it is difficult and relatively expensive for firms to adjust their capacity and production methods, because there are limits on the amount of particular inputs, such as capital equipment, that they can use. In such cases the supply curve will be relatively steep, and price will be determined largely by demand.
2. *The long term or long run.* This represents a clean-sheet situation where firms can adjust completely to changes in the market situation, and there are no restrictions on the quantities of various inputs that they can use. Firms can employ the most efficient combination of inputs to produce their output. In such cases the supply curve will be relatively flat and prices tend to reflect the costs of supply (assuming competitive markets).

Other periods can be identified, if the analysis calls for them, but for most purposes we shall need only the short-term and the long-term analysis, which we can think of as representing incomplete and complete adjustment to a new situation.

SHORT-TERM AND LONG-TERM EFFECTS OF CHANGE IN DEMAND

Increase in demand

The long- and short-term effects of an increase in demand are summarized in Figure 2.19.

Short term
Increase in demand ⇒ shortage occurs
⇒ firms expand output; extra output relatively expensive
⇒ price rises; higher price paid on all output
⇒ profitability rises

Long term
Increase in demand ⇒ industry expands capacity (some new firms enter)
⇒ supply rises relative to demand
⇒ price falls
⇒ profitability falls
⇒ process continues until firms receive normal profits on investment, when industry stops expanding capacity

Figure 2.19 Effects of an increase in demand in the short term and in the long term

---

EXAMPLE 2.4 INCREASING DEMAND FOR COUNTRY HOTEL ACCOMMODATION

When occupancy rates rise the country hotel operators at the time have too little capital investment to provide for the unexpected increase in demand. They are producing relatively inefficiently, because they have underestimated the amount of investment they should have made. In the short term they have to increase output using existing facilities, but their prices rise because of the increased costs caused by the temporary inefficiency in production.

Given time and in the longer term, the operators expand their investment or new operators enter the market to create the extra capacity required. Efficiency (and also competitive pressures) improve and this leads to prices coming down again, though the average firm still remains profitable.

Decrease in demand

The long- and short-term effects of a decrease in demand are summarized in Figure 2.20.

Short term
Decrease in demand ⇒ surplus occurs
⇒ firms contract output; cut out relatively expensive production (cut overtime; inefficient firms go out)
⇒ price falls; lower price paid on all output
⇒ profitability falls

Long term
Decrease in demand ⇒ industry contracts capacity (some firms leave)
⇒ supply falls relative to demand
⇒ price rises
⇒ profitability rises
⇒ process continues until firms receive normal profits on investment, when industry stops reducing capacity.

Figure 2.20 Effects of an decrease in demand in the short term and in the long term

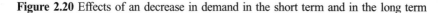

EXAMPLE 2.5 DECREASING DEMAND FOR COUNTRY HOTEL ACCOMMODATION

Country hotels operators have collectively invested too much in country hotels for the actual levels of demand. They have to pay for investment in buildings and other equipment that they cannot fully use. Most of the investment is too specialised to be used for producing something else, so they cannot sell it off or transfer it into some other use. The hotel operators are faced with higher costs than they should have. So they cut back on production, and so costs, but not by as much as they would if they could transfer some of the excess capacity into some other activity. So they suffer reduced profitability.

In the short term, a firm continues production as long as it covers its operating or variable costs, unless the cash runs out and the firm becomes insolvent or bankrupt. This is because it is better to make some surplus over operating costs rather than none at all. This is why firms continue producing even when they appear to be making losses. The losses are because the accounting system has apportioned the fixed costs of the initial investments over a period of time.

However, over time and in the longer term, the industry will reduce its investment in country hotels. Some firms sell their assets (voluntarily or else through insolvency) to other businesses. If they are sold as going concerns, still in the country hotel business, their market price falls to reflect the reduction in profits. The fall in market value reflects a loss of capital investment (which just disappears – it cannot ever be recovered). The new owners can then operate the business at lower prices because they do not need as much profit to pay for their investment. Where the value of the property falls sufficiently, the business may be sold for redevelopment as some other business. However the change takes place, we can be sure that in the longer term the industry will reduce its level of investment far enough so that it can operate profitably.

SHORT-TERM AND LONG-TERM EFFECTS OF A CHANGE IN SUPPLY

There are two general cases affecting costs of supply:

1. Costs of a particular input or inputs change. Firms will then change their methods in order to use more of the input whose price has fallen or less of the input whose price has risen.
2. The tax on the production or sale of the product change. Taxes can be levied as:
   (a) tax on value, such as VAT (percentage of selling price); or
   (b) tax of a fixed amount, such as duties on alcohol.
      The effect is similar to that of a cost increase. However, there is no change in the relative prices of the inputs used, and firms will not change their methods of production.

It is important to note, however, that the following analysis applies only to changes in costs of this particular commodity. Where costs or taxes in the whole economy increase, there is no change in relative costs. The effect is investigated for the economy using techniques of macroeconomics explained in Chapter 3.

Increase in costs of production or increase in tax rates

If the costs have risen because one input has become more expensive, firms will change their methods of production to use less of that input. This is because it has become *relatively* more expensive, even if it is still cheaper than the others. The effects of an increase in costs are summarized in Figure 2.21.

Short term

Increase in costs   ⇒ supply curve shifts up by the amount of the cost increase

⇒ price rises but by less than the cost increase

⇒ only some of the extra costs are passed on to the consumer

⇒ profitability falls

Long term

Increase in costs   ⇒ industry contracts capacity (some firms shut down)

⇒ supply falls relative to demand

⇒ price rises

⇒ profitability rises

⇒ process continues until firms receive normal profits on investment, when industry stops contracting capacity

Figure 2.21 Short- and long-term effects of increasing costs

Decrease in costs of production or decrease in tax rates

If the costs have fallen because one input has become cheaper, firms will change their methods of production to use more of that input. This is because it has become *relatively* cheaper, even if is still more expensive than the others. The effects of a decrease in costs are summarized in Figure 2.22.

Short term

Decrease in costs   ⇒ supply curve shifts down by the amount of the cost reduction

⇒ price falls but by less than the fall in costs

⇒ only some of the fall in costs is passed on to the consumer

⇒ profitability rises

Long term

Decrease in costs   ⇒ industry expands capacity (new firms enter industry)

⇒ supply rises relative to demand

⇒ price falls

⇒ profitability falls

⇒ process continues until firms receive normal profits on investment, when industry stops expanding capacity

Figure 2.22 Short- and long-term effects of decreasing costs

ELASTICITY AND ITS APPLICATION

We often do not have enough information to say how far changes in the market supply and demand affect price and quantity. However, we can use the concept of *elasticity* to assess the relative impact of these changes on price and output. Elasticity measures the sensitivity of one variable, such as quantity demanded, to changes in another variable, such as price, using the following definition:

Elasticity of X with respect to Y = Percentage change in X when Y changes by 1%.

Note that elasticity describes situations, it does not determine them. The most important elasticities that we use are the own-price elasticities of demand and supply.

(Own-price) elasticity of demand

This is often known simply as the elasticity of demand. The term own-price is used where necessary to distinguish it from other price elasticities of demand. It is defined as follows:

*(Own-price) Elasticity of Demand for a product = the percentage change
in quantity demanded of the product when its price changes by 1%.*

This elasticity of demand is a negative number, because price changes in the
direction opposite to quantity. If price goes up, this is a positive change and
so there is a positive percentage change in price. Quantity demanded goes
down, however. This gives a negative change in quantity and so a negative
percentage change in quantity. Dividing a negative by a positive always gives
a negative value. However, *we drop the negative sign in every day use* (but
only for this particular elasticity, and never in statistical studies of elasticity).

Elasticity of demand can vary from zero, when demand is completely
insensitive to price, to infinity when demand is extremely sensitive to price.
We group the different values into five cases (see Figure 2.23) because of
their differing economic implications.

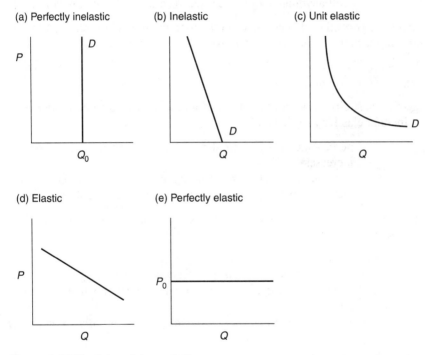

Figure 2.23 Elasticity of demand diagrams

   (a) Elasticity = 0 (perfectly inelastic demand); (Figure 2.23a).
     Quantity demanded does not change with price. Spending increases
     proportionately with price and the demand curve is vertical. This is
     unlikely in practice, because consumer incomes are limited. However,
     the short-term demand for some products, such as tobacco, alcohol
     and petrol, comes close to it, which is why they are favourite targets
     for government taxes.

(b) Elasticity is between 0 and 1 (inelastic demand); (Figure 2.23b).
Consumer spending increases when price rises. Consumers do not reduce their purchases by as much as the rise in price. The demand curve is represented by a steep line

(c) Elasticity = 1 (unit elastic demand): (Figure 2.23c). *Consumer spending stays the same as the price rises.* Consumers reduce their purchases in proportion to the rise in price.

(d) Elasticity is greater than 1 (elastic demand); (Figure 2.23d).
Consumer spending reduces as the price rises. Consumers reduce their purchases by a greater proportion than the rise in price. The demand curve is represented by a flattish line.

(e) Elasticity is infinite (perfectly elastic demand): (Figure 2.23e).
The firm has no control over the price it can charge. The firm is a price-taker or competitive firm that can sell any amount at the going price, but cannot sell anything above that price. The demand curve is horizontal.

There are two other demand elasticities that are frequently referred to: the *income elasticity* of demand and *cross-price* elasticity.

Income elasticity of demand

Income elasticity measures the effect of an increase in income on demand.
Income elasticity of demand for eating out

= percentage increase in demand for eating out when income increases by 1%

= percentage change on spending on eating out when income increases by 1%, assuming prices remain constant.

We summarize the different values for income elasticity according to their economic implications:

1. Product is an *inferior good:*
   (a) Income elasticity is less than 0: consumer spending goes down as incomes go up. Classic examples are bread and potatoes for most income levels.
   (b) income elasticity is 0: *consumer spending stays the same as incomes go up.*

2. Product is a n*ormal good:*
   (a) Income elasticity is between 0 and 1: consumer spending goes up, but the proportion of income spent on the product goes down as incomes go up. A typical example is food in general.
   (b) Income elasticity is 1: consumers spend a constant proportion of their income on the product as incomes go up.

3. Product is a *superior good:*
   Income elasticity is greater than 1: *consumers spend a greater proportion of their income on the product as their incomes go up.* A typical example is eating out.

Normal and inferior goods are called necessities while a superior good is also classed as a luxury.

Cross-price elasticity of demand

This measures the responsiveness of demand for one commodity to changes in the price of another commodity.

Cross-price elasticity of demand for accommodation with respect to travel

= percentage increase in quantity demanded of accommodation when the price of travel increases by 1%.

There are three cases:

1. *Complements*: Cross-elasticity is less than 0. The demand for the product goes down when the price of the other product goes up. Examples are travel and accommodation.
2. *Independent products*: Cross-elasticity is 0. The demand for one product stays the same when the price of the other product goes up.
3. *Substitutes*: Cross-elasticity is greater than 0: the demand for one product goes up when the price of the other product goes up. Examples are holidays in Greece and holidays in Spain.

Elasticity of supply

There is only one frequently used elasticity that we need bother about: the (own-price) elasticity of supply. This is often known simply as the elasticity of supply and is defined as follows:

Elasticity of supply of a product

= the percentage change in quantity supplied when the price changes by 1%.

The elasticity of supply can vary from 0, when supply is completely insensitive to price, to infinity, when supply is extremely sensitive to changes in price. We group the values into five cases according to their economic implications as shown in Figure 2.24.

(a) Elasticity = 0 (perfectly inelastic supply): (Figure 2.24a)
(b) *An increase in demand has no effect on the quantity supplied*. The price paid varies according to demand and is then an economic rent. The nearest case is of land in a given area where supply is fixed. However, the quality of land can be affected by the way it is maintained.
(c) Elasticity is less than 1 (inelastic supply): (Figure 2.24b).
    An increase in demand increases price proportionately more than quantity supplied.
(d) Elasticity = 1 (unit elastic supply): (Figure 2.24c)
    An increase in demand increases price and quantity supplied by the same percentage.

(e) Elasticity is greater than 1 (elastic supply): (Figure 2.24d)
An increase in demand increases price by a smaller percentage than quantity supplied.

(f) Elasticity is infinite (perfectly elastic supply): (Figure 2.24e).
Sellers will supply any amount demanded at a given price; they will supply nothing below this price. This happens when it is easy to switch the required resources into and out of producing the product. It is more likely occur in the long term than in the short term.

The different degrees of elasticity of supply reflect the supply adjustments of many industries. In the short term, supply is very inelastic, but becomes much more elastic over time.

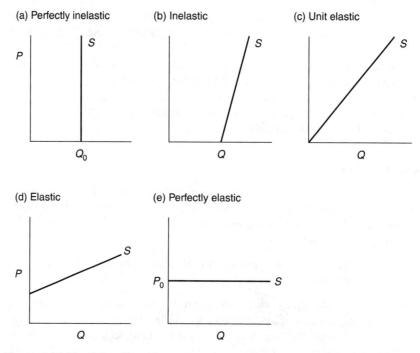

Figure 2.24 Elasticity of supply

APPLYING SUPPLY AND DEMAND

EXAMPLE 2.6: AGRICULTURAL PRICE SHOCKS

We can illustrate the application of the principles of supply and demand by considering an example from agriculture. Cases occur where the price of some commodity, such as potatoes, can rise significantly as a result of a poor harvest. This happens because, once farmers have implemented their production plans and the fields are sown, they have very little flexibility, that is the supply curve is almost totally inelastic as in Figure 2.25. The actual amount produced depends on the planned production, the weather and other factors. For instance, in Figure 2.25 P_0 is the expected price corresponding to the expected output Q_0 under normal conditions. P_1 is the actual price given the actual output Q_1. Given the inelastic demand for food, any reduction in output leads to a rise in price, unless some kind of agricultural support scheme is in operation to balance out the shortage by off-loading previous surpluses.

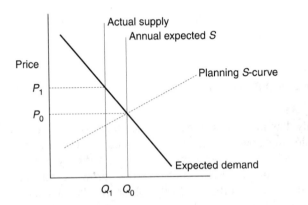

Figure 2.25 Fluctuations in price

EXAMPLE 2.7: REGIONAL VARIATIONS IN PRICE

Regional variations in price are caused by differences in supply and demand. Income per head is higher in some areas, such as London, and this shifts demand outwards. Higher income per head also increases costs of production in relatively labour intensive activities such as distribution. Higher income also implies higher land costs which, in turn, add to the costs of supply. These combined factors can explain prices being higher in London than in Manchester. On the other hand, remoteness from the main centres of production and distribution can add to costs, as in the case of Glasgow. The large expanses of cattle country in Scotland do not offset the higher costs of supply further down the chain of production.

EXAMPLE 2.8: CHANGES IN PRICE AND OUTPUT OVER TIME FOR A NEW PRODUCT

An *innovation* occurs when a new product or process comes on stream. Its price varies over time according to a number of factors. The first of these is the diffusion process. An innovation takes time to diffuse through the population. Consumers take time to accept or buy a new product. Producers take time to adapt to new ways of producing a product or to switch to producing a new product instead of an older type product. The diffusion process can be represented by a diffusion curve, showing the percentage of the population using the product or the total purchases in a period. The typical shape is shown in Figure 2.26.

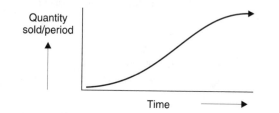

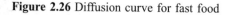

Figure 2.26 Diffusion curve for fast food

Initially demand grows slowly and then takes off very rapidly followed by a slowing down in the growth of demand. The firms who produce the product first have an advantage, but not if they produce too far in advance of the market. As the market grows firms find that their demand curve is shifting rapidly which means that they enjoy high rates of profit. However, the excess profits attract new entrants after a time and these will come in quickly. As a result, the price tends to fall fairly rapidly as does profitability.

IMPLICATIONS FOR MANAGEMENT

The most important implication of market analysis for managers is that changes in demand or supply bring changes in profitability in the short term. This leads to changes in property and company values. It also leads to changes in capacity in the long term which will tend to push profitability back towards normal levels, with corresponding adjustments in property and company values. It is important not to jump on to a bandwagon of change just *after* everybody else because the investment will be overpriced and will yield falling returns.

FURTHER READING

Begg, D., Fischer, S. and Dornbush, R., 1994, *Economics (4th edn)*. London: McGraw-Hill, chs. 2 (pp. 24–30), 3, 5.

Parkin, M. and King, D., 1995, *Economics (2nd edn.)*. Wokingham: Addison-Wesley, chs. 2, 4, 5, 6.

Introductory economics texts: sections on the market/supply and demand.

REVIEW EXERCISES

1. Show on a diagram the effect on the demand curve for holidays in Greece of:
   (a) a fall in price of Greek holidays;
   (b) a fall in income;
   (c) a rise in price of holidays in Spain;
   (d) improvement in the perceived quality of Greek holidays;
   (e) improvement in perceived quality of Spanish holidays.
   Note: does the demand curve shift in (down), out (up) or stay the same? Be careful with (a).
2. Show on a diagram the effects on price and output of a shift of the demand curve:
   (a) upwards;
   (b) downwards.
3. Show on a diagram the effect on the supply of hotel and catering services of:
   (a) a rise in price;
   (b) a fall in the cost of materials;
   (c) a rise in labour costs;
   (d) an improvement in productivity;
   (e) an increase in the tax rate on hotel and catering services.
   Note: does the supply curve shift in (up), out (down) or stay the same? Be careful with (a).
4. Show on a diagram the effects on price and output of a shift of supply curve:
   (a) upwards;
   (b) downwards.
5. Explain the effect on industry profitability in the short run and in the long run of:
   (a) increase in demand;
   (b) decrease in demand;
   (c) increase in supply;
   (d) decrease in supply.
6. Use a suitable example to show how supply and demand analysis can explain:
   (a) weekly changes in commodity prices (see *Caterer & Hotelkeeper*);
   (b) changes in price and output as a new product is introduced;
   (c) the effect of cheaper travel costs on a potential tourist resort.

Structural change PART 2

Economic trends affecting the hospitality industry $\boxed{3}$

Key concepts
This chapter analyses economic trends that affect the hospitality industry. We:

- explain how economic activity is measured;
- measure the economic importance of the hospitality industry;
- describe the trends in economic activity;
- explain their impact on household activity;
- explain the implication for the hospitality industry.

Prerequisite: Chapter 2.

DEFINING THE ECONOMY

The *economy* is a term used to denote the patterns of economic activity in a country, including production and employment, income, consumption and living conditions. In order to define the economy, we must look at (1) production, (2) consumption, saving and investment and (3) exchanges and transfers.

Production

Production converts resources, called inputs, into outputs or products that are (expected to be) of greater value

The production process is shown in Figure 3.1.

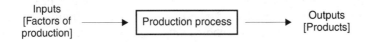

Figure 3.1 The production process

Factors of production is the traditional name for inputs, which are classified into *land*, *labour* and *capital*. We usually use the term inputs, however, as firms use different types of each factor and also many intermediate products, such as semi-finished goods and services bought from other firms.

Output consists of tangible *goods,* such as cars, and intangible *services,* such as catering, although the boundary between goods and services may be blurred in some cases. These commodities are called producer goods or services if they are sold to firms and consumer goods or services if sold to consumers.

The production process is the method or technique used to produce a product. We can also describe the production process as being capital or labour intensive according to the relative amounts of capital and labour inputs used.

EXAMPLE 3.1

Producing hospital meals using a cook–chill process uses more equipment and less labour than traditional methods of cooking on-site. The cook–chill method is relatively capital intensive and the traditional method relatively labour intensive.

We measure the amounts of capital and labour used in production by the amount spent on them. This is only approximate because increasing wages without changes in productivity means that labour costs increase and suddenly the process becomes more labour intensive!

Consumption, saving and investment

Consumption is using up goods or services.

Most services are consumed almost immediately they are produced. Perishable goods, such as fresh fruit, are consumed whether somebody uses them or not: if they are not used, they degenerate. Even long-lasting items, such as machinery, are partially consumed and lose value during the year. This loss of value is called *depreciation* in business and *capital consumption* in Government statistics.

Saving is putting aside resources for future use.

If current output (income for this year) is not used up, it is saved for future use.

Investment converts savings into products for future use.

Money saved can be used to finance investment processes to produce machinery, buildings and vehicles. These investments are part of the *capital stock* and are used to produce even more outputs in the future. As capital stock wears out, firms and households must make replacement investment to maintain the level of output. If they do not, then disinvestment occurs, and output will fall in the future.

Exchange and transfers

Exchange takes place when two individuals or organizations swap commodities of value to the other party.

It includes employment contracts and meals in a restaurant. Each exchange is a transaction that is a two-way process: time is exchanged for money; money for prepared food.

Transfers are a one-way flow of resources from donor to recipient; the donor does not receive specific goods or services in return.

Transfers include private and government pensions, grants and subsidies, and taxes.

MEASURING THE ECONOMY

The formal and informal economy

Economic activity takes place on three levels:
1. The *formal economy*, where goods and services are bought and sold in the market or are provided by the government. This provides the largest part of income, output and employment and is the easiest to measure and compare with other countries. The Office of National Statistics (ONS) publishes data on output, income and expenditure in the UK in its *UK National Accounts*, *Economic Trends* and other publications.
2. The *informal*, *hidden* or *black economy*, where goods and services are bought and sold, legally or illegally, but the sale or income earned is not recorded or declared for tax purposes. It is difficult to estimate the size of the informal economy, but based on expenditure data it has been estimated variously at up to 10% of the output of the formal economy.
3. The *household economy*, where goods and services are produced in the home for domestic consumption or traded within a group of neighbours. We do not yet have reliable estimates of the size of the household economy, but its value is probably between a third and a half of the recorded output of the country.

The formal economy

Government statistics measure economic activity in the UK using accepted international conventions. The basic principle is that:

Expenditure on the output = Value of output produced = The factor income earned.

EXAMPLE 3.2

When you buy a meal for £10.00 in a restaurant:

- your *expenditure* on goods and services is £10;
- the restaurant has produced goods and services to the *value* of £10;
- it has earned *factor income* of £10. It *distributes* this income among the various factors of production: wages for labour; profit for capital, including interest payments on money borrowed; rent for land.

Note that firms owning the land are regarded as paying rent to themselves.

We should be able to get the same value for output whether we are using data on income, production or spending. Errors in data collection however, affect the results, with the expenditure method being the most reliable.

Government statistics use the following conventions:

Measuring income by factor income earned

Factor income is the wages and profits paid to the *factors of production* (labour and capital) used to produce goods and services. Profits also include the rent paid to the factor land, as it is difficult to separate the earnings of each.

We exclude *transfer income*, because nothing has been produced in exchange.

Measuring expenditure by expenditure on final output

A firm produces either:

1. *Final output*, which does not undergo further processing by industry; or
2. *Intermediate output*, which is sold to other firms for further use in production.

We only include spending on final output because the value of intermediate output has already been include in final output. So, we include the following in *final expenditure*:

1. output produced and sold to consumers (= consumer spending);
2. investment goods such as machinery sold to firms (= investment spending);
3. goods and services produced for or by the government (= government spending);
4. goods and services for export (= exports).

The spending equivalents are given in brackets, but are reduced by the value of any imports so as not to include foreign production.

We measure final output by the price paid (whether we think it value for money or not). We can then calculate total output in the country by adding together the final outputs of the products. Where the government provides the product free of charge, its value is measured by its cost to the government.

Measure expenditure at factor cost to make it equal to the value of output and factor income

The actual amount spent is called *expenditure at market prices* and includes payment of taxes such as VAT and excise duty on petrol and tobacco. These taxes are transfer payments to the government: they do not correspond to any factor income and the customer gets nothing specific in return. So we deduct these taxes to get the *expenditure at factor cost:*

> *Expenditure at factor cost = expenditure at market prices − taxes on spending + subsidies on spending.*

Expenditure at factor cost is then equal to factor income earned.

Summary measure of output and income

Two of the most frequently used measures of output and income are:

1. A measure of factor income earned in the country:
   Gross Domestic Product at Factor Cost (GDP f.c.) = consumer spending + government spending on goods and services + investment spending + exports − imports of goods and services − taxes on spending + subsidies on spending.
2. A measure of spending power in the country
   Gross National Product at Factor Cost (GNP f.c.) = GDP f.c. + net property income from abroad.

Net property income consists of profits and royalties from investments abroad. This represents an additional, but small, source of extra spending power.

There are also frequent references to various measures at *market prices*. These are useful when studying the pattern of spending, because people decide their spending on the basis of their incomes and the market prices that they have to pay. Two such measures are Gross Domestic Product at market prices (often called Money GDP), and Gross National Disposable Income at Market Prices (referred to as Real National Disposable Income). The terms are slightly confusing at first because economics also uses the term 'real income' to compare changes in income over time after we have removed the effects of inflation or price changes.

MEASURING CHANGES IN OUTPUT

Table 1.1 of the *UK National Accounts Statistics* gives information on these national income variables as well those at market prices. It presents information in two ways:

1. *at current prices*: this measures output at the prices actually paid for the goods and services or their cost if paid for by the government;
2. *at constant prices*: this eliminates the effect of inflation by revaluing outputs at the prices that would have been paid for them if they had been bought in the base year (currently 1990), which is used for comparing different years.

Table 3.1 illustrates the difference for the years 1982 and 1992, using data from the 1993 *National Accounts Statistics*.

Output at current prices has grown considerably faster than output at constant prices. This reflects the rate of increase in prices (inflation) in the economy during this period.

Table 3.1 Output at current and constant prices

	At current prices		At constant (1990) prices	
	1982	*1992*	*1982*	*1992*
GDP at market prices (£m)	279,041	597,242	425,252	537,448
GDP at factor cost (£m)	238,385	516,027	370,493	466,564
GNP at factor cost (£m)	239,845	520,320	371,804	470,847

Source: UK *National Accounts*
Note: These data are revised annually for a period of ten years, so 1992 data will not be finalized until the year 2003.

Calculating economic growth

We measure changes in output using GDP as follows:

EXAMPLE 3.3 INCREASE IN GDP AT CURRENT PRICES (INCREASE IN MONEY GDP)

Increase in GDP f.c.

$$= \text{GDP}(1992) - \text{GDP}(1982)$$
$$= 516,027 - 238,385$$
$$= 277642$$

Percentage increase in GDP f.c.

$$= (\text{increase in GDP/original GDP}) \times 100\%$$
$$= (277,642/238,385) \times 100\%$$
$$= 116.5\%$$

This means that for every £100 of output produced in 1982, the country was producing £216.5 (= £100 + £116.5) in 1992, in money terms. However, this does not mean that the country was producing 116.5% more output in real physical terms. Much of the increase in the value of output was accounted for by inflation during the period.

We calculate the real increase in output by using the constant price estimates as shown in Example 3.4.

EXAMPLE 3.4 INCREASE IN GDP AT CONSTANT PRICES (INCREASE IN REAL GDP)

Increase in GDP f.c. at constant prices (at constant factor cost)	$= 465{,}646 - 370{,}493$ $= 95153$
Percentage increase in real GDP	$=$ (increase in GDP/original GDP) $\times$ 100% $= (95{,}153/370{,}493) \times 100\%$ $= 25.7\%$

Indices of output

We can express changes in economic variables such as GDP as index numbers, with the base figure being given as 100. For instance, if we set output in 1982 equal to 100, then the index of money output in 1992 is given by the formula:

EXAMPLE 3.5 INDEX OF OUTPUT

Index in 1992 $=$ (GDP in 1992/GDP in 1982) $\times$ 100
$= (516{,}027/238{,}385) \times 100$
$= 216.5$

Measuring average change in prices

We should be aware of the impact of inflation (= the general increase in prices) on the real value of industry output, sales or spending over time. One of the ways of measuring price increases is to measure the average price increase over all goods and services using the implicit *GDP deflator*, illustrated in the following example.

EXAMPLE 3.6 IMPLICIT GDP DEFLATOR AND PRICE CHANGES

Implicit GDP deflator for 1992 $= \dfrac{\text{GDP at current factor cost}}{\text{GDP at constant factor cost}}$
$= 516{,}027 \div 466{,}564$
$= 1.106$
$= 110.6 \ (1990 = 100)$

This means that prices had increased on average by 10.6% since 1990.

Similarly, GDP deflator for 1982 $= \dfrac{238,385}{370,493}$

$= 0.643$

$= 64.3 \ (1990 = 100)$

This means that prices in 1982 were only 64.3% of what they were in 1990.

So the percentage increase in prices between 1982 and 1992

$= \dfrac{\text{GDP deflator for 1992 GDP} - \text{deflator for 1982}}{\text{GDP deflator for 1982}} \times 100\%$

$= \{(110.6 - 64.3) \div 64.3\} \times 100\%$

$= 72\%$

TRENDS IN THE ECONOMY

Analysing changes in economic activity

Changes in economic activity, whether in an industry or in the economy, can be divided into trends and fluctuations, according to the following model:

Change in activity = Trend + fluctuations about the trend

The trend consists of changes that may come about slowly but have a major effect in the longer term. For instance, in recent decades, productivity has increased by about 2% a year, on average. This small annual change has a longer term impact, meaning that output grew by about 25% over a ten-year period. The impact on the industry may, however, be more uneven, because of the diffusion process in adopting new processes or methods of consumption (see the discussion in Chapter 2 on 'Applying supply and demand'), but the direction of change is the same. The length of the period is a matter of judgement, but we shall look at changes over a period of ten to twenty years. However, the length of time chosen affects the way we perceive data and interpret them, so a different picture could emerge if we were to take a longer time period of twenty to fifty years.

Fluctuations about the trend are changes that occur in both directions over short periods of time and may be significant. For instance, the annual rate of growth of output can vary from less than -1% to more than $+4\%$ within a few years, with a corresponding effect on the hospitality industry, although the longer term growth averages about 2% a year. We divide these fluctuations into:

1. *Macroeconomic fluctuations.* These follow a fairly regular pattern of change that repeats itself over a period of between about four to ten years, such as when the economy goes up in a boom and down in a recession. Improvements in the boom period usually match the deterioration in conditions in a recession. However, their pattern is approximate because of odd changes such as political crises, freak weather conditions or other unpredictable and one-off events.

2. *Seasonal fluctuations*. These fluctuations occur regularly and even themselves out over the week or year.

Types of cycle

In practice, the distinction between structural changes and fluctuations is partly a matter of convenience and partly a matter of the time period under consideration. There are four major types of cycle, which are also named after some of the economists who studied them:

1. Inventory (or Kitchin) cycle: a short-term, 3–5 year cycle, associated with the stocking and de-stocking (or inventory) processes in the economy and with government macroeconomic policy since the 1950s.
2. Trade (or Juglar) cycle: the classic, 7–11 year, economic cycle, associated with periodic over- and under-confidence in the economy, linked with rising and declining new fixed investment.
3. Building (or Kuznets) cycle: a long-term, 20–25 year cycle, associated with waves of building activity.
4. Longwave (or Kondratieff) cycle: 50–60 years, sometimes associated with significant waves of technological development.

These cycles occur at the same time: we could be at the bottom of a longwave cycle and yet be at the top of a short-term inventory cycle. This could partly explain the situation of the 1980s and 1990s where unemployment in the boom was still higher than in the depression of the 1950s and 1960s, when the economy had just come off the top of the longwave.

ECONOMIC GROWTH

Defining economic growth

The growth in real output over this period is shown in Table 3.2.

The data show that GDP at market prices and at factor cost move closely together, and over the longer term the increases are similar to those in GNP at market prices. The data also show that the economy was growing faster in the 1950s and 1960s and growing more slowly after that. However, there were also significant changes in the rate of growth during those periods that are consistent with the existence of the major cycles (except for the longwave, for which we need data over a couple of hundred years).

Sources of economic growth

The income of a country can be expressed by the following equation:

Income in the country = income per person × number of people in the economy

Table 3.2 Index of Output (1990 =100)

	Gross National Disposable Income at market prices	Gross Domestic Product market prices	Gross Domestic Product at factor cost	% change in GDP in previous five years	% change in GDP in previous ten years
1949	35.8	35.3	35.6		
1954	40.7	40.6	41.0	15.2	
1959	46.2	45.5	45.5	9.9	27.8
1964	55.5	54.7	54.9	20.7	33.9
1969	63.0	62.1	63.0	14.8	38.5
1974	68.8	70.7	71.1	12.9	29.5
1979	77.7	78.5	78.5	10.4	24.6
1984	82.9	81.9	81.9	4.3	13.8
1989	99.9	99.6	99.4	21.4	26.6
1994	105.8	103.6	103.5	4.1	26.4

Source: Economic Trends Annual Supplement.

So, income goes up when either:

1. income (GNP) per head (per person) increases, while the population stays constant; or
2. the population increases, while income (GNP) per head remains constant.

When income per head goes up, people consume more goods and services. However, they change their pattern of consumption, because they spend a smaller proportion of their income on the basic necessities of life. On the other hand, if the population goes up but real income per head stays the same, consumption per head remains the same. Larger populations may encourage shared consumption of certain types of goods (such as roads) and the larger market allows some goods to be produced more cheaply, so that people may feel better off. However, these effects are small in relation to the changes in consumption patterns that come from higher income per head.

REASONS FOR ECONOMIC GROWTH

There are two reasons for economic growth:

An increase in factors of production used

The economy can increase the amount of inputs used per head of the population. For instance, investment in education increases the amount of human capital by improving the quality of labour. This is equivalent to increasing the effective number of labour units that are used in the future.

Similarly, people can invest more of their income in physical capital stock per head and so increase output per head in the future. The principle of diminishing returns (☞ chapter 1) reminds us, however, that the extra investment should be put into the right areas so that the return stays high.

Improvement in productivity

Increases in factor productivity occur when each unit of capital or labour or land produces more than before. This is because of technical progress (or technical change), which has played a significant part in economic growth, though how great is a matter yet to be settled empirically. Technical change is either:

1. *embodied* in new plant and machinery, in which case firms have to invest in new equipment to take advantage of the improvements; or
2. *disembodied*, where productivity improvements become generally available through the development and diffusion of new management and worker skills.

General effects of technical progress

Technical progress can affect methods of production. Assuming the relative prices of the inputs stay constant, technical progress can be:

1. *labour-saving*: that is, it causes more capital-intensive methods of production;
2. *capital-saving*: that is, it causes more labour-intensive methods of production;
3. *neutral*: that is, it does not affect the capital–labour ratio.

Technical progress can be neutral even where machines have taken over from human labour, because firms substitute a smaller number of higher quality and more expensive employees for cheaper and less well qualified ones. Labour with the appropriate skills represents more *human capital* than unskilled labour and is paid correspondingly more. If all markets were equally competitive (which they are not, unfortunately) a worker who earns twice the wage of another worker represents twice as many 'labour units' as the lower paid worker.

STRUCTURAL CHANGE IN THE ECONOMY

The varied range of different activities in the economy are grouped into *sectors*. The term 'sectors' is used in three different ways:

1. It groups together economic organizations that undertake similar activities, such as:
   (a) the household sector (or the personal sector in *UK National Accounts*);
   (b) the business sector (company sector in *UK National Accounts*);
   (c) the government sector (public sector in *UK National Accounts*);

(d) the foreign sector (includes imports and exports and the flow of money and financial capital into and out of the country).

We can further subdivide these sectors as convenient. For instance, the business sector is often divided into the industrial and commercial sector and the financial sector.

2. It can refer to part of an industry, such as the fast food sector of the hospitality industry.
3. It may cover a group of related industries according to some common features or underlying characteristics. In this sense we identify three important sectors:

    (a) *Primary sector*: this includes all industries concerned with extraction and cultivation of natural resources, including agriculture, forestry, fishing, mining (coal, minerals, oil).
    (b) *Secondary sector*: this includes all industries producing goods, such as manufacturing, construction and public utilities such as gas, water and electricity.
    (c) *Tertiary sector*: this includes all industries that are considered to be producing services, such as banking and finance, hotels and catering, public administration and so on.

Some writers also identify a fourth sector (*quaternary*) to include modern high technology services such as telecommunications. This, however, is not particularly important here and so we stay with the basic three sectors.

We should be able to decide the meaning of the term 'sector' from its context. In this section we are using sector in the third sense. Initially, and historically, the division of the economy into different sectors for a purpose had certain philosophical implications. Several early economists considered real production to subsist only in primary industries. Later, this was extended to include manufacturing. It is only within the last hundred years that services have come to be regarded as constituting real economic output and even today there is a bias in many public policy discussions against services. The distinction between sectors is useful, however, because we can see certain patterns of development in these sectors as economies grow.

Long-term changes in economic structure

The long-term pattern of development in the three sectors (primary, secondary and tertiary) is similar in many of the industrialized economies of Europe, North America and Japan.

The primary sector declines fairly rapidly in importance to about 5% of GDP as the economy grows, although it remained a substantial part of the economy in some countries until quite late in their development, as in the United States. The decline in the UK was much earlier, more marked and went further than in many countries and is now less than 4% of output, of which only about half is from agriculture.

The secondary industries grow to a peak of between 45% to 60% of output, depending on the economy. As economies become more advanced, there is a decline in the relative contribution of the secondary sector. Germany and Japan in particular, however, reached a higher point in their secondary industries and the dip came later in those countries. In the UK, secondary industries have fallen from about 40% in the 1960s to about 30% in the 1990s. Manufacturing fell in the same period from roughly 30% to 20% of output, with the other 10% or so being construction and utilities.

Advanced economies are service economies, with over 50% of employment in service industries, even when industrial output is still climbing. In some countries such as the UK this proportion has reached over 60%, with the USA leading the way, well in advance of Western Europe. In the UK, the tertiary sector accounted for approximately 53% of total output in the 1960s but by the 1990s had risen to 66%. Significantly for UK problems, however, employment in services grew from about 48% of the total to over 70%, indicating a long-term problem of improving productivity and raising living standards across the whole population.

There may, however, be some process of re-industrialization at higher levels of output. In the UK, for instance, industrial output has increased significantly since the depression of the early 1980s even though industrial employment has remained low.

The major changes in the structure of the UK economy in the last thirty years have been:

1. a continued decline in the so-called production sector of the economy and a corresponding increase in the relative importance of services;
2. the growth of the oil industry at the expense of manufacturing industry, not services;
3. major growth in service industries in the 1980s, particularly in transport and telecommunications, financial and business services, personal social services, retailing, the hospitality industry and tourism.

Producer and consumer services

Besides the general government services of public administration and defence, there are two main types of services: producer and consumer services. Producer services are provided for businesses and include most information technology, business services, finance and banking among others. Their role is to help businesses by supplying procedures and processes more efficiently than can be done by the firms themselves. They can do this by the larger scale of their operation, giving them the flexibility with which resources can be switched between firms to keep costs down. Consumer services are provided for the final consumer and include personal services, hospitality services, social services and retailing. The line between producer and consumer services is sometimes hazy particularly in areas such as finance, distribution and hospitality services. Producer services are more likely to be standardized using capital intensive methods of production and/or using highly skilled labour, though some consumer services may also operate in this way.

ECONOMIC TRENDS AND THE HOSPITALITY INDUSTRY

Measuring the importance of the hospitality industry

The contribution of an industry to the economy is its net output or value added.

Net output = Gross output − value of bought in goods and services
= Value of work done
= Payments to labour and capital used.

The total output of the economy must, of course, equal the sum of the net outputs of all industries in that economy. The contribution of a firm to an industry is logically measured in the same way. The Standard Industrial Classification (SIC) system divides the economy into different industry groups or orders, each with one or more sub-orders, corresponding to an industry or sector of an industry.

Each firm or organization is then classified to an industry or industry sector according to the highest percentage of output produced. Therefore, that particular industry may include output that is quite different from what people may interpret as its major product. It also means that some output will be assigned to some other industry because it is not the major output of that firm. Thus, contract caterers are assigned to the hotel and catering industry, because their major output is catering. But works canteens run by firms themselves are classed with the steel industry, the engineering industry or whatever class the firm belongs to.

In practice, government data relating to the hospitality industry use two classifications. The one most frequently used in publications relating to the industry is based on the earlier 1968 SIC and this is used in Table 3.4. This provides greater detail for the different sectors of the industry and allows better comparison over the longer period.

The relative contribution of an industry to the economy is measured by its net output or value added relative to GDP. However, the data here relate to turnover including VAT and other taxes, so that what we are measuring is the relative importance of the industry gross output in relation to final spending only, either GDP at market prices or in relation to final consumption expenditure (equal to consumer spending plus government spending on goods and services plus exports net of imports). If we wish to make comparisons on a factor cost basis, we need to remove the effect of purchases and taxes on spending (information on which is given in the respective *Business Monitors*).

Table 3.4 The Hospitality Industry (SIC (1968) Classification)

		1977		1994	
SIC	Sector title	Enterprises	Turnover (incl. VAT) £m	Enterprises	Turnover (incl. VAT) £m
8841	Hotels and other residential establishments	15,714	1,603	12,994	6,090
8842	Holiday camps, caravan and campsites	1,419	201	2,095	1,610
8851	Restaurants, cafes selling food for consumption on the premises	12,982	915	16,764	4,816
8852	Establishments selling food for consumption wholly or partly off the premises	22,696	759	27,147	5,242
8860	Public houses	41,661	3,150	38,049	2,050
8870	Clubs (excluding sports and gaming)	16,995	1,022	15,743	1,200
8880	Catering contractors	1,123	298	2,424	2,180
	Total	112,650	7,948	115,180	23,188

Source: *Business Monitor*, SD025 (1977); *Business Monitor* PA 1003, 1994; Keynote UK *Catering Market*, 1995.

TIME, COST AND ECONOMIC CHANGE

The key to understanding the changes in the hospitality industry during the last twenty years or more lies in three factors:

1. changes in technology;
2. changes in patterns of working;
3. changes in household activity.

To understand how these factors have affected the hospitality industry, we introduce the concepts of utility, user cost and the cost of time.

Utility

Economics uses the term 'utility' to describe an individual's level of welfare or satisfaction. A person's utility comes from the activities he or she undertakes. These activities include employment, home production (such as meal preparation and DIY), and leisure activities. Individuals allocate their time, which is scarce, and other resources amongst the different activities available, according to the relative costs and benefits produced. These depend on personal wealth; the opportunities for work in the market, as indicated by relative wage rates; the alternative uses to which people can put their time; and domestic technology, including skills and hardware available.

User cost and the cost of time

We do not have enough time to do all that we would like to do, so that time has a real cost. This varies with the uses to which we can put time. So higher income earners have a higher cost of time, but other factors may also affect the value of time in particular circumstances, such as the period of the day or week.

The User Cost is the total cost of buying and using a product or doing an activity.

User Cost   =   price of the product
                  + transaction costs, including all dealing or similar costs
                  + access costs, including time costs of travel
                  + time costs in using the product or doing the activity

The concepts of time and user costs are particularly important for understanding how changes in household activity have occurred and how they have affected the hospitality industry.

ECONOMIC GROWTH AND HOUSEHOLD CHANGES

Households

A household is a group of people sharing certain basic domestic arrangements in common, traditionally meals, although today's households seem to eat together less often. The members of the household increasingly act independently of rest of the household, but they still do so within the collective framework of the household. This means that we can apply the same principles of behaviour to the household as we do to an individual. So we can say, as a first approximation: *that a household does an activity more (less) often when the perceived benefit relative to the perceived cost increases (decreases).*

However, we must be aware that the relative positions of the individual members change over time and so the balance of activities also changes. There are also natural changes associated with the life cycle that affect the consumption and working patterns of individual households.

The effect of economic growth on household behaviour

As we get better off, we need more time to spend our extra income. However, we do not have any more time as there are still only 168 hours in a week. Time then becomes relatively scarce. We deal with this problem in the following ways:

1. We use our time more effectively. For instance, we sleep less. The lighter work that people do these days means that less sleep is required to recover from the working day, so a small amount of waking time can be generated. We also spend time searching for better ways to save time.
2. We take some of our extra income in the form of leisure, as a shorter working week or as longer holidays. For the last 100 years or so, people have done both, with more emphasis being on reducing the working week.

In recent years, however, people in the UK have tended to take extra holidays rather than have a shorter working week. This has an impact on those sectors catering for holidays, but does not reduce the pressure on time during the working week.

3. We reduce the time-intensity of our activities relative to the amount of money we spend on them. In other words, we change our activities so that we spend our money more quickly. Leisure activities become more active and more expensive. For instance, we take a larger number of expensive holidays than previously, spending greater amounts of money at the same time.

4. We spend less time on household production by substituting market goods for time in domestic production. We do this in two ways:

   (a) We buy or lease domestic equipment such as washing machines and vacuum cleaners to make household production more capital intensive and release some time for other activities.

   (b) We buy services in the market place. For instance, we save on meal preparation time by using convenience foods (part or whole meals) from the supermarket or else by eating out. This means that much of the extra eating out is convenience eating. Also, we switch to more expensive leisure activities that are on average further from home and this increases the level of convenience eating.

Each of these indicators shows that households become less concerned about saving cost and more concerned to save on time. We often do jobs at home because it is cheaper to do so, rather than because we particularly enjoy them. Most people would prefer not to prepare meals, clean and wash, but they do so to save money because they cannot afford to buy in the services they would require. However, as incomes go up, the value of time goes up and they need to spend less time on these tasks.

Changes in economic conditions also affect the relative importance of different types of household. Those types of households that are best suited to long-term economic conditions increase in relative importance, whereas those that are unfavourably placed decline in importance.

For instance, there has been a marked decline in the proportion of families with children, the average size of the family and an increase in the proportion of single person households. This is illustrated in Tables 3.5 and 3.6.

One factor in this trend has been the increasing expense of rearing children. More material and educational spending is required for a child to function in normal society. The time cost of rearing children has increased, because mothers can earn much more than previously through working in the market. Similarly, the production of convenience meals, household appliances and increases in the housing stock all make it relatively cheaper for single people to live by themselves in separate households.

The impact of the changing role of women

The changing position of women in the formal economy during the last thirty years has had a major impact on household activity and through it on the

Table 3.5 Household size in the UK

Size	% in each category			
	1961	1971	1981	1991
1	14	18	22	27
2	30	32	32	34
3	23	19	17	16
4+	34	31	29	23
No. households (millions)	16.2	18.2	19.5	21.9

Source: Social Trends

Table 3.6 Structure of households in the UK

Household type	% in each category			
	1961	1971	1981	1991
1 person/2+ unrelated adults	16	22	27	36
Married couple without children	26	27	26	28
Married couple/single parent with children	57	51	49	44

Source: Social Trends

hospitality industry. The increase in real wage rates makes it more expensive for women not to work in the market, in terms of wages lost for each hour not worked. Consequently, the proportion of women working, particularly married women and those with families, has increased. Table 3.7 shows changes in *activity rates* for the UK, that is the percentage of the group (men or women) that are in work or actively seeking employment.

Table 3.7 Economic activity rates (%) Britain

Age	Males			Females		
	1971	1981	1991	1971	1981	1991
16–19	70	72	70	65	70	69
20–24	88	85	86	60	69	73
25–34	95	95	94	46	56	70
35–44	96	96	95	60	68	77
45–54	96	95	91	62	68	73
55–59	93	89	80	51	53	55
60+	83	69	54	29	23	34

Source: Social Trends

Men have not changed their working patterns significantly, apart from the substantial decline in activity rates for those over 50. However, activity rates for women have increased for all age groups, particularly between the ages of 20–54. The dip in activity rates for the 20–34 age groups has now been translated into a bulge extending to the 35–44 age group, the age group corresponding to the significant years of marriage, child-rearing and divorce.

The proportion of women who work full-time increased significantly by the early 1980s and has remained fairly constant at about 55% of those in work. What has been of significance has been the impact of economic change on working mothers:

1. The most important determinant of a mother's work pattern has been the age of her youngest child. During the 1980s, there was a significant increase in the proportion returning to work, in the hours worked and in the proportion who returned to work full-time directly. This is shown in Table 3.8.

Table 3.8 Employment Rates (%) for Mothers by age and number of children

Number of children	1981			1989		
	All	full-time	part-time	All	full-time	part-time
1	49	21	28	59	27	32
2	48	15	32	60	19	40
3+	38	12	26	44	13	31
Age of youngest						
0–4	22	6	16	39	13	26
5–10	45	17	28	65	21	44
11–15	67	30	37	74	33	41
16–18	70	36	34	74	38	36

Source: *Employment Gazette*

2. The greatest increase in activity has occurred among the better educated, who also earn relatively more and who have become a greater proportion of the potential female labour force, as shown in Table 3.9.

Table 3.9 Education and activity rates

Qualifications	1981			1989		
	All	full-time	part-time	All	full-time	part-time
above A-level	57	25	32	78	38	41
A-level	43	17	26	59	24	35
O-level	45	17	29	59	22	37
Other	44	16	28	54	20	34
None	44	16	29	49	16	33
All	46	17	29	57	21	35

Source: *Employment Gazette*

3. The presence of children in the household has a declining impact on activity rates for women generally, as shown in Table 3.10.

Table 3.10 Activity rates and children in the household

Percentage of women who are	1981		1989	
	With child(ren)	Without children	With child(ren)	Without children
In full-time work	17	50	21	50
In part-time work	29	16	35	20
Unemployed	5	6	6	6
Inactive	49	28	37	24

Source: *Employment Gazette*

The increase in women working in the market has had three effects.

1. As women work more in the market, so they want to spend more of their leisure directly in the market. The substantial increase in their earnings has enabled them to demand the right to spend their money and leisure time in the market place. Consequently, leisure spending has become less adult male-oriented and the style of spending has changed. So, for instance, there is pressure on pubs to become less of the male recreation reserve than formerly, otherwise they will lose out to other forms of leisure spending.
2. The increasing participation of married or family women in the workforce has meant that the total adult time available for domestic activity has decreased. Men have not reduced their working hours to compensate, partly because of higher average wages, but also because there has not been much redistribution of household tasks, with meal preparation, cleaning and washing done predominantly by the woman. This has put pressure on the household to save on domestic time through more sharing of other leisure activities and has encouraged more joint family activity in the leisure market.
3. The increasing earnings of women have increased their independence and security. This has reduced marital stability, increasing the number of single person households. The increasing value of time in the market has raised the cost of the non-working time devoted to child-rearing and has, together with the greater capital inputs required, reduced average household size. The smaller household size makes market consumption relatively cheaper for the household as a group, in relation to income per head.

ECONOMIC GROWTH AND THE HOSPITALITY INDUSTRY

Increasing capital intensity of operations

The way economic growth takes place affects production operations. The structure of the economy would only stay the same if all industries increased their productivity at the same rate as the increase in demand. However, the shift in demand towards services has increased faster than supply and the demand for goods rises more slowly than the supply. So services require more resources, which increases their relative prices, while goods require fewer resources, which reduces their relative prices.

Also, the increasing productivity of capital is equivalent to an increase in the quantity of capital relative to requirements. This reduces the price of capital relative to the price of labour. So capital-intensive methods of production become relatively cheaper than before, and this puts pressure on the service sector to become more capital intensive. This means that even in relatively low-paid industries such as hotels and catering, firms are looking to reduce their use of labour. In the hotel sector, for instance, the design of new hotels makes them less labour intensive in both general operations and in the specific services provided. Highly labour intensive activities such as room service become even more expensive to operate. This can be seen in the relative growth of hotels of two-, three- and four-star category, where room service is either not available or is exceedingly limited, often to the provision only of early morning continental breakfast at relatively high prices compared with similar restaurant meals. Even checking-in procedures are being streamlined and the use of automated procedures is gaining ground. One implication of this is that the proportion of managerial and administrative staff relative to operative staff will increase, and staff will have to be reskilled in newer technologies. This ultimately leads to higher pay levels, as these staff embody higher amounts of human capital.

Increased standardization

Firms can make best use of capital by having large scale production units, as larger capital units are, in practice, relatively cheaper to run. Firms can also increase the effective scale of their operations through standardization of the product, as this allows large production runs and cuts down on both management costs and costs incurred in switching production runs.

However, service firms need to bring their products to the customer. This limits the size of any production run because of the scale of local demand. Restaurants, however, can get round some of these limitations by transferring some production off-site to central production units. This also increases standardization of the product and allows better control of quality. Hotels do this by converting themselves into meeting stations so that business people converge on the hotel instead of using it as a stopping point.

Reduced perishability of hospitality products

Firms also have to reduce the perishability of their products to cope with peak demands and restore the balance between production and consumption. Consumption varies during the day, week and year, despite increased leisure time. We tend to spend much more at weekends and on Friday evenings. Production however, has become more concentrated, with people being reluctant to work weekends. They have to be paid higher wages to continue working when other people are relaxing. If firms do not increase wage rates, they will end up having to recruit poorer quality staff. Either way, the cost of supplying at peak periods goes up. The only way to keep costs, and therefore prices, down is to produce during the main production period, when most people are at work. Firms can only do this if they can reduce the perishability of the product, so that it can be stored and held until required.

So, burger operations send most of the work out to the factory, with the restaurant merely being a finishing station. Similarly, restaurants buy in frozen gateaux and portion packs as a way of reducing perishability and hence risk. It is cheaper to do this than to risk having to prepare on the day, in addition to other operating advantages.

Changing consumption patterns

Another feature of the changing economy has been the way consumers have changed their use of accommodation and food services. For instance, in eating out, pizza sales have increased faster than burger sales. We could explain these changes by saying tastes have changed. However, we would then need to explain why tastes have changed the way they have. We can instead explain many of these as coming from the changing economic pressures on households and the impact of changing technology. Time, as we have seen, is becoming relatively scarce. So consumers react by reducing the time-intensity of their activities.

EXAMPLE 3.6

One way of doing this is to simplify domestic meal production processes, by using convenience foods or by eating out. Convenience foods cost more money, but they may be cheaper for the household to use, when the value of the time saved in producing fairly complex meals is included (even for sandwiches, in many cases). In the longer term, consumers also save time because they do not need to acquire the skills necessary for the intricate work involved. Competition between food manufacturers encourages them to reduce the costs of production. Modern technology and their control processes also allow manufacturers to produce similar but differentiated products that use much the same process without increasing the cost. The greater variety of foods available increases the value of convenience meals relative to their cost. So households buy convenience meals more often.

The miniaturization of technology into the home as fridges, freezers, microwaves and other equipment means that domestic meal production becomes more geared to industrialized products and alters the level of services bought in the market. For instance, the consumer can reproduce the basic burger in a bun from a fast food restaurant, because the product can be bought directly as a frozen burger in a bun bought in the supermarket and regenerated at home; or the constituent products can be bought separately. So restaurants have to satisfy

---

consumer demand for variety by upgrading the kind of food product offered. Pizza still (for the time being) represents a relatively complex product to produce at home. However, given modern catering methods, it becomes much simpler to produce at the catering establishment. Consequently it has gained in popularity, with consumption growing faster than the burger.

FURTHER READING

Begg, D., Fischer, S. and Dornbush, R., 1994, *Economics (4th edn)*. London: McGraw-Hill, chs. 2 (2.1–2.6, pp. 16–24), 20, 30.

Griffiths, A. and Wall, S. (eds.), 1995, *Applied Economics: An Introductory Course (6th edn.)*. London: Longman, ch.1.

Parkin, M. and King, D., 1995, *Economics (2nd edn.)*. Wokingham: Addison-Wesley, ch. 22 (pp. 615–25).

REVIEW EXERCISES

1. Use information in the official annual publication *UK National Accounts (Blue Book)* (Table 1) (obtainable from the Economics journal section of your library) to complete the following table:

	At current prices		At constant (19..) prices	
GDP *at market prices*				
GDP *at factor cost*				
GNP at factor cost				

Alternatively compare any recent ten-year period.

Comment on the difference in growth in money terms and in real terms.

2. Use the *UK National Accounts* to find out how the relative importance of different industries in the economy have changed during the period 1984–94.

4 Structural change in the accommodation, food and drink sectors

Key concepts

This chapter analyses the impact of structural changes in the economy on the various sectors of the hospitality industry. It applies the analysis of the previous chapter to changes in the markets for hotel accommodation, eating and drinking out. We:

- assess the changes in tourism relevant to the hotel market;
- analyse changes in the hotel market;
- analyse changes in the market for eating out;
- analyse changes in the market for drinking out.

Prerequisites: Chapters 2 and 3.

A NOTE ON SPENDING AND INCOME

Changes in spending at actual prices paid (or current prices) are a mixture of changes in the real quantity of goods and services produced and of their prices. If we are measuring changes in the quantity produced (or real output), we calculate spending at *constant prices*. This means that we revalue the goods and services people buy at the prices they would have paid if they had bought those goods and services in some particular year (the base year). This chapter is concerned mainly with changes in the relative shares in spending or sources of income, so we do not need to consider data at constant prices. However, we should retain a sense of proportion when reading data spread over a number of years, given the significant amounts of inflation during this period. Table 4.1 shows changes in prices over the period we are considering, based on the government's Retail Price Index (RPI). This measures the average change in prices of the average basket of consumer goods and services in a given year, called the base year. (The information on average patterns of consumption is collected through the Family Expenditure Survey, supplemented by other data where required, as with alcohol consumption, which people regularly under-declare.) It gives slightly different results from the GDP deflator, but the difference is relatively unimportant here. The RPI is rebased every so often depending on the rates of inflation and the extent of changes in consumer spending patterns. Table 4.1 gives summary information, taken from the *Annual Abstract of Statistics*, relating to the RPI, based on 13 January 1987 = 100. Earlier years were based on 1974 (with different consumption patterns), but these have been rebased to 1987 = 100. Table 4.1 also gives the value of £100 in each of the years in terms of the equivalent value of goods and services in each of the other years. For example, £100 in 1980 would buy a bundle of goods that would cost £223 in 1995 (cell marked with a *). In the same way, £100 in money in 1995 buys what would have cost only £45 in 1980 (cell marked with a #).

Table 4.1 Changing price level UK, 1980–94 (13 Jan 1987 =100)

| Year | Index | Equivalent purchasing power of £100 in | | | |
		1980	1985	1990	1995
1980	66.8	100	142	189	223 *
1985	94.6	71	100	133	158
1990	126.1	53	75	100	118
1995	149.1	45 #	63	85	100

Source: Monthly/Annual Abstract of Statistics 1996

These figures are based on the pattern of expenditure in 1987 and should be taken as approximate only. The comparability of data over time declines, as some items (such as food) become relatively less important and others (such as computers) more important as their prices decline.

THE ACCOMMODATION SECTOR

The hotel product

Hotels are a large and varied group of establishments that provide a variety of services based on the *provision of variable short-stay accommodation services* for tourists and also local residents.

The range and quality of the services varies greatly, but they include:

- accommodation for travellers and short stay visitors;
- food services for hotel residents and local customers;
- event accommodation for business meetings, conferences and social functions (this includes meeting rooms, food and drink and overnight accommodation, if required);
- leisure activities such as health and fitness centres; casinos and dancing;
- retail services for a variety of products.

Hotels are often associated with food as well as accommodation, but the provision of food services need not be part of a hotel's core activity. There are numerous examples where people buy food from associated or independent firms nearby. These include roadside lodges with nearby restaurants and the growing use of hotels with apartments.

It is also relatively easy to distinguish large hotels from bed and breakfast places, but it is difficult to draw the exact line between hotels and other short-term accommodation providers in terms of the range or quality of services provided. Roadside lodges, for instance, are competing effectively in existing and developing hotel markets. So, we look at the long-term development of the industry in terms of short-stay residential accommodation centred round tourism.

Defining and classifying tourists

Visitors to an area are usually divided into:

1. *Tourists*: those travelling away from home who stay for one night or more. They include: travellers passing through; short stay visitors; and local inhabitants who stay at a hotel after some function or event. Only about a quarter of tourist nights are spent in hotels, approximately half stay with friends and relatives and the rest stay in different types of self-catering units. The average length of stay at UK hotels varies between two and three nights according to region. Those staying in hotels have a low take-up of evening and day-time meals in the hotels.
2. *Day-trippers*: those travelling to and returning from a place within a day. The trip lasts at least three hours and excludes shopping, medical, educational and similar visits. Hotels can provide restaurant and other services, though they often have to be combined with functions such as weddings or tied in with business meetings. They may also convert trippers into tourists by providing accommodation combined with other activities, such as theatre-going. On the other hand, as transport facilities improve, people on business trips, and even non-business visitors, are becoming less inclined to stay overnight.
3. *Other day visitors*: These are unlikely to be heavy users of hotel facilities. However, in small towns and in large cities, there are many hotels that can provide food service to such visitors.

We can divide tourists into further categories where they display typically different behaviour patterns for accommodation and other services.

Purpose of visit

One useful classification is by purpose of visit. The major categories are:

1. *Business and conference travellers*: Demand comes from trade representatives, exhibitions, conferences and training requirements. Business tourism increases with the economic prosperity of the region or country *receiving* the tourists, as it attracts business people wishing to sell there. However, the conference trade also depends on competitive supply to the market and is more affected by conditions elsewhere. The advanced

industrialized countries also conduct a large amount of their foreign trade cross-trading in similar goods and services between themselves. So as foreign trade increases, the demand for business accommodation also increases.

2. *On holiday*: Holidaymakers are more likely to use cheaper accommodation, particularly self-service accommodation such as flats and cottages, than those on business. Holiday demand varies with the prosperity of the region or country *generating* the demand for tourism and the cost of holidaying in a particular location relative to its attractiveness.

3. *Visiting friends and relatives*: These visitors tend to stay more with friends and relatives and so use hotels less often. Demand is also associated with the prosperity of the originating region rather than the host region.

4. *Other or miscellaneous*: This can be a fairly large group whose demand for accommodation depends on the reason for their visit. However, changes affecting lifestyles and the standard of living affect the use of accommodation in similar (though not identical) ways.

Origins of tourists

Another useful classification is the *origin* of the tourist, as we know this affects their pattern of spending and use of accommodation. The standard categories are:

1. *local*: usually within defined administrative boundaries or within a short journey time (about an hour's car journey);
2. *regional*: from within the particular administrative region or region defined for the study, such as a particular state in the USA or a Tourist Board Region in the UK;
3. *national*: from within borders of the country being studied;
4. *international*: those coming from another state or territory.

Local, regional and national tourists are forms of domestic tourism as they take place within a country's borders. The distinction between them is a matter of convenience, based on country size and accessibility between localities. The classification can be broken down into further categories as appropriate. For instance, European and North American tourists in the UK have different requirements as regards location, activity and accommodation, and this can have significant implications for the marketing of hotels.

Trends in international tourism to the UK

Table 4.2 shows the trend in international tourism during the 1980s up to the early 1990s.

Europe still dominates international travel because there are several small but relatively prosperous countries close together that allow their residents to cross easily from one country to another. However, Europe's position is declining relative to other areas for several reasons:

Table 4.2 International tourism: Arrivals, 1980–95

	Arrivals (millions)			Average annual change %		Receipts (excluding fares) US$ 000m			Average annual change %	
	1980	1990	1995	1980–90	1990–95	1980	1990	1995	1980–90	1990–95
Europe	189.8	286.7	337.2	4.2	3.3	61.7	144.0	189.8	8.8	5.6
Americas	61.4	93.6	111.9	4.3	3.6	24.2	69.5	95.2	11.1	6.5
E. Asia/Pacific	20.9	53.1	83.6	9.8	9.5	8.5	38.8	69.3	16.4	12.3
Rest of World	15.7	25.8	34.3	5.1	5.9	7.6	12.4	16.2	5.0	5.5
World	287.8	459.2	567.0	4.8	4.3	102.0	264.7	371.7	10.0	7.0

Source: World Tourism Organization

- The nature of tourism itself, with its connotations of exploration and novelty. Europeans and North Americans have long had the income to enjoy international tourism, with Europe originally being the most accessible. We should, therefore, expect some relative decline in Europe's position. The same will apply within the various countries of Europe itself.
- The increasing income per head of Europeans, a major tourist group, which leads to them to go further afield.
- The increasing relative cost of tourism services in Europe. The most significant change has been the declining relative cost of access to distant locations, starting with the package tours to (what were at that time) lower wage areas of Europe of the 1950s and 1960s and extending to the long distance trans-oceanic flight tours of today. Technological change has been of considerable importance in these developments, reinforcing the effects of changes in relative values of tourist locations for the major tourist groups.
- The increasing income of the Pacific region, which generates more tourism within the region, especially as the infrastructure of roads and accommodation facilities develop.

Table 4.3 shows how the trends in international tourism are reflected in the numbers of visitors to the UK.

Table 4.3 Overseas visitors to the UK, by origin, 1980–95

	N. America		W. Europe		Other Areas		Total
	millions	%	millions	%	millions	%	millions
1980	2.08	16.8	7.91	63.7	2.43	19.6	12.42
1985	3.80	26.3	7.87	54.5	2.78	19.2	14.45
1990	3.69	20.5	10.75	59.7	3.58	19.9	18.01
1995	3.88	16.4	15.08	63.5	4.79	20.2	23.75

Source: Tourism Intelligence Quarterly

The long-term growth rate in visitors is about 3.8% a year, which is less than the annual 4.5% growth rate for international tourism generally. The mix of visitors by origin varies according to the level of economic activity. Longer haul visitors from North America become relatively more important when world economic conditions are improving, as in the mid-1980s and they become less important during recessionary times, such as at the beginning and end of the 1980s. However, long haul visitors have comprised a relatively stable market during the last ten years without much growth opportunity. The Western European market seems to have taken on a new spurt of growth, reflecting trends in British tourism abroad. This growth is not certain to continue as British holidaymakers start to go further afield, although they may be compensated by a growing number of tourists from Eastern Europe. As Table 4.4 shows, the proportion of visitors coming to the UK is fairly stable, with business tourism becoming more important.

Table 4.4 Reasons for visit: Overseas visitors to the UK, 1980–95

	Independent holiday		Inclusive holiday		Business		Visit friends & relatives & Miscellaneous		Total
	mn	%	mn	%	mn	%	mn	%	mn
1980	4.15	33.4	1.33	10.7	2.56	20.6	4.38	35.3	12.42
1985	4.72	32.6	1.95	13.5	3.01	20.9	4.77	33.0	14.45
1990	5.44	30.2	2.26	12.5	4.49	24.9	5.83	32.3	18.02
1995	7.16	30.1	3.26	13.7	5.83	24.5	7.50	31.6	23.75

Source: *Tourism Intelligence Quarterly* (British Tourist Authority)

There has also been a shift towards inclusive holidays, away from independent holidays. This may seem strange, as people tend to take more independent holidays as they become more familiar with a place. However, the group of visitors on an inclusive holiday is generally likely to contain a high proportion of first time visitors, who make the trip once and then holiday elsewhere. There was, for instance, a rapid growth in the number of Japanese tourists in the late 1980s, which later died back. Also a holiday need only have some linkage between travel and accommodation to count as an inclusive holiday. As these partly inclusive holidays are often significantly cheaper than a non-inclusive holiday, so we can expect them to grow in relative importance.

Tourist spending

Tourist spending has varied between 3.1% and 4.0% of GDP since 1980, as shown in Table 4.5.

The increase in the relative importance of overseas tourists in the mid-1980s and mid-1990s reflects in part the better economic conditions which encourage travel further afield, particularly by North American tourists, while better economic conditions encouraged UK residents to spend relatively more abroad.

Table 4.5 Tourism spending in the UK, 1980–95

Year	International				Domestic		All tourism	
	Excluding fares (£m)	% all tourism	Including fares (£m)	% all tourism	(£m)	(£m)	% consumer spending	(%) GDP
1980	2,961	35.6	3,753	45.2	4,550	8,303	6.0	3.6
1985	5,442	41.4	6,817	51.9	6,325	13,142	6.0	3.7
1990	7,785	38.4	9,810	48.4	10,460	20,270	5.8	3.7
1995	11,885	42.9	14,910	53.9	12,775	27,685	6.2	4.0

Source: *Tourism Intelligence Quarterly* (British Tourist Authority)

The changing mix of tourists

The same variability is seen in spending by tourists according to their origin, as shown in Table 4.6.

Table 4.6 Earnings from overseas visitors to the UK, by origin, 1980–95

	N. America		W. Europe		Other Areas		Total
	£m	% total	£m	% total	£m	% total	£m
1980	509	17.2	1,248	42.1	1,204	40.7	2,961
1985	1,709	31.4	1,823	33.5	1,911	35.1	5,442
1990	1,944	25.0	3,338	42.9	2,503	32.2	7,785
1995	2,370	19.9	5,362	45.1	4,152	34.9	11,885

Source: *Tourism Intelligence Quarterly* (British Tourist Authority)

The differences in spending patterns is important because of the variability of tourist origins, as shown in Table 4.3. Note that the shift in tourism from the higher spending North American visitors towards the lower spending West Europeans is not fully compensated for by the increase in tourists from further afield. We should also note that spending by North American tourists is moving more in line with their number, indicating a switch to less expensive trips.

As Table 4.7 shows, foreign and domestic tourists spend their tourism money differently, but their spending on food and accommodation are converging, as we would expect from the growth in tourists from nearby Europe.

Changes in tourism by UK residents

It should be noted that much of the data on UK residents' tourism are gathered from tourist board surveys. The nature of the surveys means that we should treat the data with caution. There were also significant changes to the surveys in 1984 and 1989 which makes comparison over longer periods less reliable.

Table 4.7 Tourist expenditure pattern (%), 1991–95

	Foreign (%)		Domestic (%)		All tourists (%)	
	1991	1995	1991	1995	1991	1995
Accommodation	32.3	36.1	36.0	37.0	34.9	35.5
Eating out	22.5	22.0	25.0	24.0	24.1	23.5
Shopping	27.1	24.5	13.0	14.0	18.9	18.9
Other	18.1	17.4	26.0	25.0	22.1	22.0
Total	100.0	100.0	100.0		100.0	

Source: Tourism Intelligence Quarterly (British Tourist Authority)

Table 4.8 shows the long-term trend in UK residents' tourism.

Table 4.8 Tourism by UK residents

	UK total			Non-UK total			All tourism		
	Trips Mn	Nights Mn	Nights per trip	Trips Mn	Nights Mn	Nights per trip	Trips Mn	Nights Mn	Nights per trip
1973	132	590	4.5	11.7	165	14.1	143.7	755	5.3
1974	114	535	4.7	10.8	145	13.4	124.8	680	5.4
1979	118	525	4.4	15.5	205	13.2	133.5	730	5.5
1980	130	550	4.2	17.6	228	13.0	147.6	778	5.3
1993	90.9	375.9	4.1	23.6	253.3	10.7	114.0	629.2	5.5
1994	109.8	416.5	3.8	27.5	287.8	10.5	136.7	704.4	5.2

Source: Tourism Intelligence Quarterly; British Tourist Authority.

Table 4.8 includes pairs of adjacent years to show the volatility of tourism as the economy fluctuates. These data indicate long-term trends, although they do not tell the whole story, especially the full effects of booms and slumps in the economy. However, they show that the large increase in income per head over the period has not increased the number of trips or the number of nights per trip. There has, however, been a shift away from UK tourism towards foreign tourism, even discounting the increase in international business tourism during this period. As Table 4.9 shows, there has been a substantial increase in long (four or more nights) holidays abroad, while the average spending per night abroad is more than twice that in the UK.

Table 4.9 Long holidays* in Britain and abroad: Adults and accompanying children

	Number of Holidays (millions)					Holiday Spending (£m)				
	Britain		Abroad		Total	UK		Abroad		Total
	Mn	%	Mn.	%	Mn.	£m	%	£m	%	£m
1980	36.50	75.3	12.00	24.7	48.50	2,420	40.8	3,510	59.2	5,930
1986	31.50	64.3	17.50	35.7	49.00	3,050	31.2	6,740	68.9	9,790
1994	32.00	59.5	21.75	40.5	53.75	4,450	26.7	12,220	73.3	16,670

Source: Tourism Intelligence Quarterly (British Tourist Authority)
*Long holidays are defined here as 4 or more nights

The growth in consumer income, however, is an important economic factor in these changes:

Growing consumer income has increased consumer tourism

For many decades, consumers have been taking part of their increases in income in the form of more leisure, either as a shorter working day or week or as more holidays a year. Since the 1980s, in the UK, the working week has not changed substantially, if anything it has increased, but the average number of days holiday per year has been increasing.

As women have increased the amount of time they spend working, household income per head has increased significantly more than leisure time. This increases the relative cost of time and encourages consumers to reduce the time-intensity of their activities. They do this by switching to relatively more expensive activities, such as tourism, where they spend more money per day of leisure. So, although the percentage of people taking holidays is fairly constant, the average number of days holiday per head has increased significantly since the 1980s.

There has also been a substantial number of workers, particularly men, taking early retirement. Although their incomes have fallen, these people are at a stage of their lives where they enjoy lower levels of financial commitment and more freedom, resulting in a new leisure market, although with a different time–money combination.

Growing consumer income has increased the number of holiday trips and reduced the average length of a holiday

The time spent on a particular holiday, like other activities, is subject to *diminishing marginal utility* (Chapter 1). As the cost of an extra day is likely to be relatively constant, holidaymakers will restrict the length of any given holiday. This is true even if tour companies offer only a fixed number of alternatives, such as seven- or fourteen-day holidays. Holidaymakers will then take an extra holiday rather than increase the number of days spent on existing holidays. This accounts for the significant increase in second holidays and extra short breaks.

Growing consumer income has encouraged consumers to go on more distant and more active holidays

Consumers have also increased their participation in activity holidays, reflecting the opportunity to spend more in relation to time. Also, second holidays tend to have a different character from the first, again reflecting the diminishing marginal utility of time spent in any particular type of activity. Each trip incurs a certain level of fixed costs, so that taking more holidays increases the amount of spending in a given time. Going further afield is an easy way of increasing expenditure per day, even though these extra holidays tend to be relatively cheaper. For instance, in 1991, UK residents spent on average £37 per night, but £26 per night for trips within the UK and £55 per night for trips outside the UK . By 1994 these figures had changed to an average of £44 per night, with £35 per night in the UK and £64 per night abroad (*Tourism Intelligence Quarterly*). The narrowing of the gap occurs because there has been increased spending per night on domestic holidays in real terms and static spending per night abroad. These changes partly reflect the move towards more active domestic holidays and more frequent, and so relatively cheaper, holidays abroad.

Tourist use of hotels

Consumer tourism

As the data in Table 4.10 indicate, there has been some switching from staying with friends and relatives, but hotels have become relatively less important than self-catering accommodation.

Table 4.10 Accommodation used (%), British holidays* in Britain

	1984	1985	1991	1992
Serviced accommodation (Hotel/Motel/Guest house)	28	33	30	30
Friends/Relatives	24	23	19	20
Self-catering	45	49	53	53
Total	103	103	103	104[†]

Source: Tourism Intelligence Quarterly, 1993 (British Tourist Authority)
*4 or more nights
[†]Total exceeds 100% because more than one type may be used

However, Table 4.11 also suggests that people are more likely to use hotels on second holidays, largely because of the reduced use of holiday camps.

Table 4.11 Accommodation used, British holidays* in Britain,1992

Accommodation	Percentage using on	
	Main holiday	Additional holiday
Hotels	24	26
Holiday camps	12	7
Friends/relatives	17	24
Other	53	47
Total	106	104

Source: Tourism Intelligence Quarterly (British Tourist Authority)
*4 or more nights

There are similar trends in holiday tourism abroad as shown in Table 4.12. We can explain these trends by the effect of economic growth on the relative user cost (Chapter 3) of hotel accommodation:

Table 4.12 Type of accommodation used (%), holidays abroad of 1+ nights

	1984	1985	1991	1992
Serviced accommodation (Hotel/motel/boarding house)	66	62	54	54
Friends/relatives	17	18	20	18
Self-catering	25	29	38	38
Total	108	109	112	110

Source: Tourism Intelligence Quarterly (British Tourist Authority)

Economic growth raises the price of serviced accommodation relative to unserviced accommodation

Serviced accommodation is more labour-intensive than unserviced accommodation and will remain so unless the provision of meals and other services provided become considerably more capital intensive. The general upward trend of wage rates will be reinforced by increasing time-sensitivity as alternative employment makes people less willing to work unsocial hours. Hotel operators may mitigate some of the price increases by increasing the capital-intensity of operations. This, however, reduces the value of the services offered and still represents an effective price increase to the consumer. Thus the user cost of hotels relative to unserviced accommodation increases.

Economic growth increases the time costs of hotel consumption relative to that of unserviced accommodation

Consumers are increasing the degree of active leisure, including holidays, particularly associated with the use of the car. The demand for holiday accommodation services becomes increasingly ancillary to activities and the demand for different types of holiday accommodation varies with income and total user cost, including time costs. The activities pursued may require greater flexibility in time, place and variety of eating and resting than can be provided for by hotels. Hotels, on the other hand, are under pressure to save labour by cutting down on slack time in operations and concentrating on a limited range of services or those geared to specific parts of the day. This makes self-catering more attractive as advances in food-processing, storage and regeneration make them available on a small scale. Consumers increase the use of restaurants and takeaways that are more conveniently situated in time and space.

The costs of adjusting from any activity to eating will make time constraints more keenly felt and reinforce changes in behaviour. Consequently, people will use accommodation more frequently, particularly for short breaks, but they will tend to use it more simply.

Consumers upgrade the accommodation used

The purchase of tourist accommodation is not really different from that of any other product. Consumers upgrade their expectations from accommodation in line with their standard of living and lifestyle, except for that associated with adventure, outdoor activity or other unusual physical activity. However, improving quality is rather costly and subject to diminishing marginal utility, so that there will be a limit to how far they will be prepared to go. Consumers would rather pay for good accommodation that is more in keeping with their lifestyle than pay for supposedly luxurious accommodation which is inconsistent with their lifestyle. This can be seen in the quality improvements in UK hotels from the 1970s onwards where en suite facilities and improved basic facilities have been the norm rather than excessive luxury.

More even loading of consumption

Accommodation services are a constantly available but non-storable product. The continuing pattern of high and low demand requires large amounts of capital stock that are used only in the peak period and are under-utilized at other times. This puts increasing cost pressures on operations and raises the price at peak demand periods. So producers and consumers have had to adapt to even the loading on facilities. Hotels have had to improve their load-pricing techniques to encourage off-peak use of facilities: cheap weekend break packages encourage non-business demand; and off-season conference and other offers to organizations encourage business demand.

Consumers have also changed their consumption patterns. An increase in income increases the amount of holidays taken. However, it also increases the relative cost of an extra day's stay. The *marginal utility* or extra value of another day's holiday is usually declining for anything other than a short stay. Beyond a certain point, consumers find it relatively more satisfactory to switch the extra day to a second holiday where the relative value is higher. The marginal utility of a holiday declines as the number of days increases, so that people can increase their satisfaction by spreading holidays over the year. The relatively high price of hotels has encouraged them to holiday abroad or use other accommodation in the summer, while a cheaper package cost has encouraged them to use hotel holidays in the off-season. There has also been a growing business base to hotel usage which is more evenly spread throughout the year. These factors help explain the changing occupancy pattern for English hotels and is illustrated in Table 4.13 for the twenty-year period 1972–91. The period has been divided into two sub-periods of ten years each to even out the effect of booms and recessions in the economy on occupancy levels.

The average for the month during each ten-year period is calculated as a simple average of figures for the month. We should not be too precise about the details, because there are problems with the accuracy and compatibility of the data used. However, the data show a definite levelling out of demand over the year. There has been a shift away from hotels in the peak season, but the off-peak months from October to April, except January, all show large increases in occupancy and the shoulder months of May, June and September have levelled off. The trend seems to be continuing into the 1990s. During the four-year period 1992–95, average annual room occupancy fell by over five percentage points, probably because of the effects of the recession.

Table 4.13 Monthly room occupancy, England 1972–91

Month	1972–81			1982–91			Av. 72–81 − Av. 82–91
	Low	High	Average	Low	High	Average	
Jan	31	41	37.5	31	44	37.7	0.2
Feb	37	45	41.6	37	50	45.5	3.9
Mar	39	48	45.3	42	53	49.5	4.2
Apr	44	55	48.3	42	58	51.8	3.5
May	48	61	55.6	48	61	56.7	1.1
Jun	53	70	63.8	56	68	63.7	−0.1
Jul	56	76	70.6	60	71	67.3	−3.3
Aug	63	78	72.4	64	69	67.3	−5.1
Sep	62	75	69.9	63	74	70.3	0.4
Oct	49	61	56.8	50	67	61.5	4.7
Nov	40	49	45.9	41	57	51.3	5.4
Dec	31	39	36.1	32	45	41.3	5.2
Year	46	57	53.4	47	60	55.7	2.3

Source: English Hotel Occupancy Survey (English Tourist Board; BDO Hospitality Consulting)

However, the months from May to September showed falls of between four and seven percentage points, while the period October to April showed falls of between two and six percentage points.

Community hotels

The large amounts of capital invested in land and buildings often results in the under-utilization of certain facilities at various times during the week or year. Other facilities can also be added relatively cheaply, such as dining rooms, meeting rooms and ballrooms, because a significant part of the cost of building them separately has already been included in the building of the hotel. This allows hotels to provide extra services to the local community. Location on or by main routes helps hotels serve tourists effectively. It also provides accessibility for the local community and improves competitiveness. One such area of development has been in leisure provision, such as health and indoor sports activities. These require significant, but relatively small, static space requirements, but can be used flexibly through different pricing structures so that their use is spread over the day.

CASE STUDY: NO LEISURE, NO HOTEL

Vaux Group, the Sunderland-based brewer, owns the well-established Swallow hotel chain. The group has 35 mid-market, business-oriented hotels. The company has embarked on a programme of upgrading and disposal to keep its product up to date. In January 1996 it put five of its Swallow hotels up for sale: those in Darlington, Doncaster, East Kilbride, Newcastle-upon-Tyne and Wakefield.

According to Peter Catesby, managing director of Swallow Hotels, the hotels were all profitable, but were being sold because they do not have leisure clubs and they are unable to have leisure facilities attached to them. Proceeds of the sale would fund two new hotels, one in Liverpool and one near Huntingdon.

Source: Scheherazade Daneshkhu, UK Company News: Vaux To Sell Five Swallow Hotels, *Financial Times*, 1 February 1996, p. 26.

THE EATING OUT SECTOR

Trends in eating out

Spending on food in the UK increases as income per head increases, but the proportion of income spent on food declines (the income elasticity of demand for food is less than one). (This occurs in other countries as well and illustrates Engel's law , named after the nineteenth-century statistician who propounded it.) This is illustrated in Figure 4.1.

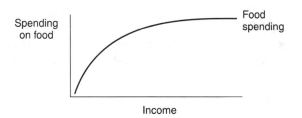

Figure 4.1 Variation in food consumption with income

The consumer increases his spending faster than physical consumption of broad commodity ranges, such as meat, fruit, vegetables. He pays a higher price per unit:

- for better or more desirable items, such as steak instead of mince; or
- for more value-added service in convenience foods that require relatively simple finishing processes for him to complete.

The growth of eating out

The proportion of income spent on eating out in the UK has remained fairly constant at about 3.5–4%, but it increased from 16% to 20% of food expenditure between 1978 and the early 1990s, despite the recession (Payne and Payne, 1993). An explanation for this can be found in the changes in household activity and technology that have followed the substantial growth in productivity and real wages in the industrial economy since the 1950s.

Women have increased their labour force participation: more of them now go out to work and they work for more hours a week than twenty years ago

(Chapter 3). This is particularly true for women in their child-bearing and child-raising years. However, men have not reduced their working hours to spend more time on household tasks, which makes time scarcer for the traditional household. The large increase in the number of people living alone also increases time scarcity, because there is no one to share household tasks with. Consequently, households have moved away from time-intensive patterns of consumption. They avoid the more complicated or inconvenient tasks of preparing meals at home by eating out more, buying in ready meals (from food stores) or having meals delivered (Chapter 3). This means that:

- eating out becomes much more of a convenience than a social activity;
- people eat out more simply;
- sales of fast food and delivered meals increase faster than sales of traditional cafe and restaurant meals;
- the continuing developments in format and technology maintain the early technological lead of the USA in fast food and other eating concepts, as other countries also move towards simpler eating processes;
- the suburbanization of resaurants increases in response to the need for convenience eating.

Patterns of eating out

There have also been significant changes in the frequency and distribution of eating out, as shown in Table 4.14, based on data from the National Food Survey.

Table 4.14 Meals eaten outside the home (per person per week), 1979–90

	Meals per person per week				Percentage change	
	1979	1980	1989	1990	1979–89	1980–90
Lunch	1.81	1.77	1.89	1.93	4.4	9.9
Other meals	1.39	1.46	1.95	1.83	40.2	25.32
Total	3.20	3.23	3.84	3.76	20.0	16.4

Source: Cullen, 1994 from National Food Survey

The table illustrates three important facets of eating out:

- The long-term trend is upward.
- The lunchtime market has grown only slowly – probably reflecting the slowly increasing participation of women in the workforce over this period. However, the substantial increase in other meals out reflects social changes caused by the changing income and household activity structure.
- There are significant fluctuations about this trend as income fluctuates over the economic cycle. Data are given for two overlapping ten-year periods in order to reduce the effect of economic fluctuations (Table 4.14). Not unexpectedly, the 1990 recession had a bigger impact on non-lunch meals.

Changes in the type of meal eaten out

Changes in lifestyles have meant that eating out has become integrated into the whole pattern of food production and consumption. A household changes its meal pattern and structure to avoid expensive time costs, which can vary at specific times, and market purchase costs. For instance, breakfasts have changed as eating habits within the home have become simpler to save time, organizational and technical ability. This slows down the growth of the breakfast market and also shapes the way the market will develop. Younger, more active and time-conscious people will follow the American trend for snatch-and-go, hurry-to-work early morning breakfasts, while the more leisured, older customer will go for more substantial breakfasts or brunches later on in the morning.

Choice, search and experimentation

The way we behave and what we do depends on the interaction of our preferences (or tastes) – what we would like to do – and our resource constraints such as income and relative prices of products – that limit what we can do. Preferences are conditioned by social groups, who often behave according to habits that reflect the way they have adapted to the resources generally available to them. However, as a society we believe that our welfare can be improved by searching for new ways to organize our activities and experimenting with the new or improved products or services that become available. So we can also expect *changes in* taste as people engage in search activity. For instance, new knowledge may also affect our preferences, as with the case with red meat in the diet. However, our taste changes will depend on:

- *The extent of the information gathering process undertaken*. However, the amount of time and money we spend on searching for new ways of organizing our lives depends on how valuable we expect the new information to be, although this is something we can never truly know beforehand.
- *Our attitudes towards change*. If we are reluctant to change, we react to changing conditions by trying to assimilate them to some pre-existing model. On the other hand, we can look forward, proactively adapting our existing lifestyle to some new model.
- *Switching costs of changing old habits*. These switching costs are greater for older individuals and more traditional households, because they have large amounts of unexhausted physical and psychological capital tied up in their existing consumption patterns. Young people, however, do not have these problems and so are more likely to experiment with new ideas and be readier to change their eating habits.
- *The state of the economy and expectations about the future* as this affects people's willingness to experiment. Economic optimism, as in the boom of the mid-1980s, encourages people to improve consumption by

increasing value relative to cost through new ways of consumption. Economic pessimism, as in the early 1990s, encourages people to look for cost reductions in existing consumption, since the return is likely to be greater, with the release of resources for extra consumption elsewhere.

However, many of the *apparent* changes in tastes can be explained better by changes in incomes and the relative prices of products that have affected consumer lifestyles.

The perishability of meals out and the time-sensitivity of the services means that eating out becomes more expensive (Winston, 1982). In order to keep cost increases down, firms reorganize production to reduce the time-sensitivity of the service provided. Consumers, on the other hand, respond by reducing their dependence on the catering market by using domestic capital to reduce the time-intensity of food consumption or by using complementary or convenience products. Technical progress has made smaller and cheaper units of capital available and reduced the scale of production required for its efficient use. We see this in the declining real prices and improved performances of domestic food storage and processing equipment, such as freezers and microwaves. It has also improved the manufacture and supply of complementary processed food (such as ready prepared meat portions and sauces), reducing both the time and skill required to produce a basic range of meals. Consumers can increase the range of easily-prepared meals at home – from burgers in a bun with chips to complex ready meals – fairly conveniently.

Caterers must therefore develop products that reflect those time-intensive activities that can done cheaply on a large scale or use skills that exceed the consumers' own abilities.

Consumers still want to eat simply, however in terms of time and convenience, and this increases the relative importance of snacks, sandwiches and American-style fast food. Catering firms must constantly reassess their products in the market to reflect these factors and provide customers with the variety they require by continually upgrading the kind and complexity of the meals they provide.

EXAMPLE 4.1

'Between 1986 and 1990 the hamburger sector of the fast food sector increased its market share from 17% to 21%, while pizza/pasta increased its market share from 5% to 14%. Fish and chips, Chinese and Indian suffered a decline in their share' (*source: Caterer & Hotelkeeper*, 7 Nov. 1991, pps 36–39).

This quote reflects changing consumer technology. As consumers want variety, they upgrade their catering purchases to relatively more complex products (such as pizzas). However, the time and convenience factors weigh against producers with inappropriate locations or methods of production.

EXAMPLE 4.2

Garage shops have developed a market in hand-held hot snacks. These snacks use simple finishing processes to provide the consumer with a product that appears complex to make.

EXAMPLE 4.3

Supply changes have emphasized low cost standardization with easy on-site differentiation, as provided by hamburger, pizza and sandwich bars. However, even hamburger restaurants have had to adapt and provide alternatives such as chicken (although in a compromised form as chicken burgers and nuggets) and pizza.

We can also expect *changes in tastes* as people engage in search activity. Changes in tastes depend on the three factors:

Individualism in eating out

Over the longer term, household structures change to enable the household to access various activities more effectively. Households produce goods and services, such as meals, at home as an alternative to buying them in the market. As market opportunities expand, individuals reduce their commitment to activities, such as home production of household-specific goods and services. Instead, they increase their market consumption. However, competitive, technically advanced, well developed markets are oriented to individual, impersonal transactions. We do not buy chunks of meat that take a long time to prepare for a large family group. Instead, we buy meat that has been conveniently prepared by modern production processes that turn them out in small, individualized quantities. In this sense, household-centred consumption loses the relative advantages of bulk purchase and so becomes increasingly expensive. This makes eating out relatively cheaper.

However, modern technology and changing relative costs also individualize consumption activity. Eating out does not provide significant economies of scale, and so the incentives towards cellularization of household members is particularly strong in relation to eating patterns This allows the autonomy of tastes to develop. This, in turn, allows mealtimes to be incidental to other activities for individual members of households. With increasing and more diverse leisure opportunities, for instance, eating together may impose unacceptably costly time constraints (Cullen, 1994).

The growth of the family market

As there is less time and incentive for preparing meals and eating them together at home, there is a reappraisal of family living. As women go out to work more, time becomes increasingly scarce for the household as a collective unit and the wife increases her demand for more direct leisure time in the market. However, the household must maintain the intangible but real economic benefits of family activity. Consequently, the household reorganizes through joint function activities such as increased leisure shopping and family meal consumption in restaurants or takeaways/home deliveries. These meet both needs by increasing the proportion of time in communal activity both directly as an end in itself and indirectly as a family activity-related event. In spite of the move towards individualism, food provision in pubs, fast food and roadside catering recognizes the increasing importance of family eating out.

Food courts provide for the predetermined choices of individuals in a particular environment and allows for differences within groups. They are also useful because they provide places for mass randomization of experiments.

Another factor in changing food patterns is the relative power positions of the individuals in the household. Economic analysis has usually treated household decision-making as unitary, but recent studies have questioned this. For instance, Browning *et al.* (1994) show that the wife's share in household expenditure depends on her relative market earnings and age. This supports the view that the more a woman works in the market, the more she wants to organize her time in the market.

We can extend this view to the role of children in spending. According to Becker *et al.* (1977), the cost of family specific investment, including children, increases with wage rates. In advanced economies, people do not need to invest in children as a way of transferring resources to their old age. So people must decide to have children for consumption purposes, in effect for the stream of psychic benefits they provide. If people continue to have children despite their increasing cost, then children must also be increasing their contribution to the family. This increases the relative bargaining power or 'pester power' of the child. This is particularly so at school leaving age, since this raises the cost (and so the value) of maintaining a child in the family home.

The combination of these factors increases the degree of individualism in the household and in particular in eating out. So where family eating out is increasing, it will be increasingly child-centred.

Social and convenience eating

Social eating may be seen as an end in itself, where the meal serves as a focal point for an occasional social gathering. It is often seen as a luxury item related to restaurant usage. Convenience eating, on the other hand, consists of meals and snacks that enable more time and effort to be spent on earning money or engaging in other leisure activities. It is usually identified with fast food and other popular catering, so that the more rapid growth of fast food and its increasing share of the market indicates a trend towards convenience eating.

However it is difficult to maintain that distinction between social and convenience eating as people increasingly eat out as part of their normal weekly or monthly routine. In such cases even restaurant meals can largely be for convenience. For instance, Frisbee and Madeira (1986) applied Becker's theory of household activity to show that Canadian dual income couples used restaurants more for convenience than as a luxury (or for social purposes). They predicted that behaviour would vary with the level of *earned income* (from employment and self-employment) and *unearned income* (from investments). When earnings from employment rise, the cost of time spent in meal preparation also rises. Time becomes increasingly expensive and couples spend proportionately more to save time. If people were using restaurants for convenience (time-saving), they would spend a greater *proportion* of their income on eating in restaurants as their earned income rises. On the other hand, an increase in unearned income reduces the relative importance of time saving in relation to work activities and so we would expect the proportion of income spent on eating in restaurants to fall. The results of their study showed that dual-income couples were eating out in restaurants for convenience rather than as a luxury.

In practice, we can regard social eating as eating out that is not connected with any specific activity. However, there are two different kinds: formal social eating – indicated by dressing up – and informal social eating – indicated by not dressing up.

Formal social eating is more often undertaken by the older age groups, who eat out as part of a planned routine that only slowly adjusts with changing circumstances, such as income levels or the general price of eating out. Older people are not as active in seeking new information and balance new information against the force of habit, which result from income and expenditure information gathered earlier in life.

Informal social eating, on the other hand, is associated mainly with the younger age group. This group are more market oriented and make greater use of eating out and home delivery in planning total food. This accounts for a significant amount of the increase in meals out, but it is not readily distinguishable from convenience eating.

As households and individuals reduce the time-intensity of their activities, they reduce their demand (in relative terms) for formal social eating. Changes in household structure have adversely affected young people's ability to cook and they find it inconvenient (financially or timewise) to prepare meals at home. So they tend to use home delivery for social eating.

These trends mean that most eating out is activity-related 'convenience eating'. However, what the customer wants and how he or she behaves varies with the type of activity, because the relative cost of time varies with the time of day. Also, convenience and social (sometimes family) elements can be mixed, as, for example, in shopping trips, where important leisure activities are also social occasions.

THE DRINKS SECTOR

Drinking behaviour

Trends in drinks consumption

Marketing activity and social behaviour identify three main categories of drinks, with their sub-categories:

1. alcoholic drinks: including beer and lager; cider and perry; wines; spirits;
2. soft drinks: fruit juices; carbonated drinks (such as lemonade); bottled water;
3. hot drinks: tea; coffee; food drinks.

The physical consumption of drinks has remained fairly steady in the UK at about 1.65 litres (3 pints) per head per day (Key Note, *Drinking Habits*, 1994). This, of course refers to marketed drinks. It does not include ordinary tap water, because the consumer does not pay according to the amount consumed. We cannot measure physical consumption accurately, but the data suggest that our physical requirements are fairly limited.

Spending on drinks, on the other hand, has increased in real terms, though to a lesser extent than consumer spending generally. For instance, drinks still accounted for 8.8% of the consumer budget in 1993 compared with 9.5% in 1980, despite an increase of 25% in consumer spending in real terms. This contrasts sharply with the decline in the proportion of the consumer budget spent on food over the same period. This implies that the consumer has been switching to more highly valued or more costly packaged drinks, in accordance with the changing work and leisure activities of society.

Table 4.15 gives data on spending adjusted for organizational and foreign tourist spending.

Table 4.15 Total spending on drinks (£m): UK 1980–93

UK consumer spending	1980		1993	
	At current prices (£m)	% of drink spending	At current prices (£m)	% of drink spending
Beer	5,320	41	13,835	39
Spirits and other alcohol	4,635	36	11,850	33
Total alcohol	**9,955**	**77**	**25,685**	**72**
Soft drinks	1,556	12	7,240	20
Hot drinks	1,489	11	2,600	7
UK consumer	**13,000**	**100**	**35,525**	**100**
Total UK market	14,500		39,500	

Source: Key Note, *UK Drinking Habits*, 1994.
Note: Households consistently understate their spending on alcohol in the government's Family Expenditure Survey, where selected households record their expenditure in diaries over a monthly period. As a result, alcohol consumption is based on customs and excise data. Market research organizations supplement these data by their own research.

Factors affecting drinks consumption

Physiological and dietary factors affect the total amount of fluids consumed, and the availability of plain tap water may affect demand. However, consumption patterns are affected by changes in demand and supply factors. Demand has been affected by changes in age, social grouping, household work and leisure. Supply has been affected by changes in technology, the relative prices of inputs and the political environment.

- Changes in population size and structure affect total consumption over a longer period of time. The UK population is slowly increasing and will therefore not have much effect. The structure, however, has been changing towards an older population with a higher proportion of retired people. This reduces the demand for alcohol, particularly beer, because of the lower consumption of this product by this group.
- The market for hot drinks is associated with fairly specific activities: domestic life, work-related consumption and longer-distance travel, especially by car. Time constraints and relative inconvenience limit the consumer willingness to purchase. These present no real competition for alcoholic drinks.
- Traditional alcoholic consumption is increasingly inconsistent with modern lifestyles, particularly in relation to driving. The increased enforcement of prohibitive legislation exerts a downward pressure on demand.
- Soft drinks are associated with domestic and leisure activities. They are generally preferred to alcoholic drinks by younger, more active adults (Key Note, *Drinking Habits*, 1994). The rising importance of leisure pursuits undertaken away from home also encourages soft drinks expenditure because of the convenience element. The relative prices of the more expensive convenience-size containers may be falling through improved technology and competition, particularly in relation to hot drinks. Although social groups CDE drink more beer, their basic preference is for soft drinks or wine. Higher income managerial and professional groups also prefer wine and soft drinks (see Key Note, *Drinking Habits*, 1994).
- Drinking patterns are affected by their position as social markers. Internationalization and differentiation will be more readily accepted by the younger age groups and by the more affluent.

Alcohol consumption

Alcohol has always been an important part of food and drink consumption. During the last thirty years its value has grown significantly. It now accounts for one in every sixteen pounds of consumer spending. Meanwhile the proportion spent on food has fallen to just over three times the spending on alcohol.

Beer has historically been the dominant drink in the UK. It is still the major alcoholic drink and accounts for over half the consumption by volume of alcohol. However, the beer market has been static or in decline since the 1950s, with only some moderate increases in consumption during certain periods. This is confirmed by the data on quantity consumed in Table 4.16. However, it should be noted that percentage changes in consumption must be considered approximate because

1. the data are subject to error;
2. different alcoholic strengths may make totals from different categories misleading.

Table 4.16 Alcohol consumption in UK 1980–92

	Consumption (litres per head)		
	1980	1992	Percentage change
Beer	147.2	127.0	−14
Spirits (at 40%)	5.6	4.6	−18
Cider and perry	5.1	9.4	84
Wine	10.2	16.5	62
Total	168.1	157.5	−6

Source: adapted from Key Note, *UK Drinking Habits* 1994.

The beer market itself has changed, with traditional mild beer becoming almost obsolete. Its share of the draught beer market fell from 60% in 1960 to 10% in 1990. It has, in effect, been replaced by lager, which, according to Key Note, accounted for only 1% of beer sales by volume in 1962, but 33% in 1982 and 51% in 1992.

Until fairly recently, beer used to be drunk mainly by males in a very large number of male-oriented, drink-dominated public houses or pubs, with a smaller provision from hotels and clubs and off-licences. However, the considerable socio-economic changes of recent decades have led to significant changes in the market and led to the growth of female and family markets. Moreover, an increasing proportion has been bought through off-licences and supermarkets for home consumption. Wine is also increasingly drunk at home and is strongly associated with meals.

Another significant trend is that spending on alcohol has been growing more slowly than on soft drinks. This implies that the place of alcohol in the growing leisure market and in the wider socio-economic functioning of society is limited.

Drinking out and drinking in

Drinking out, particularly as regards alcoholic consumption, has chiefly been a social activity. As such it has been affected by the same fundamental change in social and leisure activity, at home and elsewhere, that has affected the rest of the hospitality industry.

Pubs and alcohol

Public houses, or pubs, are a recognized social institution providing mainly for social drinking. As Key Note (*Public Houses*, 1996) point out, they are not formally defined. 1995 industry estimates put the number of pubs between 51,000 and 65,000 out of 82,000 holders of full on-licences that allow customers to drink on the premises.

Pubs have been the main outlet for the sale of alcohol, particularly beer. In turn, the main product of pubs has been the sale of alcohol, particularly beer, for consumption on the premises. The consumption of alcohol has been increasing, but the consumption of beer is static. This has meant that the pub sector has seen the decline of its traditional product without necessarily being able to latch into the newer consumer demands.

The long-term lack of growth in the beer market has encouraged the pub sector to develop alternative sources of revenue, especially gaming and food service. The food service element has been helped by the availability of longer opening hours in the 1990s. The change in the law was itself a response to the longer term changes in consumer lifestyles which required greater flexibility in services provision.

- The increase in income per head has produced more leisure opportunities. Consumers are also searching for more efficient and effective ways of spending leisure. They increasingly see drinking as a means to social activity rather than as a social activity in itself. Social drinking becomes increasingly secondary to other leisure activities, increasing the diversity of locations for consumption.
- The increased economic activity of women has meant that they want to increase their leisure participation in the market. So traditional drinking places have to become less male-oriented in order to provide for the new market.
- The increased relative scarcity of time has meant that family households, particularly young ones, require a greater amount of communal leisure activity. This is forcing a change in the mix of traditional drinking places, with a greater proportion of them accommodating children and becoming activity-oriented.

The basic desire for alcohol can be satisfied by drinking at home. Technical improvements in canning and the labour intensity of hospitality services is increasing the relative cost of drinks in pubs, clubs, bars and cafes, as shown in Table 4.17. This in turn encourages the growth of off-site drinking outlets, as shown in Table 4.18.

The figures presented in Tables 4.17 and 4.18 indicate a relative decrease in supply. Home consumption is also encouraged by the increasing relative cost of entertainment and the ability of the household to produce its own in-home entertainment. This is indicated by, for instance, the large number of hours spent watching television. This is itself a consequence of the significant cost of the capital equipment involved and the high initial cost of channel rental (for satellite and cable television) and the low marginal cost of watching programmes.

Table 4.17 Retail prices of alcoholic drinks (1987 = 100)

| | On-trade prices | | Off-trade prices | | | | |
	Beer	Wines and Spirits	Beer	Wines and spirits	Catering	Entertainment and recreation	All items
Jan 1987	100	100	100	100	100	100	100
Jan 1990	119.9	116.1	111.9	109.8	121.2	128.8	119.5
Jan 1993	158.2	151.6	137.5	139.5	151.7	174.4	137.9

Source: Key Note, *UK Public Houses*, 1994.

Table 4.18 Percentage (%) on- and off-licence sales (volume)

	On-sales of beer (%)	Off-sales of beer (%)
1987	82	18
1995	71	29

Source: Key Note, *UK Public Houses*; Breweries and the Beer Market, 1996

The response of consumers clearly shows that the hospitality industry is seen as a means to recreation rather than an end recreation in itself. A longer term threat, however, to the on-licence market of pubs, clubs and bars is that people's current consumption patterns are at variance with their preferences according to a Gallup Survey carried out for Key Note (Key Note, *UK Drinking Habits*, 1994). When allowed to state multiple preferences (in a rather loose sense of the term), soft drinks and white wine come out ahead of lager, bitter and spirits, among almost all age groups and social classes. In order to show the intensity of preferences and to give a more balanced view of preferences, Table 4.19 shows aggregated stated preferences.

Table 4.19 Drinks preferences, % stating a preference, aggregated

	All Adults	Men	Women	16–24	25–34	35–44	45–64	AB	C1	C2	DE
Soft drink or mineral water	65	56	73	76	73	64	56	84	76	59	51
White or red wine	63	56	63	50	74	76	66	91	79	57	40
Lager, bitter, cider, stout	75	95	45	93	97	81	59	79	80	75	66
Spirits	54	24	48	54	56	54	59	63	62	46	52

Source: Derived from Key Note, *UK Drinking Habits*, 1994

Any distortion is towards preferences for beer and spirits, but the message remains the same. The concept of pubs as beer drinking places is getting out of date. There is obviously a strong beer and spirit market, but there is a considerable latent demand for pubs as places of refreshment that need not depend on beer drinking. This suggests that different types of public house product need to be explored for the future and can also partly explain the trend away from pubs. In addition, the continuance of the majority of pubs as beer-centred depends on the maintenance of a macho culture, as even a high proportion of lower class beer drinkers are capable of switching habits. It is also consistent with the 'alcopop' explosion, which allows young people in particular to indulge their preferences for soft drinks and alcohol together.

Pub trade

The traditional role of pubs as primarily drinking establishments is unlikely to be affected for quite some time; but the sector has been affected by the ongoing socio-economic trends referred to. There has been a significant and substantial increase in food service in pubs and pub restaurants, as shown in Table 4.20.

Table 4.20 Food and alcoholic drink as percentage of pub sales

	1982	1993
Alcoholic drink	77	69
Food and refreshments	16	25
Other	17	16

Source: Key Note Report: *Public Houses*, 1994

Rising incomes have increased the consumption of wines rather than beer. In turn, the growth of wine consumption has been associated with food consumption, at home or outside. The growth of one- and two-person (especially non-retired) households has provided a new market of people who lack the time or skill for meal preparation. The structure of the household has been changing and the housewife has become more market-oriented, increasing the need for family-oriented food and drink services and also better meal provision for the working husband or wife. Pubs and catering establishments also need to broaden the range of services provided beyond just food and drink as hospitality markets become more activity-related.

Pubs have been in an ideal position to fill some of these gaps. They have been able to make use of existing licences which allow the development of alcohol related food services. Modern technology allows pubs to make use of very limited space to provide increasingly sophisticated food services. The suburban location and the design of many pubs give them the space to provide integrated food, drink and leisure services for families. The large breweries in particular have responded by developing new products to fill the market gaps that have appeared in catering. The concentration of ownership in brewing and the substantial ownership of pubs by large firms enables considerable capital to be utilized in a targeted way, using advanced technology. They have made large capital injections into catering to develop several chains of pub restaurants, often associated with large scale branding.

Breweries and the changing pub sector

Breweries are in the business of producing beer, although some have a sideline in other alcoholic products. Pubs, as discussed above, have been the main outlet for the sale of beer which is their main product. The close two-way relationship between the product, beer, and its major outlets, the pubs, has existed for over 100 years in the vertical domination of the supply chain by the major suppliers of beer, the large breweries. However, changes in economic and social structures have affected these relationships in recent decades.

The decline of the traditional dark beers and the corresponding increase in lager consumption has allowed the growing influence of foreign suppliers, whether directly or through licensing of production in the UK. The relative decline of beer and spirit consumption and the large growth in wine consumption have threatened the traditional roles of brewers and pubs in consumer markets. In response, the larger brewers have embarked on a programme of diversification.

Breweries have also developed new markets, investing accumulated profits in allied industries or sectors. They have, for instance, increased their investment in off-licences, hotels, restaurants and leisure services. They have done this where socio-economic trends and technological developments have given them significant opportunities to establish a significant market or technical lead or to acquire major assets. For instance, Bass have acquired Holiday Inn Hotels and Whitbreads have established or franchized a number of restaurant chains, as well as developing their hotel and off-licence interests. There has also been a significant drive to establish pub catering, where the local market allows it, as profit margins are higher.

CONTRACT SERVICES

The spread of contract services

Contract services cover both catering and what are now called hotel services. In the past they have formed distinct sub-sections of a particular sector. The trend towards deregulation and privatization in the UK and elsewhere in the Western world over the last fifteen years had a major impact on catering and accommodation services in the public sector. Compulsory competitive tendering of these services in health, education and welfare institutions had resulted in a significant growth of private contractors in these sectors.

According to Key Note, contract catering has increased its share of the UK market from 7% in 1991 to 9.3% in 1995. Table 4.21 shows the rapid changes in the sector during 1991–95. Traditional industrial and commercial contracts still account for over 45% of the units operated and over 40% of the meals provided. However, the main areas of recent growth have been the public sector, such as education, health and welfare institutions, and public catering in travel and recreation. For instance, state education units increased from 3% in 1990 to 32% of all units in 1995. However, the smaller independent school sector, with about one tenth of education outlets, provided about 60% of education meals.

Table 4.21 The UK contract catering market 1991–95

	1991				1995			
	Outlets	%	Meals (mn)	%	outlets	%	Meals (mn)	%
Business and industry	7,775	74.7	322	50.0	7,474	48.0	465	42.7
Healthcare	337	3.2	38	5.9	397	2.6	81	7.4
State education	450	4.3	30	4.7	4,957	31.8	172	15.8
Independent schools	620	6.0	81	12.6	578	3.7	99	9.1
Local authorities	463	4.4	31	4.8	451	2.9	18	1.7
Ministry of Defence	190	1.8	55	8.5	393	2.5	92	8.4
Public catering	324	3.1	62	9.6	1,006	6.5	134	12.3
Construction sites, oil rigs and training centres	246	2.4	25	3.9	311	2.0	28	2.6
Total	10,405	100	644	100	15,567	100	1,089	100

Source: Key Note, Contract Catering, 1996

Over the last ten years, large operators have increased their dominance of the industry. These firms have also moved towards the integration of catering and other ancillary services (as with hotel services in healthcare). There is also the tendency to ally with major brand names in the delivery of services. For instance, Compass has tied up with Harry Ramsden's, Burger King and Pizza Hut, as well as developing its own brands, such as Upper Crust. This reflects the effects of increasing technology on consumer mobility and the standardization of consumption patterns.

FURTHER READING

The ideas for this section have been in a series of papers over a number of years. They are in:

Cullen, P.F., 1985, 'Economic Aspects of Hotel and Catering Industry Changes', *International Journal of Hospitality Management*, Vol. 4(4), pp. 165–71.

Cullen, P.F. and Foxcroft, E.G., 1987, 'Economic Features of Efficient Catering Service Production', *Service Industries Journal*, Vol. 7(2), pp. 340–52.

Cullen, P.F., 1994, 'Time Tastes and Technology: The Economic Evolution of Eating Out', *British Food Journal*, vol. 96(10), pp. 4–9.

These apply the concepts of Gary Becker and other economists who have developed the economic analysis of households (what they sometimes call the new home economics).

Complementary aspects of the marketing and sociology of eating out can be found in:

Riley, M., 1994, 'Marketing Eating Out: The Influence of Social Culture and Innovation', *British Food Journal*, Vol. 96(10), pp.15–18.

Wood, R.C., 1994, 'Dining Out on Sociological Neglect', *British Food Journal*, Vol. 96(10), pp. 10–14.

Wood, R.C., 1995, *The Sociology of Food*. Edinburgh: Edinburgh University Press.

Information on the various sectors of the industry can be found in various reports published by market research organizations such as Key Note, MSI and Euromonitor. The Economist Intelligence Unit also publishes various reports and the quarterly *Travel and Tourism Analyst* also contains commentaries on the hotel industry.

REVIEW EXERCISES

1. Use various editions of *Social Trends*, the Family Expenditure surveys or other sources to compare patterns of household spending in 1985 and 1995 on: leisure activities; food; meals out; alcohol.
2. Discuss where and how demand in the hospitality industry is affected by:
   (a) the changing relative cost of time in household activity;
   (b) the diffusion of technology into the household.

Fluctuations

Macroeconomic fluctuations and the hospitality industry

5

Key concepts

This chapter deals with macroeconomic fluctuations in the economy. We:

- explain how and why fluctuations occur;
- explain the features of government macroeconomic policy;
- explain how macroeconomic activity and policy affects the hospitality industry;
- explain how firms may anticipate and deal with fluctuations in the economy.

Prerequisites: Chapters 2 and 3.

BOOM FOLLOWS SLUMP FOLLOWS BOOM: STAGES OF THE MACROECONOMIC CYCLE

Macroeconomic fluctuations are the short-term fluctuations about the long-term trend in activity (see the section on Trends in the economy in Chapter 3). Figure 5.1 presents a stylized picture of these fluctuations, with the main

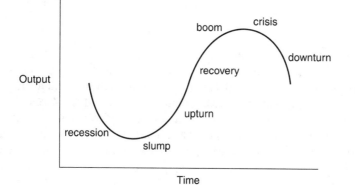

Figure 5.1 The stages of the macroeconomic cycle

stages of the cycle noted.

Long-term growth in the economy means that the UK has suffered only mild and very short-lived drops in real output since 1960. However, there have been frequent stop–go cycles, where rising output has been followed by a period of very low or no growth and rising unemployment, which we identify as the period of recession and depression (or slump).

The *unemployment rate* is the percentage of the available workforce that is unemployed. In the 1950s and early 1960s, this varied between 1.1% and 2.3% of the workforce. Since the mid-1960s, the unemployment rate has risen considerably, reaching peaks of over 11% (over 3 million) at the worst points of the cycle in 1986 and in 1993. This was about twice the rate at the best points of the cycle in 1989/90.

AGGREGATE DEMAND AND SUPPLY

The level of economic activity depends on the aggregate demand for and aggregate supply of *final* goods and services (see the discussion on Measuring the economy in Chapter 3.). These are represented by the

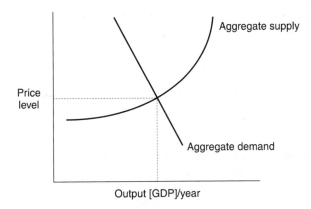

Figure 5.2 Aggregate demand and supply

aggregate demand and supply curves in Figure 5.2.

The demand and supply curves are similar to the market demand and supply curves of chapter 2, but they refer to total output and average prices in the economy. The resulting output is measured by Gross Domestic Product. This can be at constant factor cost. If we make the necessary adjustment for spending taxes or else at market prices. Price is measured by an index of prices which is designed to show how prices have changed on average.

Aggregate demand

Aggregate demand is the amount of money that various groups want to spend on final goods and services. It consists of:

- Consumer spending (C): on goods and services. This varies with the level of income, but is the actual proportion of income spent over the economic cycle. (Note: official statistics include the spending by households and non-profit institutions under consumer spending. However, spending on house purchases (net of sales) is classed as consumer investment and is included under investment.)
- Investment spending (I): this includes investment in fixed assets (plant machinery and vehicles) and inventory investment in stocks and work in progress.
- Government spending on goods and services (G).
- Exports (X).

So we write aggregate demand as $C + I + G + X$.
Aggregate demand increases when:

- people's expectations about future income increase – they are then willing to spend more
- the prices of domestic (UK) products fall relative to imports – people want to buy more home produced goods and services; and
- the rate of interest falls – firms are willing to invest more and consumers borrow more to finance extra spending.

Aggregate supply

Aggregate supply is the value of final output that firms are prepared to sell plus the value of imports. The money that is paid out to firms goes in wages and profits, taxes, and some is saved. As these are all part of the supply process, we split these money flows into three parts:

1. *Taxes that businesses and consumers pay to the government* (T). These include various sales and production taxes; income tax, national insurance payments to the government. We also include here taxes on capital such as capital gains tax and inheritance tax, because they effectively reduce the level of demand relative to supply in the economy (which is equivalent to raising supply relative to demand).
2. *Savings* (S). These include the retained profits that are directly invested in the business and consumer savings.
3. *Consumer spending* (C). This remaining factor income, after taxes have been paid and social security and other payments have been received, must all be spent, and so it is the same as consumer spending.

We now also add in as part of supply, a fourth element:

4. *Imports* (M). These represent the payments to foreign suppliers for goods and services received.

We can write aggregate supply as: C + S + T + M.

Aggregate supply depends on the available capital stock and supply of labour. The curve drawn in Figure 5.2 shows that increasing output leads to small increases in price when there is surplus capacity in the economy, but leads to large increases in price when there is little useable surplus capacity. This means that prices can rise significantly if demand increases quickly, because firms may not be able to put unemployed labour or capital to use quickly.

The balance in the economy

As we apply the principles of demand and supply analysis to the whole economy, we can identify different states of the economy:

1. Aggregate demand and supply are in balance when consumer and other spending is the same as the amount firms plan to spend on production, including normal expected profit. That is when

$$C + S + T + M \quad = \quad C + I + G + X$$
or $\quad S + T + M \quad = \quad I + G + X$

   Savings, taxes and imports are known as *leakages* from the economy, as they reduce the level of demand in the economy relative to supply. Investment, government spending and exports are known as injections.

   Where injections and leakages balance, the economy grows according to the rate of technical change.

2. If aggregate demand is greater than aggregate supply, price and output rise according to the amount of useable spare capacity. However, prices have been rising for many years, partly because of the shift to services (see Chapter 3, first section). So increases in aggregate demand push up prices even faster.

   Conversely, if aggregate demand is less than aggregate supply, output falls while prices tend to rise more slowly than before.

In practice, demand and supply are unlikely to be exactly in balance for the following reasons:

1. *Domestic saving reduces demand; investment spending and credit-financing increase demand.* The Financial Sector, which includes banks, building societies, pension funds and insurance companies, should match the supply of funds (savings) with the demand for funds to finance large consumer purchases and business investment. However, savings and investment may be different because:
   (a) *Financial institutions may lend or invest money overseas or not invest at all.*
   (b) *Banks can create money.* Banks need only a small proportion of the cash deposited with them to service their customers' cash requirements. The banks invest the rest or lend it on to firms or consumers who spend the money mostly by cheque or other credit transfer. The bank credit effectively functions as money, even though there is no increase in cash in the system. Hence banks can increase or decrease

the level of investment or fund consumer spending without a corresponding change in the level of saving.

2. *Taxes reduce demand and government spending increases demand in the system.* If the government balances its budget, the economy should be in balance. However:

   (a) *government taxes and spending can affect saving and investment in the economy.* For instance, people tend to save out of disposable, after-tax income. So increasing income taxes reduces people's savings and increases the level of demand.

   (b) *government borrowing usually increases the amount of money in the economy.* The Bank of England, a government department, acts as the UK's *central bank*. The Bank of England manages the financial system and effectively underwrites the bank credit to the government. This means that any government borrowing from the banks leads to extra credit and so money in the system. We should note that a growing economy needs extra money to finance the increase in everyday transactions, but if the government increases the amount of money too much, the level of demand will increase further.

3. *Exports increase demand but imports reduce demand by providing alternative supply.* Outflows of money have to balance inflows over time, but *exports may not balance imports in the short term.*

Interest rates and economic activity

Changes in the rate of interest also affect economic activity. The rate of interest is the rental price of money and it varies according to the demand or supply of funds (Chapter 2). However, the government manipulates the rate of interest in the money markets in order to control the level of money and spending in the economy. Banks, in particular, borrow very short term (some of it overnight) to lend longer term. The Bank of England controls the rate of interest at which they make these very short-term borrowings and this affects the various rates of interest throughout the economy. This in turn affects the amount of money in use.

The government cannot completely control both the rate of interest and its level of borrowing at the same time. Normally, government borrowing competes with other users of funds and increases the rate of interest. (When serious, this is known as *crowding out* of investment). However, the government (through the Bank of England) can arrange to borrow from the banking system in such a way that new money is effectively created. This keeps the rate of interest down, but increases the money supply. Aggregate demand increases more in the second case.

Balance of payments and the economy

The balance of payments is the difference between the spending by non-residents on goods and services produced in the UK (exports) and the spending by UK residents on goods and services produced abroad (imports). When exports are less than imports, either borrowing from foreign creditors increases or more foreign investment must come into the country. Short-term foreign creditors must be paid soon and this leads to more demand for foreign currency in exchange for sterling or a greater supply of sterling to exchange against foreign currency. This causes a fall in the value of the pound against foreign currencies (such as the dollar), known as *a fall in the exchange rate* or *depreciation of the pound*. This increases the cost of imports but makes UK exports seem cheaper. This, in turn, reduces the growth of imports and encourages the growth of exports and increases total demand in the economy.

However, interest rates can rise instead (or be increased by the government) to attract foreign depositors into the country. This leads to some reduction in real, physical, investment. It also keeps the exchange rate up and so does not benefit exports or reduce imports.

WHY FLUCTUATIONS IN OUTPUT OCCUR

One reason for fluctuations is that injections, particularly investment, actually depend on the level of output expected. When an investment, government spending or exports increases, this increases demand in the economy. Firms do not have the appropriate amount of equipment to produce the extra output efficiently, so they begin to increase their investment. They need quite large increases in investment to make up the difference, since it requires about £4 to £5 of equipment to produce about £1 of goods or services. In practice, firms only make part of the required investment at one go, because of caution and lack of funds.

As firms increase their investment, output and income rise still further and this encourages more investment. However, as the shortfall in capital stock is made up, there comes a point when the rate of investment starts falling. Other factors, such as a shortage of investment funds (which pushes up the rate of interest) or bottlenecks in production or importing equipment from abroad, also eventually reduce the rate of investment. In practice, the UK growth rate is less than 2% per annum on average. It cannot sustain an annual growth rate of 3–4% for more than a couple of years. The rate of growth slows down and so reduces the need for more investment. The economy may then stop growing and, as investment starts falling, reverse into decline.

The downward trend continues until the level of investment stops declining (some minimum levels of investment are always required). When this happens the level of income starts rising again.

GOVERNMENT MACROECONOMIC POLICY

Macroeconomic policy objectives

The government uses various *macroeconomic policies* to control the fluctuations in economic activity. Underlying these policies are various objectives that are based on a mixture of ideology, electoral considerations and outside pressures, such as those from the European Union on movement towards a single European currency. These objectives can be generally stated as:

1. control inflation (target 3%);
2. control unemployment;
3. improve the rate of growth;
4. control the balance of payments;
5. limit Public Sector Borrowing to 3% of GDP;
6. limit national debt (total accumulated government borrowing) to 60% GDP.

The control of inflation and unemployment are the two major goals. Controlling the balance of payments is important because balance of payments problems have in the past been a major block on economic growth. The balance between unemployment and inflation is one that varies between political parties and the relative importance attached to each affects the policies the government pursues. Objectives 5 and 6 are additional EU criteria for implementing the single currency.

Inflation

Inflation is defined as a continuing rise in prices. In the UK, these price changes are measured by the Retail Price Index, based on the average rate of change of prices of items in the average shopping basket of the average consumer, although this does not fully measure all inflation (see Chapter 3, Measuring changes in output, and the first section of Chapter 4).

There are three reasons why prices continue to rise:

1. *Excess demand in the economy.* This causes prices to rise until the excess demand is eliminated. However, the rise in prices generates extra money income, some of which will be spent within the country. This increases demand still further in the next period (about three months) but this knock-on effect peters out as leakages in the system make the successive increases in income smaller.
2. *Cost increases occurring independently of demand.* Increases in the prices of imported goods and services and trade union pressure on wages can cause continuing price increases, but can also cause unemployment. This may lead to further government spending that effectively validates the price increases. However, rising budget deficits will limit both government spending and further price increases.
3. *Structural change in the economy, allied with wage rate inflexibility downward.* Excess demand in some areas leads to a rise in prices, but excess supply in other areas causes unemployment not falling prices. As a result, average prices continue to rise.

Unemployment

The UK has over 58 million people in it. About 28 million are economically active, that is, in employment or actively seeking employment, with about 25–26 million employed and 2–3 million actively seeking work, according to official government statistics. Alternative definitions, such as those used by the International Labour Organization may give a somewhat higher total. Those in employment may be fully employed (with or without overtime working) or under-employed, on short-time working. Unemployment is caused by the following factors:

1. *Seasonal factors*: For instance, some tourism and hospitality workers are only in employment for part of the year. Other workers are laid off temporarily because of bad weather. This unemployment requires government measures to improve alternative or complementary employment. Unemployment data are seasonally adjusted to eliminate this element.
2. *Supply side factors:*
   (a) *Frictional unemployment.* This includes people temporarily out of work or between jobs. It can be reduced by improving communication flows in the labour market.
   (b) *Structural unemployment.* This includes workers who have the wrong skills or are in the wrong area because changes in the economic structure have led to the loss or decline of traditional industries. The government needs to help such people with retraining or with relocation.
   (c) *Long-term unemployment.* This includes people who have been out of work for a long time and are unlikely to get another job or retrain. The number of long-term unemployed has been increasing over the last thirty years because the general increase in unemployment makes it difficult for such people to get into the labour market. The government needs to reduce these numbers through retraining programmes.
3. *Demand factors.* Demand deficient or cyclical unemployment is caused by a general lack of demand for labour. The government can improve the situation by stimulating demand in the economy.

In practice, it is difficult to slot people into the different categories. Instead, we get some idea of the relative size of the problem by categorizing the unemployed by the length of time they have been unemployed: less than 8 weeks is regarded as frictional unemployment, while more than 26 weeks is regarded as long-term, including structural unemployment. This gives a rough idea only, because the number in each category rises when the total level of unemployment rises.

Constraints on macroeconomic policy

Government fiscal and monetary policy is constrained by the international economy.

The UK economy is not independent of other economies, particularly as regards interest rates and the level of exports which both affect the level of demand in the country.

Government policy to improve the working of the economy has to take account of the following three constraints:

1. The UK economy is a very open economy

This means that a substantial part of UK output and consumption depends on international trade. The UK exports about 30% of its output and imports 30% of its consumption. This figure has been growing over the last thirty years. In 1970, only about 22% of output and consumption was internationally traded. *This links economic growth and cycles to world levels of economic activity and reduces the ability of the government to control its own economy.*

2. There is international capital mobility

This means that funds can move about freely between countries. Capital mobility increased significantly during the 1980s as countries relaxed financial controls, especially in the West. Developing countries have also allowed greater freedom of capital movement, which has increased investment in those countries substantially when there have been low returns on investment in industrialised countries. *International capital mobility makes it difficult for the real rate of interest in the UK to differ much from the real interest rate in world financial markets.*

The actual rate of interest is called the *nominal* or *money rate of interest*. The real rate of interest is the nominal rate adjusted for inflation:

real rate of interest = nominal rate of interest – rate of inflation.

EXAMPLE 5.1

The nominal rate of inflation = 5% per annum; and
the annual rate of inflation   = 3%:
then the real rate of interest = 5% p.a. – 3% p.a. = 2% per annum.

The following example shows the effects of this on the UK.

EXAMPLE 5.2 EQUALIZATION OF REAL INTEREST RATES

Suppose the German interest rate   = 4% p.a. and
the German rate of inflation   = 1% p.a.
then the real German rate of interest = (4 – 1)% p.a.   = 3% p.a.

⇒ The real UK real rate of interest should also be 3% per annum.
⇒ If the rate of inflation in the UK is 4% per year, then the UK rate of interest should be:

$$= \text{real rate of interest} + \text{rate of inflation}$$
$$= 3\% \text{ p.a.} + 4\% \text{ p.a.} \quad = 7\% \text{ p.a.}$$

So, if the government wants to keep a lower rate of interest of 5% it will have to either:

1. reduce the rate of inflation to 2% p.a.; or
2. allow the value of the pound to depreciate by 2% a year against the German mark.

If the German real rate of interest rises, there will be a movement of money from the UK to Germany which will eventually cause UK interest rates to rise.

3. Each policy change generates signals to consumers and businesses

The way these signals are received and interpreted affects business and consumer confidence and so their investment and consumption behaviour. The problem for the government is that the same measure could be interpreted differently on different occasions. Making sure that businesses and consumers interpret the signals correctly is more a political than an economic problem. The policy measures have some economic effects, but these could be swamped by the political effects on the confidence factor.

Expressing macroeconomic objectives

Macroeconomic policy regulates the level of demand and supply of goods and services in the economy. Hence, there are two basic policy programmes: demand management and supply management.

Demand management regulates the level of demand in the economy by controlling the various elements of demand (net of taxes), namely: consumer spending; investment; government spending; and exports (net of imports – these are usually considered together as a net amount).

Supply management means improving the supply in the economy so that greater amounts are supplied at lower prices by improving productivity and labour supply – reducing the rate of increase in labour costs; and also by reducing other costs.

Demand responds quicker than supply to changes in current income flows and expectations about the immediate future. Supply, however, is more affected than demand by past decisions about investment in physical and human capital. Hence, demand problems can be dealt with more quickly, while supply side problems take longer to deal with. So macroeconomic policy is more concerned with controlling the level of demand in the economy, although supply side economic management was much in vogue in the 1980s in Britain (and also the USA).

Demand management

The government can manage demand through three different policies.

Monetary policy

This controls the amount of money and credit, including the rate of interest and bank lending, in the economy. The interest rate is the price paid for the use of money. Different rates of interest reflect differences in supply – such as risk, administration costs and competition – and demand for various uses. Financial markets, where large financial institutions such as banks, insurance companies and pension funds operate, have much lower rates of interest than consumer credit markets.

The essential feature of money is that it is a highly liquid asset, that is, it can be easily and quickly exchanged for goods or services of the same nominal value. All assets can be classed according to their liquidity. Some, such as land, are highly illiquid and converting them into other assets of the same value is neither quick nor easy. There are, however, many financial assets that are very liquid and often perform the functions of money and this makes monetary control more difficult. Consequently, the government employs two concepts of money: narrow money and broad money. Narrow money is close to what we would call money, while broad money includes a range of bank deposits and easily utilized credits. The government tries to use definitions that give fairly good relationships between money and the level of economic activity. However, the relationships tend to break down when the government has been manipulating a particular variable for some time. Consequently the government has changed its definition of broad and narrow money a few times during the last twenty years.

Expansionary monetary policy occurs when the government expands money supply faster than before. Interest rates then begin to fall. This leads to some movement of money out of the country and downward pressure on the exchange rate. If the government allows flexible *exchange rates*, the value of the pound goes down. This increases the prices of imports in pounds and reduce the prices of exports in foreign currencies. So imports go down and exports go up, which reinforces the effects of lower interest rates on demand at home.

However, the UK government has pursued an anti-inflationary strategy based on the long-run control of the growth of the money supply. Crudely put, the long-term growth rate of the UK economy is about 2% per annum. This means that on average for every £100 of goods and services produced last year the economy now produces £102 at last year's prices. If the money in the system has also grown by 2%, then for every hundred pounds of purchasing power last year there is now £102. Hence there is £102 of money demand for every £102 of goods and services available. This means that supply and demand balance and there is no need for prices to rise.

However, if the government increases the money supply by 5%, there is now £105 of money for every £102 worth of goods and services available. Demand exceeds supply and so prices rise. The approximate rise in prices is given by the equation:

$$\% \text{ Rate of inflation} = \% \text{ Increase in money supply} - \% \text{ Increase in productivity}$$
$$= 5\% - 2\%$$
$$= 3\%.$$

In practice, there is a time lag of about a year and the relationship does not strictly hold in the short term and when unemployment may be significant. However, it gives some idea on how costs and price may behave in a year's time.

Fiscal policy

This uses government spending and taxation to control the economy. The main instruments of fiscal policy are:

- direct taxation on income and wealth, including corporation tax;
- indirect taxation on spending and production;
- spending on investment and consumer goods and services;
- grants (including pensions and other direct subsidies) to consumers;
- grants and allowances to investors.

If the government balances its budget, so that spending is the same as taxation, it returns the same amount of money into the system as it took away in taxes. However, the level of demand may still increase, depending on the way the government gets its taxes.

People plan their spending and savings according to their *disposable income* (in this context disposable income is equal to income after income tax has been paid). When income tax goes up consumers' disposable income is reduced and so is the amount they save. Similar effects on savings occur when the government taxes major items of domestic capital such as washing machines and cars (called *consumer durables*) that people partly finance out of savings. The result is that, if the government spends all the tax, the total amount of spending in the economy rises and there is an increase in aggregate demand.

However, taxes on *non-durables*, such as alcohol and tobacco, do not affect consumers spending. So there is little impact on demand, although the tax increases the retail price index, which we use to measure inflation.

There will be also be some structural change in the economy, because demand increases in some sectors and falls in other sectors.

A major consideration in policy is the need to control the public sector borrowing requirement or the annual increase in government debt. This is because increased borrowing either raises interest rates or increases the money supply, which affects the rate of inflation in about 1–2 years.

Fiscal policy must also take into account the international dimension. For instance, an expansionary policy may have the government increasing spending faster than taxes, and then

- aggregate demand increases;
- but this may bring interest rate rises as government borrowing increases and firms require more finance for investment;
- interest rate rises may bring foreign depositors in, as long as confidence is maintained;
- however, the government needs to make sure that the exchange rate is not allowed to appreciate too fast. Otherwise exports become too expensive and imports too cheap, leading to a reversal of the increase in demand.

The opposite would happen for contractionary monetary and fiscal policy.

We can see that fiscal policy has to be linked with stable exchange rates, and monetary policy with flexible exchange rates. The choice of a fixed or flexible exchange rate is often determined politically and is complicated by the need not only to keep in step with other countries in the EU, but also with the possibility of floating against the US dollar and other currencies.

Administrative policy

This uses direct controls over market activity, to alter the level of demand or supply in the system. They are tried from time to time, usually in a desperate attempt to control the economy after other measures have failed. Commonly used controls include wage controls (particularly over public sector pay rises), price controls, and limits to bank credit. They tend not to last long because the system tends to break down.

VIEWS ON MACROECONOMIC POLICY

Many economists believe that the government can reduce unemployment through increasing demand, but at the cost of increased inflation. The government then has to choose between different target combinations of unemployment and inflation. The government should actively use demand management techniques, particularly fiscal policy. On the other hand there are many economists who believe that the reduction in unemployment will not last. They argue that there is a natural rate of unemployment that is determined by the level of structural change, frictional and seasonal unemployment. If the government raises demand to reduce unemployment, it encourages workers to press for higher wages which will lead to higher price rises and more unemployment. According to this view, the government should keep inflation down to improve long-term employment. Monetary policy is then more important. They should also aim to reduce unemployment in the long term by measures to improve the working of the labour market.

The two views are somewhat crudely labelled Keynesian (pronounced *Kaynzian*), after the economist Keynes, and Monetarist, respectively, although there are other schools of thought that apply a mixture of these ideas and some others.

THE IMPACT OF THE MACROECONOMY ON THE HOSPITALITY INDUSTRY

Investment and operations problems

Fluctuations in income, employment and interest rates affect demand and supply conditions in the hospitality industry. They also make investment planning more difficult. An investment may be appropriate for the long-term trends in the market, but the timing may be wrong. Investments such as building a hotel take time to come on stream, that is, to bring in customers and cash. If a firm brings an investment on stream when the economy is going into a recession, it may have to pay for equipment that is not being utilized because demand is low. This may jeopardize the profitability of the investment and the ability of the company to meets its obligations.

For most sections of the industry, the proportion of consumer spending that goes on the industry does not change a great deal throughout the various stages of the cycle. Business spending varies with the level of business activity, which in turn is related to the level of consumer spending. So demand for the industry varies throughout the economic cycle, though the industry tends to follow the economy into and out of recession with a slight time lag.

Sales to overseas consumers are affected by the prevailing rate of exchange. However, demand from foreign business tourists varies with the level of economic activity in this country.

The state of the economy also affects the pattern of hotel usage. In periods of low economic growth, people travel less often but stay longer and use higher priced accommodation. This can be seen from Table 5.1 for UK tourism as the UK moved from boom in 1987–88 into recession in 1990–91.

Table 5.1 UK tourism trips, days and expenditure, 1987–91

	1987		1991		Percentage change	
	UK	*Total*	*UK*	*Total*	*UK*	*Total*
Trips (mn)	131.6	147.2	94.4	111.1	−28.3	−24.5
Days (mn) (1+ nights)	493.0	670.4	395.6	598.9	−19.8	−10.7
Average stay (days)	3.7	4.6	4.2	5.4	13.5	17.4
Spending (£m)	6,771	13,051	10,470	17,368	54.6	33.1
Spending/trip (£)	51.5	88.7	110.9	158.8	115.3	79.0
Spending/ day (£)	13.9	19.3	26.0	29.5	87.1	52.9

Source: Key Note, *Hotels*, 1992

While the number of trips in the UK fell, trips abroad remained constant, giving a smaller total decline in the number of trips. Average stay however, increased for trips in the UK and spending per day increased substantially above the rate of inflation. This pattern is repeated in the division of holidays into long and short breaks, shown in Table 5.2, as the economy moved from 1988 boom to 1990 recession and the slow climb out in 1992.

Macroeconomic policy changes will affect hospitality firms in two ways: directly and indirectly.

Table 5.2 Long and short break holidays by UK adults 1988–92

	Long breaks (5 days or more)				Short Breaks (4 days or less)			
	Trips (mn)		Spending (£m)		Trips (mn)		Spending (£m)	
	UK	Abroad	UK	Abroad	UK	Abroad	UK	Abroad
1988	34.0	19.9	3,740	9,112	34.5	2.0	1,325	248
1990	25.9	18.9	3,414	10,067	31.4	2.4	1,526	336
1992	28.5	19.4	3,583	10,614	34.3	2.2	1,077	351

Source: *Caterer & Hotelkeeper*, 19 March 1993

Direct impact

Firms will experience a direct impact when the government uses the industry or a closely related industry as an instrument of policy. For instance, the government may decide to increase its hospital or road building programme to increase the general level of spending in the economy. This would have an immediate impact on the construction and civil engineering industries.

However, this is rarely the case with the hospitality industry. The last significant use of the industry in this way in the UK was through the Development of Tourism Act in 1969, in order to help deal with the chronic balance of payments problem. Tourism was seen as a way of increasing the export of services, and possibly encouraging people to holiday within the UK instead of going abroad. Reports indicated an increasing shortage of good standard accommodation. Hence the government gave generous incentives for improving existing accommodation or building new high standard accommodation. Although we could consider this as investment for structural change, it can be regarded as part of macroeconomic policy as well, for two reasons. First, it was intended to have a fairly limited life (which it did), with a limited intended expenditure. Second, it was designed specifically to deal with one of the policy objectives, that of reducing the balance of payments deficit.

Indirect impact

Firms experience an indirect impact of government macroeconomic policy when the direct effect of policy decisions has a knock-on effect on the hospitality industry. For instance, if a change in government policy brings an increase in consumer disposable income, this leads to an increase in demand in various sectors of the hospitality industry.

In analysing the effect on the industry, we should look at the effect on demand and supply.

Demand

For most sectors of the industry, demand follows roughly the level of economic activity in the economy as a whole. However, those segments of the industry serving the foreign market will be affected by variations in the exchange rate. This will apply especially to three-, four- and five- star hotels, particularly in London and near international airports, that depend heavily on the foreign market. It will also apply to some extent to those restaurants that are dependent on foreign trade in these areas.

Supply

The costs of production and delivery are affected by the rate of inflation, taxation levels and to some extent by variations in the exchange rate.

The cost and availability of finance should be considered separately, since they may be affected differently by changes in the general level of activity.

Table 5.3 shows how the recession has affected the level of individual bankruptcies and company insolvencies in the industry. It shows that the worst time tends to come as the economy is moving out of recession. There are several explanations for this:

- the greater the length and severity of the recession the greater the financial strain on firms;
- firms expand activities too fast for their depleted funds during the upturn in the market;
- the reviving markets allow creditors to recoup more of their money from ailing businesses.

Table 5.3 Bankruptcies and insolvencies, 1989–93

	1989	1990	1991	1992	1993	1994
Bankruptcies of all self-employed	5,863	8,489	14,609	19,525	18,561	15,114
Of which hotel and catering	719	867	1,481	2,366	2,437	2,102
Company insolvencies	10,456	15,051	21,827	24,425	20,708	16,728
Of which hotel and catering	371	489	748	1,010	912	777

Source: Annual Abstract of Statistics, 1996

CASE STUDY: THE HOTEL INDUSTRY IN RECESSION: BOOM TO SLUMP: 1988–92

The following shows how attitudes changed as the recession began to affect the hotel industry.

1988

1987 had been a boom year with hotel prices increasing by 30%. The market was optimistic and this led to considerable investment by foreign and domestic firms. UK companies were also using their domestic profits to expand abroad. Rapid expansion during the year also brought recruitment problems. Nine new hotels were being built in and around Birmingham and nine more were being planned, with an expected job demand for 10,000. Four new hotels opened in Reading, with houses being bought to accommodate staff, some of whom were recruited from abroad. The country house hotel sector continued to grow, although there were signs of market saturation with average gross operating profit of 15% about half that of a large modern hotel.

Occupancy rates increased to 75% and large hotel chains increased rack rates by 10%, although overseas visitors in the early summer were 2.3 % lower than the previous year, with North American tourists down by 8.2% (because of rising prices?). US visitors increased later in the summer as the dollar became stronger but optimism declined later in the year after the sharp and *unexpected* (!!) rise in interest rates, with the pound rising in value causing demand to fall.

1989

Optimism continued at the start of the year, with planned investment of over £480 million on new hotels and more being spent on refurbishment. Small hotel groups such as Select Country, Resort Hotels, Ptarmigan Hotels and Parkdale Holdings were also growing through acquisition. Country House Hotels continued to boom, with 100 new projects planned. However, the high prices paid by some small operators had led to barely adequate profits and some firms were withdrawing from the market.

By May, high interest rates were beginning to affect the property market, although many hotels at the upper end of the market were selling for high prices. The pound sterling began a downward slide against the Deutschemark and the US dollar. This increased the inflow of US and German tourists who favoured the higher tariff hotels (as we would expect), and helped them achieve consistently higher occupancy rates than other hotels. In September, Stakis announced plans to build a chain of 20 upmarket Country Court business hotels in the south of England over a three-year period. In October, Whitbread relaunched its Coaching Inns as Lansbury Hotels and bought more hotels for its division as part of a £500 million expansion plan for the company.

1990

Confidence in the hotel industry remained high during the first part of the year, despite high interest rates and a falling property market. Investment was at its highest for 15 years by June with £1.4 billion being spent, half of the 2.9 billion investment in tourism including timeshares, marinas, heritage and sport facilities. By the end of June, 105 hotels were under construction, with 25 of them in London. The English Tourist Board predicted continuing expansion in the budget, three- and four-star markets.

Although the recession was well under way in the rest of the economy, with falling average spending, this was not reflected in the hospitality industry. The *Caterer & Hotelkeeper/American Express* Business Barometer Survey found high interest rates and inflation as areas of concern, but hoteliers were confident that business would improve by the end of the year. There were plans for increased investment: 31% of hoteliers planned refurbishment investment; 38% reported increased turnover, but this was in money not real terms. Most hoteliers reported good or increasing corporate business with a high proportion of direct bookings, although there was some uncertainty over the conference market. More attention was given to the relaxing of East–West tensions than to the Middle East crisis.

However, confidence declined later in the year. By August, demand in the top hotels in London, particularly for business luncheons and conventions, was suffering from the fluctuating oil prices, a weak dollar and the effect of falling share prices on British companies. Hotel operating profits were badly affected by poor market conditions and suffered substantial drops in real income. London occupancy rates fell by 11 percentage points, largely because of the decline in high-yielding weekday bookings.

The average middle to upper grade hotel in England outside London and in Wales increased room rates above the 10.1% inflation rate. However, corresponding London hotels achieved only 5.1% increase. Rooms and food and beverage income increased less than costs and produced less revenue growth than other services such as phones and shops. This reflected the overcapacity developing in London as a result of the 1980s' boom. Lower tariff hotels, however, saw a marginal increase in occupancy.

Some hotel companies, including Stakis, Country Club and Resort Hotels reported greater trading margins. However, receiverships in the hotel industry were among the worst in the country, having increased from 45 in 1989 to 135, an increase of 200% compared with 35% for the country as a whole.

Many heavily borrowed smaller firms went under. The common theme was the crippling cost of loans taken out when base interest rates had been half what they now were. The biggest collapse was the 28 hotel Baron group with debts of £140 million. High interest rates also hit more broadly based leisure companies: Leading Leisure went into receivership; Mecca Leisure also tried to stay afloat by selling assets, including hotels, but eventually had to sell out to Rank Organisation for £540 million.

By the end of the year the property market had plunged, lowering the value of many hotels and providing long-term investment opportunities for some investors, particularly for those with low levels of debt. For instance:

- Mount Charlotte, the second largest hotel group after THF, had paid £645 million for Thistle Hotels in 1989. This had severely affected its profit profile, and caused a significant drop in share values, which had not recovered because of the recession. This allowed an almost casual takeover of the company by Brierley Investments. Queens Moat Houses took over Norfolk Capital for an apparent bargain of £184 million. Periquito Hotels was set up with five mid-market hotels.

- John Jarvis set up Jarvis Hotels by buying the 412 strong Embassy chain from Allied-Lyons for a bargain £186 million.
- THF bought Crest Hotels from Bass for a bargain £300 million.

1991

In March, 80% of hotels believed business would improve over the next six months. Extra marketing activity was being undertaken. However, only 35% of hoteliers reported that bookings were up compared with the previous year, but many hotels were retrenching: 39% of hotels had reviewed buying policies; 43% were reducing stocks; 39% were increasing pressure on suppliers; 10% had made redundancies; 14% had cut wages.

By July, most four- and five-star hoteliers thought that it would be 12 months before the industry recovered. Almost 60% had abandoned or postponed expenditure on capital improvements, but not many had reduced spending on advertising, marketing and training.

One commentator estimated banks and finance houses had lost £100 million in the previous 18 months, with receiverships putting £300 million pounds worth of hotels on to the market.

By September, a survey showed business confidence was more modest, although interest rates had fallen and were now of less concern than 6 months previously. Half felt that the worst of the recession was over. Only 9% thought that the recession would not be over for another 12 months. High interest rates, falling consumer spending and inflation continued to worry companies. More hotels had undertaken additional, unscheduled marketing. Local advertising, special prices and discounts, listings in guides were popular. The emphasis was on tactical measures such as reviewing buying policies and reducing stock, but a significant number had also increased prices. Towards the end of November, there was evidence that the conference market was hardening up with smaller discounts being given. Room occupancy for September was 64% compared with 70% for 1990. Problems in the 5-star sector were aggravated by the appearance of more hotels in the London market, as investments and refurbishment came on stream. The only real note of optimism was from the budget sector.

Sources: Caterer & Hotelkeeper: Trading Places, Review of Hotels '88, 22/29 December 1988, pp. 24–25; Hotel Sector Building Boom, 22 August 1990, p. 11; High Hopes for Economic Recovery, 20 September 1990, pp. 27, 29; The Way We Were, 20/27 December 1990, pp. 25–26; Receiverships Up 220% as Recession Bites, 10 January 1991, p. 25; UK Trends, 18 July 1991, p. 14; Barometer notes Realistic Attitudes, 10 October 1991, p. 16; Industry Thinks Its Way out of Recession, 23 May 1991, p. 28; A Year of Living Dangerously

1991, 19/26 December 1991, pp. 24–29; 1992: Goodbye to All that, 18/25 December 1992, pp. 28–31; Recovery on Course as Room Occupancy Rises, 24 March 1994, p. 23.

ANALYSIS

An important element of this cycle for hoteliers seems to have been short-sightedness. Little seems to have been learnt from the previous major recession in 1980–81. There is the attitude that 'it will not happen to me' even up to the middle of 1991 when the recession was deepening elsewhere, with many hotels planning major investments based on continuing demand rather than planning strategically for development after the recession. The property boom of the late 1980s had led them into a fool's paradise. The commentators quoted summed up neatly what many hoteliers realized only too late. However, some hotel groups had been protecting their position by raising money from shareholders to pay off debt. Others such as Friendly Hotels had raised capital and reduced debt by selling hotels and leasing them back. This enabled them to pick up bargains from hotels.

PREDICTING MACROECONOMIC CHANGES

Hospitality firms can use various sources of economic information to reduce risks, avoid pitfalls and cope successfully with fluctuations in activity. The most convenient to use are the economic activity indicators published by the government. An economic activity indicator is an index number for a particular variable whose behaviour is similar to that of the economy as a whole. The index number expresses the level of the particular variable as a percentage of its value in some base year.

EXAMPLE 5.5

The index number for consumer credit now is 120 (1990 = 100). This means that consumer credit is (120–100)% = 20% higher now than it was in 1990.

Similarly, if the index number for consumer credit now is 120 (1990 = 100) and last year it was 110, then the growth in consumer credit since last year is given by:

growth = ((index now − index last year)/index last year) × 100%
= ((120 − 110)/110) × 100%
= 9.1%.

Consumer credit is a good example of a *leading indicator* or variable that changes ahead of economic activity as a whole. An increase in credit means that consumers are wanting to spend more money. When producers perceive this increase to be continuing, they increase output and so employ more people.

In fact, The Central Statistical Office (CSO), publishes four sets of indicators:

1. *longer leading*, where changes takes place about six months ahead of the economy;
2. *shorter leading*, where changes take place about three months ahead of the economy;
3. *coincident*, where changes take place about the same time as broader economic activity;
4. *lagging*, where changes tend to take place after changes in the economy as a whole.

The CSO decides where data series fit best. Each series is converted into real values (eliminating the effects of inflation), smoothed and detrended using time-series analysis techniques. The standardized series are amalgamated with others in the same category to give the four composite indicators. Notice that the series have been detrended, that is, the long-term growth has been removed. This allows us to see the short-term cyclical pattern more clearly so that we can judge whereabouts on the short-term cycle the economy is. You should also note that the series do not all tell the same story all of the time so there is still some art left in interpreting them.

Managers can assess the impact of macroeconomic change by using the following approach.

1. Look at forecasts published by different institutions

The Treasury, the National Institute for Economic and Social Research, and various University Business Schools all publish surveys, and summaries of them are published in newspapers. The forecasts differ, because they reflect different assumptions about how the economy works. These differences often reflect political ideologies, so that it is useful to know something about the background of the forecasters, according to whether they are some brand of Keynesian or Monetarist. Keynesian economics tends to favour fiscal techniques of demand management. Monetarist economics tends to view monetary control as important and sees fiscal measures as having limited value in demand management.

2. Look at economic activity indicators

These will give some indication of which way the economy seems to be going. Remember that international constraints are important in open economies and that boom follows slump follows boom.

3. Be sensitive to political factors

Be aware of which indicators the government pays particular regard to, as these may change if the government changes and may even do so during an existing government's period of office. Important indicators that affect government policy are:

- *The rate of inflation*: If it goes up (down), the government may implement contractionary (expansionary) policies such as higher (lower) interest rates or higher (lower) taxes.
- *Retail sales*: Rapidly rising (falling) sales may lead to contractionary (expansionary policies).
- *Balance of payments* (= export – imports). If the deficit is rising, there will be pressure on the pound. This will lead to increases in interest rates or expenditure or credit controls.
- *Government Borrowing (Public Sector Borrowing Requirement)*: If this becomes too high a proportion of GDP, the government will raise taxes or cut spending.
- *Growth of the money supply*: The government sets a target band rate of growth (say 2–4% a year). If the money supply increases faster than this, the government will act to reduce the rate of growth of the money supply. In particular, broad money supply is determined by:

  new government borrowing + increase in bank lending to the private sector – increase in private lending to the government.

- The government can act to change any of these with knock-on effects on firms.

IMPLICATIONS FOR MANAGEMENT

Dealing with the recession

Firms should take the regularity of the recessions into their long- and medium-term planning so that they avoid unnecessary problems. They should:

- Forecast the time path of the recession using the cyclical indicators described above. Identify the cyclical hazards to the firm, and prepare preventive action to deal with them.
- Plan product lines and rebranding so that the growth of the market is relatively high during the downturn period so that there is a buffer against the general fall in demand. This allows further capital expansion to occur when property prices and interest costs are lowest at the end of the recession.
- Keep assets flexible. Avoid unnecessary diversification of activities. Many large and small firms have to undergo a period of restructuring to divest themselves of peripheral business caught up in the periods of expansion.

- Control liquidity so that the core business can survive without requiring large cash injections during any recession.
- Control borrowing so that a 50% increase in interest rates and a 50% cut in operating surplus will still leave debt interest covered; leave a clear margin that allows for a fall in property and other values which affect the security offered to lenders.

FURTHER READING

Economics textbooks cover, to varying degrees, aspects of the macro-economy of the country in which they are published. There are also applied economics texts that include more institutional detail. These are useful because their commentaries avoid the use of diagrams. These include:

Griffiths, Alan and Wall, Stuart (eds.), 1995, *Applied Economics: An Introductory Course (6th edn.)*. London: Longman.

REVIEW EXERCISES

1. Identify the various stages of the short-term (inventory) cycle. Indicate the typical problems hotel and catering firms face at each stage.
2. Discuss the implication of the following for the hospitality industry:
   (a) government borrowing goes up;
   (b) government prints money;
   (c) government borrowing increases beyond expected levels;
   (d) imports rise faster than exports;
   (e) US interest rates go up;
   (f) German interest rates go up.
3. Briefly explain how economic activity indicators may be used to guide investment planning by hotels.

Discussion topic

4. Use an example from a recent issue of *Caterer & Hotelkeeper* to discuss how a firm has responded to changes in the level of economic activity.

6 The hospitality industry and the local economy

Key concepts

The hospitality industry usually derives its existence from the demands of visitors and residents for its services. The presence of hospitality establishments may also lead to further developments in the area. In either case, hospitality managers or their local association have an important part to play in the local development, benefiting not only their own businesses, but also the town. This chapter analyses the interaction of the hospitality industry in a locality or region with its surrounding area. We:

- analyse the concept of the tourism life cycle for an area;
- analyse the interaction of the hospitality industry within a locality;
- explain the concept of the multiplier and its application in impact studies;
- evaluate the role of the hospitality manager in local development.

Prerequisite: Chapter 5.

TOURISM LIFE CYCLE AND LOCAL DEVELOPMENT

Chapter 2 introduced the concept of the diffusion process in the market for a product over time. We can also apply this diffusion process or product life cycle concept to the development of a tourist locality, based on the work of Butler (Butler, 1980; Cooper, 1991). The general pattern of change in the locality as a resort is described in Figure 6.1.

Stage A represents the initial stages of discovery, exploration and development. The area's facilities are only appropriate to local needs at this stage of development and access is geared to the purposes of local trade. This makes travel to the area relatively expensive and restricts tourism to independent tourists who put a high value on novelty, isolation or cultural experimentation. These tourists are prepared to accept the rudimentary local facilities and can afford either the time or the money required to travel there. As people come to know more about the area, the trickle of visitors becomes a steady stream that encourages local suppliers to develop facilities to cater for the increased visitors, although government regulation and provision of facilities remains largely at the local level.

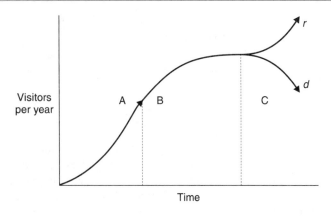

Figure 6.1 Life cycle of tourist resort

At some point, however, the market enters a period of rapid take-off as the stream of visitors becomes a flood. Demand outstrips the ability of local businesses and local government to fund the investments required to cope. The rapid rise in profitability encourages outside organizations to come in and national government takes a more active role in developing and regulating tourism. At this stage, the apparent benefits of tourism and its disbenefits increase. Increased demand brings increased employment in what are often relatively low employment regions. However, there are side-effects, such as peak period congestion and overloading of the service structure, that impose economic costs on local residents who may not be involved directly or indirectly in tourism. These side-effects are unpriced, that is, the tourists who effectively cause these problems do not compensate those who suffer.

Stage B covers the period of consolidation as the area becomes part of the standard tourist market. Tourism is still increasing but the rate of growth slows down until eventually it virtually ceases. As the rate of growth slows down, the profitability of further private investment and public funding tends to decline as well. The perceived quality of the area for tourists declines as the area's social and private capital decline.

At Stage C the resort enters a period of stagnation and eventual decline as tourists move on to other areas, represented by the downward arrowed path (marked *d* in Figure 6.1). The majority of visitors to the area come from a smaller proportion of its former markets. This segment is also declining because of natural ageing. The general range of facilities continue to decline in quality because of the unprofitability of further investment.

Local authorities need to consider a sustained effort at *rejuvenation* in order to move along an upward path (*r* in Figure 6.1) instead. They could, for instance, develop new attractions that meet the changing patterns of leisure, such as activity holidays or conference or other business usage. However, the concern should be for the quality of the tourist mix rather than number, with an emphasis on the net contribution to the area, taking into account the decline in value of existing tourist accommodation and other facilities. Inevitably it is in the interests of local hospitality operators to actively co-operate with local government bodies in monitoring changes and developing strategies for maintaining tourist flows.

CASE STUDY: TURNING THE TIDE AT THE SEASIDE

The severe decline in traditional UK seaside holiday markets by the late 1980s has forced the various resorts to adjust to a new role. Scarborough had seen its traditional markets of the industrial areas of Nottinghamshire, Yorkshire and Durham severely decline, though its fishing, food and manufacturing industries still remain. Since 1990 Scarborough has been trying to win back the holidaymakers, by promoting itself as the heritage and natural beauty centre of North Yorkshire. The borough includes the towns of Filey and Whitby and according to David James, Scarborough's Director of Tourism and Amenities, the town is not so much a holiday destination as a touring base. More than 70% of visitors come by car and there are many attractions within an hour's drive, such as York and the old fishing villages of Robin Hood's Bay and Staithes, as well as the startling coastline. Further away are Castle Howard and Flamingoland, as well as the Yorkshire Dales and Moors.

The type of customer too has changed. Some hoteliers find it hard to accept that the traditional week or fortnight market has collapsed. Others like Trevor James, owner of the eight-room Lynton Hotel, recognize that the town should market itself to the three- to four- day top-up holiday market after people have been abroad. He was one of the twelve hoteliers who went for an RAC listing in 1994 to promote themselves to the touring market.

Meanwhile, Eastbourne, on the south coast, has been gently shaking off its image as an old-fashioned town for grey-haired old ladies. The local authority and industry have brought new amenities, including the Sovereign Harbour Development. The council also works with the Eastbourne Hotels Conference Consortium members to provide twice-yearly study tours for conference organizers. The conference facilities are limited and dated, but Graham Bean, general manager of the Hydro Hotel and Chairman of the Conference Consortium, maintains that the traditional feel suits many organizations and they are close to many of the hotels.

Julian Martyr, managing partner of the 87-bedroom Langham Hotel, says that the hoteliers have to change the product they offer as the market moves towards the more interest-based conference and activity holiday markets. The competition is now world-wide. The Langham specializes in activity holidays, especially bowls. Other hotels concentrate on conferences. However, many have had to invest in private bathrooms. This is too expensive for many of the small guesthouses and bed and breakfast establishments and about 100 have closed since 1989.

Source: B. Gledhill: The Tide is Turning, *Caterer & Hotelkeeper*, 18 May 1995, pp. 56–59; D. Goymour: Sea Changes, *Caterer & Hotelkeeper*, 27 April 1995.

ANALYSIS

These cases illustrate the changes that traditional resorts have had to make towards activity related tourism, such as activity holidays and conferences, and also to develop themselves as second holiday centres. Both cases illustrate the need to recognize tourism trends and for local hoteliers to work with the local authority and other private industries to promote and develop the area together.

MULTIPLIER ANALYSIS OF THE LOCAL IMPACT OF TOURISM

In Chapter 5, we saw that the economy is in balance when aggregate demand equals aggregate supply. This happens when the level of injections of spending into the economy equals the level of leakages of spending out of the economy. That is where:

(injections) $\quad I + G + X = S + T + M$ (leakages)

where I = Investment; G = government spending; X = exports; S = savings; T = taxes; M = imports.

If aggregate demand is greater than aggregate supply, then output, income and employment rise in real terms if there is spare capacity available. As income rises, savings, taxes and imports all rise until leakages balance injections. The economy then grows according to the rate of improvement in technology.

Tourism spending by people from outside a region is an export of that region because it brings money into the area. So we can adapt the foregoing analysis and apply it to the impact of tourism on output, income and employment in the area (Archer, 1982; Fletcher and Archer, 1991).

The multiplier

Any injection into an economy increases income by more than the amount of the injection. This effect is known as the multiplier effect. The size of the income multiplier is given by:

Income multiplier = $\dfrac{\text{increase in income}}{\text{increase in injection}}$

Its value is given by the formula:

Multiplier   = $1/c$,
where c = the marginal propensity to leak
                  = proportion (between 0 and 1) of extra income that is saved, taxed or spent on imports.
                  = proportion of extra income saved + proportion of extra income taxed + proportion of extra income spent on imports.

Thus, if the marginal propensity to leak is $\frac{2}{3}$, the multiplier is $1 \div \frac{2}{3} = 1.5$.

The reason for this is that £1 of tourism spending by non-residents creates extra income in equilibrium of Y.

This income, Y, creates further spending of £$(1 - c)Y$ and leakages of £cY. If the economy is in equilibrium, then leakages must equal injections. So:

£cY = £1.
Therefore extra income,
Y = £1.$(1/c)$,
so the multiplier is $(1/c)$, which is greater than 1 because c is less than 1.

THE MULTIPLIER PROCESS

The multiplier expresses the relationship between the level of income or output and the initial injection into the economy. Some tourism multiplier researchers have called this the *normal multiplier*, because many studies have used different measures of the multiplier instead.

The *equilibrium value* of the multiplier shows the final effect after leakages and injections are again in balance. However, we can use the *dynamic multiplier* to show the effect of the initial spending after a certain period.

Figure 6.2 shows how the original spending grows as people re-spend the money they earn.

The initial tourism spending has a direct effect or first round effect on the local tourism industry. The direct output effect is the increase in final demand (that is output for sale to the tourists). Some of this extra output goes in wages and profits to the industry. This is the direct income effect. The direct effect is less than the change in tourism spending (including travel), because the government levies various sales taxes. In economic terms, however, this is the difference between measuring output at market prices and measuring it at factor cost. For this reason we should measure income generated before deducting taxes on income and profit.

However, foreign firms or firms outside the region may provide some of the tourist services (such as travel). This is equivalent to importing the service and reduces the net value of the exported services.

The increase in output or income has indirect effects on other industries. As wages and profits are re-spent, this creates further demand in the system

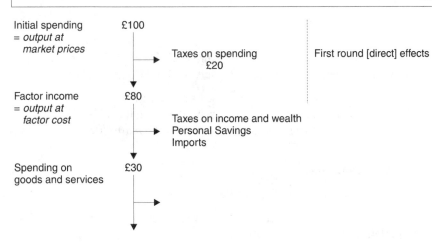

Figure 6.2 The multiplier mechanism

and so further output. Once again, we can distinguish between the output effect (output at market prices) and the income effect (output at factor cost)

Some writers also point out that the providers of tourist services, such as hotels, increase their demand from their suppliers and this increases the output in the supplying industries. These industries also increase their demand for goods and services from their suppliers. We can note the subsequent effects on these suppliers as a so-called indirect effect of tourism. However, these extra outputs are intermediate output (Chapter 3). *We must not add them to the total output* because that would be double counting. We can however, see the net effect by looking at value added or net output in each local industry. This would reduce the so-called direct effect by the value of intermediate inputs used.

For this reason, we must be very careful when looking at claims for the direct and indirect effects of tourism to make sure that the values are true values.

Some of the extra income from tourist spending is leaked from the local economy in the form of income and corporation (profits) taxes, savings, imports and by firms and workers from outside the area remitting some of the wages and profits to another area of the country or abroad.

However, some of the income is re-spent in the area and creates further local income. Businesses and local government are also likely to invest in improving or adding to existing facilities and equipment to provide for the higher level of activity in the area. This investment will also add to demand and contribute to the multiplier effect. The extra income generated from the second and subsequent round of re-spending is called the *induced effect*. In practice, it probably takes about a year and a half for most of the effects to work through the local economy.

Note that the convention is to state the total multiplier effect on the region as the direct effect plus the indirect effect plus the induced effect. If this convention is used, the direct effect is the net output only at the *first round* of spending.

MULTIPLIER STUDIES

The variety of approaches used to measure multipliers makes for confusing reading. So we need to interpret the results carefully depending on:

- *the type of multiplier*: what they seek to measure;
- *the form of the multiplier*: how the multiplier is defined;
- *the method and information used to measure the multiplier*.

The type of multiplier

There are two *main* types of multiplier:

1. *Value multiplier.* This summarizes the effect on some money value. The important kinds of multipliers are:
   (a) *Output multiplier.* This is the ratio of the change in total output to the initial tourist expenditure.
   (b) *Income multiplier.* This is the ratio of the change in income in the region to the initial tourist expenditure. The calculations for this multiplier usually exclude wage and profit income which is repatriated by foreign workers or companies.

   These multipliers are given as pure numbers. Studies may also give multipliers relating to specific variables such as government revenue.
2. *Employment multiplier.* This measures the increase in full-time equivalent employment resulting from an increase in tourist spending. The study should make clear how it is measuring the multiplier as there are different ways of calculating it. The employment multiplier must state the units such as number of full-time jobs per £100,000 of tourism spending.

The form of the multiplier

The appropriate form of the multiplier relates the change in final output to the initial increase in spending. This is called the *normal multiplier* to distinguish it from other forms of the multiplier. Two popular measures that have been used are:

1. the ratio of direct plus indirect income to direct income;
2. the ratio of direct plus indirect plus induced income to direct income.

These forms of the multiplier are economically unsound and are of little use in formulating good policy. The multiplier should express income generated in relation to the initial change in spending.

The method and information used to measure the multiplier

There are basically two ways we can gather the information to calculate the multiplier:

1. The *Input–Output* method. This uses an *input–output table* for the local economy showing:
   (a) the purchases made by the various industries in the economy from one another;
   (b) payments for wages, profits, imports, and taxes;
   (c) consumer purchases, government spending, investment and exports.
      There are standard mathematical procedures for calculating the impact of an increase in demand that allow us to track spending through successive rounds and calculate the multiplier. This method requires the collection of a large amount of information and is both time consuming and costly.
2. *Ad hoc multiplier.* This is a quicker and cheaper method that uses information on spending and leakage patterns. We calculate the multiplier using the standard formula $M = 1/c$, where c is the marginal propensity to leak. The more we can disaggregate the model and measure the propensity to leak according to where the spending takes place, the more accurate our model will be. This may seem a cruder approach than using input–output data, but it is very much cheaper and quicker, and is effectively of more use where the technical structure of the economy is changing rapidly.

Adjustments to the multiplier

The multiplier is an attractively simple way of quantifying the impact of tourist activity on a region or locality. However, it is derived from a simple income–expenditure (or expenditure–income) model in macroeconomics and so the multiplier has to be handled with care to deal with the limitation of that model. For instance:

- The effects only continue if the increased level of injections is maintained.
- The income–expenditure approach assumes that there is spare capacity in the economy, so that any increase in demand is immediately matched by an increase in supply, without a rise in prices. This can be resolved by adjusting the calculations for capacity constraints (Wanhill, 1988).
- Leakages out of the system are affected by the marginal propensity to consume (= 1 − marginal propensity to save). This is known to vary over the economic cycle and consequently the model has to allow for this.
- Investment and government injections may be induced by changes in income. These not only alter the level of income, but can cause fluctuations in the local economy.
- The value of the multiplier varies according to area and the methods used. However, the value of the normal multiplier should lie within a band about the general multiplier for the country. In the UK this is about 1.5, again depending on the initial injection, the direction of spending and other actors such as the tax regime. Values for other forms of the multiplier will be correspondingly higher.

Application of the multiplier

The model is essentially a short-run adjustment model. It is not appropriate for understanding the long-term growth of the area, as this depends on the development of a balanced economy which will require a sufficient mix of skills to maintain a balanced population, without migration from an area. Too much tourism or the wrong kind of tourism may damage the long-term growth of the local economy. For instance, multiplier studies reflect the fact that people staying in hotels generate more local income than people self-catering, who in turn provide more income than day-trippers. However, each type imposes its own costs in traffic congestion and uses of the infrastructure and local services, that impose real economic costs on those who do not derive any direct benefit from tourism.

FURTHER READING

Archer, B., 1982, 'The Value of Multipliers and Their Policy Implications', Tourism Management, Vol. 3(4), pp. 236–41.

Cooper. C.P., 1991, 'The Life Cycle Concept and Tourism', in Cooper, C.P. (ed), *Progress in Tourism, Recreation and Hospitality Management, Vol. 3, London: Belhaven Press.*

Fletcher, J.E and Archer, B.H., 1991, The Development and Application of Multiplier Analysis, in Cooper, C.P. (ed), *Progress in Tourism, Recreation and Hospitality Management, Vol. 3, London: Belhaven Press.*

Hughes, H.L., 1994, 'Tourism Multiplier Studies: A More Judicious Approach', *Tourism Management*, Vol. 15(60), pp. 403–6.

Competition

Costs and market structure $\boxed{7}$

Key concepts

Market structure refers to the number and size of firms, which limit the freedom of action for any firm in setting prices or in product specification. This chapter analyses the different market structures and their relationship to the cost of production (or *cost structures*) of firms in an industry. We:

- classify markets according to their structure;
- explain the meaning and nature of economies of scale, scope and experience;
- analyse economies of scale and scope in the hospitality industry;
- analyse the implications of these economies for market structure.

Prerequisites: Chapters 1 and 2.

MARKET STRUCTURE

Industries and markets

An *industry* is a collection of firms producing similar products. (Theoretically, they have high cross-elasticities of demand (see the discussion of Elasticity and its appplication in Chapter 2).) Firms often produce more than one type of product, so for the purpose of official statistics they are allocated to an industry according to their most important product (in terms of sales). Some hotel companies own pubs and restaurants, and vice versa. This means that the hotel industry is not the only supplier of hotel services. At the same time, the industry supplies more than hotel services. We analyse the development of a company according to its products but analyse its competitive position in the separate markets in which it operates.

Profits

Profits are the surplus after all expenses have been paid (Chapter 1). They are the return on the capital invested in the business. *Normal profit* (or *opportunity cost of capital*) is the level of profits investors require so that they continue to invest funds to replace worn out equipment and maintain the current level of production. Firms can make more than normal profits, called *supernormal profits*. They can also make less than normal profits, in which case they are making *economic losses*, even if they appear to be making an accounting profit.

The average level of profits depends on the acceptability of their product in the market, their costs of production and the degree of market competition. Competition reduces the power of the supplier because customers can buy elsewhere. A firm can make more or less than normal profits in the short term, but cannot do so in the long term if there is strong competition in the market:

- If the general level of profits is too low, competition between firms forces some of them out, leaving the remaining firms with a better level of profits.
- If the general level of profits is too high, new firms enter the market and compete away the excess profits.

In effect, the industry adjusts its capacity so that, in the long term, firms on the edge of entering or leaving the industry can expect to make only normal profits (Chapter 2). Firms cannot keep prices higher than necessary in the long run and must tie them down to the costs of production.

However, where there are only a few firms in the market, consumers have less flexibility and individual firms may be able to raise prices and make extra profits, called supernormal profits, in the long term. We look at the firm's ability to control price through an analysis of market structure, according to the number of firms in the market or market structure.

Market structure

We classify markets according to the number and position of buyers and sellers, as in Table 7.1.

Table 7.1 Market structure: Classification

Number	Sellers	Buyers
One	Monopoly	Monopsony
Two	Duopoly	Duopsony
Few	Oligopoly	Oligopsony
Many	Imperfect competition	
With differentiated products/inputs	Monopolistic competition	
Many, with identical product/input	Perfect competition	

Note: *Bilateral monopoly* is the term for one buyer and one seller.

Monopoly

A monopolist is the only firm selling the product, with no close substitutes. It can raise its price and reduce output to increase profits, depending on the elasticity of demand for its product. However, excessive profits encourage other firms to enter the industry or produce substitute products, unless the monopolist is able to prevent entry into the market through superior efficiency or *barriers to entry*.

Oligopoly

The small number of firms in oligopoly means that any action by one firm has a noticeable effect on the others. If a firm cuts its prices to sell more, its competitors' sales will decline and they will react by reducing their prices. Oligopolists can collude together to keep prices high and restrict output, although this is illegal in most countries. Collusion can vary from tacit agreement by sharing information on costs of production, to organized cartels with explicit detailed agreements about market sectors and market shares. The firms can, instead, compete by giving undisclosed discounts or engage in open price wars, or use non-price competition, for instance, through service programmes.

Perfect competition

The individual firm cannot control the price at which it sells the product. The firm has a perfectly elastic demand curve and price is determined by market demand and supply.

Monopolistic competition and imperfect competition

There are many firms in the industry, but each one has some limited control over price. Imperfect competition occurs because of the limitations of the market itself, such as location. Monopolistic competition, on the other hand, occurs when producers deliberately differentiate their products so as to raise prices above the perfectly competitive level, by exploiting consumer loyalty to the product.

However, we can treat price differences, for instance between hotels in the same town, as reflecting specific quality differences within a given price–quality structure. This allows us to use supply and demand analysis for discussing changes in the general level of hotel prices.

Dominant firms

There is a trend in many industries, including the various hospitality sectors, for larger firms to increase their share of output, with many small firms operating on the fringes. In such cases, the large and small firms are usually supplying different, though closely related, segments of the market. The large firms can still control the price that smaller firms can charge, and so we can treat them as extensions of monopoly or oligopoly.

Factors affecting structure of industry

Larger firms become more important in the long run in open competition when they are more effective in creating customer value. This can happen for three reasons:

1. They adapt better to structural and cyclical changes in the economy (Chapters 3 and 4).
2. They are better at integrating the production and marketing of service products (discussed in chapter 10).
3. They are more efficient (produce at lower cost) because of
   (a) economies of scale;
   (b) economies of scope;
   (c) experience economies.

In reality, small firms can learn from big firms and so it is unlikely that the first two reasons will of themselves continue to increase the dominance of large firms. However, the third reason would make it difficult for small firms to remain competitive in the long run. The next sections deal with these economies and their implications.

ECONOMIES OF SCALE AND SCOPE AND EXPERIENCE

Economies of scale relate to the costs of production, so we introduce the following definitions:

Average cost (AC) (or unit cost) = *Total costs of production ÷ Number of units produced.*

Production costs are lowest in the long run (Chapter 2), when firms can adjust their actual capacity to the most efficient level. So we define:

Long-run average cost of production (LRAC) = Lowest average cost possible with the given technology.

We also define the following:

Rate of output = Amount produced in a given period of time (such as a year).

Period of production = Number of years over which output is produced or a facility (e.g. hotel) *is operated.*

Economies of scale

We then define the following:

Economies of scale exist when the long-run average cost falls as the rate of output increases.

No economies of scale exist when the long-run average cost is constant as the rate of output increases.

Diseconomies of scale exist when the long-run average cost rises as the rate of output increases.

In each case, the total period of production (number of years in operation) remains the same.

This concept is illustrated in Figure 7.1.

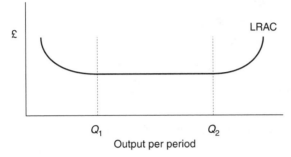

Figure 7.1 Economies and diseconomies of scale

Economies of scale exist up to output Q_1 where minimum average cost is reached. This is also the minimum efficient scale of production (m.e.s.). Firms producing a smaller rate of output than the m.e.s. are at a long-run competitive disadvantage, since they can be undercut by larger firms. They have to compete on factors other than price.

There are no economies of scale between Q_1 and Q_2, as long-run average cost is constant. Firms of any size between Q_1 and Q_2 can exist without suffering cost disadvantages.

Beyond point Q_2 there are diseconomies of scale, as the rate of output is too high to be as efficiently controlled. Such firms can only compete effectively in the long run if their size enables them to gain some monopolistic advantage in the market by closing off the market to competitors.

Types of economies of scale

Economies of scale can exist at the level of the industry, the firm or the production unit. We analyse each in turn:

Economies of scale external to the firm, internal to the industry

These relate to the effect of industry size on costs for each firm.

External economies of scale exist when the long-run average cost of production in each firm falls as the output rate of the industry increases.

If external economies exist, a new hotel in an area would reduce the costs of production for all the other hotels in the area. This could happen if, for instance, a larger local industry meant that specialist suppliers of goods or services could set up in the area. Specialist suppliers reduce costs because they tailor the product to their customers' requirements. External economies encourage the localized concentration of industry, although other factors such as climate and accessibility may be important.

Economies of scale internal to the firm (internal economies)

These relate to the activities of the firm independently of other firms.

> *Economies of scale internal to the firm exist when the long-run average cost of the firm decreases as the rate of output of the firm increases.*

Each firm is classed as an enterprise, where it is a company or where an individual or partnership run a business. Each enterprise has one or more establishments (plants, or production units), identified by separate addresses or locations. For instance, each Jarvis hotel is an establishment in the Jarvis Hotels enterprise. So we distinguish two kinds of internal economies:

Establishment (plant or unit) economies of scale

> *Establishment economies of scale exist when the long-run average costs of the establishment fall as output rate of the establishment increases.*

Figure 7.1 illustrates this case, where the cost curve refers to different sized establishments.

Example 7.1

A 100-bedroom hotel has a lower average cost per guest than a 50-bedroom hotel, provided they both operate at the same normal occupancy rate and for the same period of time.

Enterprise (firm) economies

> *Enterprise economies of scale exist when the long-run average costs of each establishment falls as the rate of output of the enterprise increases.*

Example 7.2

A hotel company has two hotels. It opens a third hotel. Average cost per guest night falls.

Figure 7.2 illustrates this situation, where the cost curve for each establishment shifts downwards as extra establishments are opened. AC_1 is the average cost curve when there is just one hotel in the group. AC_2 is the average cost curve for each hotel when there are two hotels in the group.

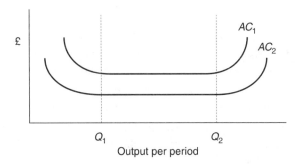

Figure 7.2 Enterprise economies of scale

Long-run implications of internal economies/diseconomies of scale

We can see the implications of economies of scale for the size of firms and establishments by applying the *survivor principle* (Stigler, 1958). This states that the firms which are of most efficient size have a greater or increasing proportion of industry output over time. The effect is shown in Table 7.2.

Table 7.2 Long-run implications of internal economies/diseconomies of scale

		Establishment		
		economies of scale	*no economies of scale*	*diseconomies of scale*
Enterprise	Economies of scale	**Large, multi-unit firms with large units**	Large, multi-unit firms, units of varying size	Large multi-unit firms owning many small units
	No economies of scale	Independent or multi-unit firms with large units	**Firms of different sizes, with small or large units**	Firms of different sizes with small units
	Diseconomies of scale	Large independent units	Firms of different sizes with small units	**Small firms with small units**

Evidence suggests that establishment and enterprise economies go together. For instance, larger hotel chains such as Swallow and Forte have been steadily eliminating smaller hotels from their portfolio since the 1980s, selling them off to smaller operators or enlarging them. On the other hand, small seaside and country hotels tend to be independently owned. In effect, we tend to see industries moving towards one of the configurations down the centre diagonal of the matrix.

Economies of scale are probably affected by location, with larger hotels and hotel chains becoming relatively more important in London and the large cities, while not being important in seaside and country places. This is because the higher density and more even demand of the city markets enable the hotels to take advantage of economies of scale.

Economies of scope

A number of firms increase the size of their operations by increasing the range of products as well as increasing the output of individual product lines. These firms may be able to take advantage of economies of scope.

> *Economies of scope exist when increasing the rate of output of one product reduces the average cost of other products produced by the firm.*

Economies of scope in an establishment increase the size of the establishment; economies of scope in the enterprise increase the size of the firm. There are also diseconomies of scope. If there were not, then firms would find it cheaper and more profitable to produce wide ranges of goods and services rather than just a small collection of them. Many industries in Europe and America in the 1990s, including the hospitality industry, saw cases where large firms tended to demerge, that is hive off large parts into separate firms or sell off subsidiaries, such as the hotel and restaurant chain Forte selling off contract caterer Gardner Merchant in 1992, which later merged with the French caterer Sodexho in 1995.

Experience economies

Economies of scale and of scope apply to all firms in the industry and depend on the conditions of production at the time. Experience economies, however, as the name implies, relate to the experience of a particular firm.

> *Experience economies exist when the average cost of production falls as the total historical output of the firm increases.*

In other words, the more the firm has produced in the past, the cheaper it can produce in the present. The experience curve is illustrated in Figure 7.3. It is an empirically observed phenomenon that was first used by the Boston Consulting Group in planning business strategy.

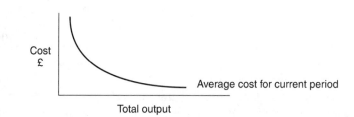

Figure 7.3 Experience economies

Larger firms have a cost advantage over smaller firms, because of their accumulated experience. When the market is relatively static or slowly growing, competition between firms tends to intensify and in these situations experience counts. However, the benefits of experience may decline fairly rapidly as historical output increases, so that firms should aim to expand their market share rapidly early on and establish a strong position for the future.

SOURCES OF ECONOMIES OF SCALE AND SCOPE

We now look at the reasons for economies of scale – that is, why they occur, and the sources of economies of scale – that is, where to look for them.

Reasons for economies of scale

Economies of scale exist because for the following reasons:

1. Increasing returns to scale in the production process. A firm may be able to double output without having to double the inputs it uses. For instance, small capacity machines are relatively more expensive than larger ones, because of differences in the relative amounts of material and time required to make them. Similarly, doubling the number of hotel bedrooms requires less than double the amount of public space to avoid congestion and less than double the number of staff to avoid long queues for services.

   Capital equipment also suffers from indivisibilities because, once it has been leased or bought, it has to be paid for, whether it is being fully utilized or not. This may make capital intensive methods too expensive at low levels of output.

   On the other hand, very large units can suffer decreasing returns to scale because managerial ability, co-ordination or resources are strictly limited.
2. Falling input prices. That is, firms may be able to get discounts for buying large quantities.

Sources of economies of scale

Economies of scale can occur at different stages of the production process. The traditional five sources of economies of scale are: purchasing and production; management and personnel; marketing; finance; risk.

Purchasing and production

Large scale production can lead to lower average costs because:

- Any indivisibilities usually occur at lower levels of production.
- There may be increasing returns to scale in production.

These are usually establishment economies. However, some economies can exist at the establishment and the enterprise level:

- Large purchases reduce processing costs per unit for suppliers and enable them to reduce prices.
- Standardization of production processes across establishments increases the standardization of production equipment and materials required. The firm may get suppliers to tailor the equipment and materials to the firm's needs, thus improving quality and reducing inspection costs.

The firm will get the most out of these economies when all its establishments produce exactly the same products. However, this may not be appropriate, because local markets may require different products.

Management and personnel

Large organizations with standardized operating procedures can produce more cheaply because:

- Training costs are reduced.
- Managers are more easily transferred between different units in the organization. This reduces disruption costs when managers leave or do not meet requirements.

Marketing

Large firms can advertise and promote products more cheaply per unit produced because expenditure increases more slowly than the number of separate units. These can be establishment economies, particularly in respect of local promotion, or enterprise economies.

Finance

Some finance economies are closely linked with the size of the establishment but most are enterprise economies. Raising large sums of money is usually cheaper because of the relatively lower processing costs.

Risk

Any venture or undertaking has risks attached to it. Risk means the variability of possible outcomes, that is to say different events may result from a given action. The more variable the outcome the greater the risk. Example 7.3 shows the difference in risk for two hypothetical cases:

EXAMPLE 7.3

An investor is considering buying one of two takeaway restaurants:

Store A has: a 50% chance of making £20,000 profit a year
a 50% chance of making £30,000 profit a year

Store B has: a 50% chance of making £0 profit a year
a 50% chance of making £50,000 profit a year

The expected profit of each store is given by the equation:

Expected profit = average profit
So for store A, expected profit = 50% of £20000 + 50% of £30000
= £((.5 × 20,000) + (.5 × 30,000))
= £25,000 a year

And for store B, expected profit = 50% of 0 + 50% of £50,000
= £25,000 a year

The takeaways are equally profitable, with the same average £25,000 a year. However, takeaway A is a safer bet, because its profits are less variable. Takeaway B has more variable profit and so is the riskier project.

Risk is a bigger problem for smaller firms because:

- They are less likely to get and keep the required share of the market to keep costs down.
- They are less likely to have accumulated sufficient financial reserves to tide them over bad years, particularly in the early years of operation. If there is an economic recession, the larger firms probably seem a safer bet for lenders. If poor results are seen to result from poor management, larger firms can often satisfy their lenders and shareholders through a change of management. Smaller firms have more difficulty changing their management and more difficulty in persuading lenders that this will improve their position.

ECONOMIES OF SCALE AND SCOPE IN THE HOSPITALITY INDUSTRY

We now look at some examples of different organizations in the hospitality industry and see to what extent they take advantage of economies of scale and scope.

EXAMPLE 7.4. A LARGE HOTEL CHAIN (SUCH AS SWALLOW HOTELS)

This organization utilizes enterprise economies of scale:

- *Purchasing and production.* The company can use economies of scale in this area if production is standardized across the whole chain so that large quantities are bought. Where local hotel managers are allowed discretion as to what is produced, the economies of scale are reduced. However, if the manager has to select from a standard range of products, there are still economies of scale in those products. The company obviously has to balance economies of scale against local market preferences.

  Production economies essentially relate to the size of the establishment and so there are unlikely to be production economies as such. However, large companies tend to manage large establishments, which probably have significant production economies of scale.

- *Personnel and management.* There are significant economies in the training and deployment of managers and other highly skilled personnel. A large part of the manager's skills are company specific. Standardization of training reduces costs of training. It also reduces the disruption if a manager leaves or proves unsuitable as the company can develop a reserve pool of management relatively cheaply.
- *Marketing.* External national marketing is cheaper per hotel, since market research and promotion can cover more than one hotel at a time without a significant increase in costs. Cross-marketing of hotels can also be done at small cost, particularly where the brand awareness is high.
- *Finance.* The company can raise capital more easily because of its size. The firm can also take advantage of the lower cost of internally generated funds, by concentrating the profit from all hotels into a rolling process of development at successive units.
- *Risk.* The chain has the advantage that a poor result from one hotel can be offset by good results elsewhere, unless there is a general recession. The company can also test new ideas on one unit, without committing the whole firm. Any failures that tend to occur normally can be more easily off-loaded.

EXAMPLE 7.5. A LARGE DIVERSIFIED COMPANY SUCH AS WHITBREAD (BREWERIES, RESTAURANTS AND HOTELS)

Most of the advantages are similar to those in Example 7.1, but have to be scaled down according to the relative size of the different operations. There will also be economies of scope particularly in personnel, marketing and finance and risk. However, diversified companies are not always more successful and can get over-stretched, especially during recessions. They also tend to dilute management skills. Such organizations frequently have to refocus their activities, often redefining core activities and sometimes selling off major areas of business as Forte did with Gardner Merchant contract caterers.

EXAMPLE 7.6. A FRANCHISED ORGANIZATION SUCH AS BURGER KING

A franchised organization has two components: the franchisor, Burger King, and the group of franchisees, independent firms operating under licence that trade under the Burger King name. A franchise may also have master franchisees who subfranchise units to other franchisees, as with Burger King's UK operations.

Note that where the franchisor (Burger King) employs a manager to run one of its units, that unit is an establishment within the Burger King enterprise. However, where the unit is run by a franchisee, that unit is part of a separate enterprise, owned by the franchisee.

The typical franchise requires an entrance fee plus a share of turnover.

The franchisor gets the following economies of scale:

- *Purchasing and production*. The large scale purchase of supplies is more stable. Supplies can be produced to the own company's specification and so reduce costs.
- *Management and personnel*. The company can oversee the development of the brand using a smaller and more accessible management structure, because the franchise contract encourages franchisees to work efficiently. This is particularly appropriate where the establishments are scattered over the country (discussed in Chapter 4).
- *Marketing*. The benefits come in both product development and promotion, aided by the wider branding of the product.
- *Capital*. The franchisor expands its operations using other people's capital and gets a return through royalties and entrance fee payments by the franchisee. The royalties help pay for promotion and product development. The franchisor has to ensure that the net royalty returns still leave the franchisee with higher returns than he or she could get from investing on his or her own account.
- *Risk*. The franchisees are risking their whole businesses. So the franchisor cannot pass the risks on because the franchisee would not pay to have them. This means that the franchisor can only spread capital risks over a wider number of activities, by reducing the risks to the franchisee. This happens where the franchisee trades an unknown and high risk venture (his or her own idea) for a well-known and lower risk venture).

Franchisees benefit by being able to convert small businesses into effective parts of a large one. This reduces their costs through the following economies of scale:

- *Purchasing and production*.
  (a) The franchisee can take advantage of the experience economies of the franchisor.
  (b) The standardized product range should give reduced cost of equipment and materials gives effective purchasing power reduction
- *Management and personnel*. The standard company training for all staff accesses experience and scale economies.
- *Marketing*. This is organized nationally by the franchisor and so gives economies of scale.
- *Finance*. Banks may regard the franchisee as a better risk, since she will have been vetted by the franchisor and is selling a branded

product with some local or national reputation. This makes finance easier to get and possibly cheaper.

- *Risk*. There is a reduction in risk as the cost of searching for suitable sites and choosing appropriate product branding will have been reduced. The franchisee accepts the risks of being a franchisee of an established brand, because he or she avoids the higher risk of having to develop a new product alone. Industry quit rates are lower for franchisees than for non-franchised operations.

EXAMPLE 7.7 TIED HOUSE

A tied house is one where the owner or tenant of a pub is tied by agreement to selling a brewery's beer and some other products to the exclusion of competitors. Although government regulations now require a guest beer to be available, they do not affect the nature of the tie. The tie gives a marketing advantage to the brewery by preventing other breweries from competing at that site. It can also sell beer and other products at higher prices. However, there are cost advantages also.

The brewer can take advantage of the following economies:

- *Purchasing and production*
  (a) The firm secures a larger market for its local brewery. This allows it to take advantage of the fairly significant economies of scale in brewery production.
  (b) Having a large number of outlets close together reduces transport costs per litre of beer.
- *Marketing*. Local marketing costs are spread over a greater volume. Costs are smaller because of local inertia and the smaller number that are floating consumers.
- *Risk*. This is reduced because it becomes more difficult for competitors, especially new rivals, to enter the local market, especially as it is difficult to obtaining licences and planning permission for new pubs.

The main advantages to the publican on the other hand are:

- *Marketing*.
  (a) The publican saves on market research costs, since the brewery actively chooses ties.
  (b) The publican benefits from the national advertising.
- *Finance*. The publican gets finance more cheaply through brewery loans.
- *Risk*. There is reduced risk from selling a well-known, branded product, although other factors such as decor, may affect the number of customers.

This case has some similarities with franchising, but the relationship is not as free on the publican's side. Also, the standardization is restricted to the individual products sold and does not usually include the pub design and range of facilities.

EXAMPLE 7.8 A CONSORTIUM OF INDEPENDENT HOTELS

A consortium of hotels is a group of hotels that freely associates for specific purposes, such as marketing or purchasing. There is a central organization that survives by selling services to members. Small hotels join the consortium in order to reap enterprise economies of scale. The advantages to the members are usually in three areas:

- *Purchasing and production.* Economies are limited by how far the hotels are standardized in their operations. This will be reflected in the degree of control exercised by the consortium on membership.
- *Management and personnel.* Where the consortium is selective in its membership, it can provide standardized training for the type of hotel training required more cheaply than from elsewhere.
- *Marketing.* This is usually the major benefit to the hotel, particularly when marketing overseas.

EXAMPLE 7.9 THE HOTEL INDUSTRY

Table 7.3 shows the division of the industry by enterprises. While there is some seepage between the hotel sector and the other sectors of the industry, it is relatively minor. However, this does disguise the situation where hotel companies such as Forte also run restaurant chains and where breweries such as Bass and Whitbread have diversified into other sectors, particularly hotels.

Table 7.3 Enterprises in the hotel industry, 1977–92

		Enterprises
Hotels and other residential	1977	15,714
	1988	13,648
	1992	12,619
Holiday camps, caravans and campsites	1977	1,479
	1988	1,636
	1992	1,910
Total hotel and catering	1977	112,650
	1988	122,281
	1992	114,050

Sources: Business Monitor

There is a long-term trend towards the reduction in the number of enterprises or businesses. The industry traditionally consisted of a large number of small independent units, but as with many other industries, there has been a decline in the one-unit enterprise and the spread of multi-unit enterprises. The growth of large chains with relatively large units has been helped by the following factors:

- Economic growth increases the pressures on the industry to adopt large scale, systematized production methods (Chapter 4).
- The demand for better quality accommodation and services has made many hotels obsolescent and needing considerable refurbishment. However, many small hotels represent inflexible capital stock as the buildings are difficult to upgrade to customer requirements. So their relative quality falls, their market position weakens and their return on investment falls, with a consequent decline in their stock.
- Consumer demand is changing towards hotel locations that support their changed travel and holiday patterns. This has left a surplus of accommodation in traditional seaside and other holiday areas, where small hotels have a relative advantage in the market.
- Businesses also require improved communication and have moved demand towards more conveniently sited hotels. The business traveller has varied needs. For some of these, hotels or motels on or just off motorways provide a better means of communication than difficult to get to city centre hotels. Motorway hotels also allow people within the UK to make short journeys for meetings that save on overnight travel. Other hotels that are convenient for airports or train stations need to be accessible from main routes. This reduces the acceptability of many establishments for business trips.
- There has been a significant increase in the proportion of accommodation provided by companies. Time and risk factors mean that many business travellers, and increasingly consumers, will rely on branded names as a way of reducing the incidental costs of travelling.

These factors force a reshaping of industry units, with considerable expenditure requirements which favour the development of large units. In particular, large firms will enjoy economies of scale in seeking out sites for new units to serve the new travelling requirements.

FURTHER READING

Reekie, W.D., 1989, *Industrial Economics: A Critical Introduction to Corporate Enterprise in Europe and America*. Aldershot: Edward Elgar, ch 5.

Market structure and market control 8

Key concepts
This chapter analyses the pricing behaviour of firms under different market structures and conditions. We:

- derive the rules for profit maximization;
- analyse the effect of market structure on a firm;
- analyse the market control policies of oligopolists;
- analyse government policy towards market structures in the hospitality industry.

Prerequisite: Chapter 2

PRICING FOR PROFIT

The price and output policy of a firm depends on its goal(s). We derive our model of price and output behaviour from the goal or principle of *optimization* or getting the best possible outcome. For most businesses this means profit maximization in the long run, where profit is the difference between revenue (or income) and cost (or expenditure).

Although shareholders in larger, impersonal organizations take little active interest in the running of the organization, they are keen to maximize their wealth as measured by the value of their shares. Share values reflect the market's view of likely future earnings, which are the profits (net of taxes) that the company will earn (Chapter 1). If they are dissatisfied with company performance, shareholders may force a change of management directly or sell their shareholdings to a take-over bidder offering a good price, as they did when Granada bid for Forte in 1996.

We now define some cost and revenue terms and find the conditions for profit maximization.

Cost terms

The principle of *opportunity* (or *alternative,* or *avoidable*) *cost* states that

> *The economic costs of an activity are those costs that occur only if the activity is undertaken.*

A firm's *costs of production* consist of two parts:

1. *Fixed costs*: These do not vary with the level of output. They are payments that have to be made for fixed inputs as a result of past decisions, such as repayment of loans for buying equipment. They occur only in the short run, when the amount of at least one input is fixed. However, they impose a financial burden on the business and may constrain its activities by reducing the funds available to finance current activity.
2. *Variable costs*: These vary with the level of output. They can be avoided by not producing and so are opportunity or true economic costs. All costs are variable in the long run.

Accountants may class a particular cost as semi-variable implying that it has a fixed and a variable component. However, this describes its mathematical structure only, and the two elements should be considered as above.

We define the following:

(Total) Cost, TC = *All expenditure incurred in producing the commodity.*

Average Cost, AC = *Total cost / number of units produced = TC/Q*

Marginal Cost, MC = *Increase in total cost as one more unit is produced*

= *Cost of n units – cost of (n–1) units.*

Table 8.1 illustrates the meaning of these terms:

Table 8.1 Cost terms

Output	Total cost (£)	Average cost (£)	Marginal cost (£)
0	0	—	—
1	16	[16/1 =] **16**	[16 – 0 =] **16**
2	30	[30/2 =] **15**	[30 – 16 =] **14**
3	42	[42/3 =] **14**	[42 – 30 =] **12**

In practice, a firm knows how its total costs (in the second column) vary with output. From these it can calculate its average and marginal costs, which are shown in columns 3 and 4 in bold type.

For output = 0: Total cost = 0.
Average cost is not defined (since 0/0 is not defined)
Marginal cost is also not defined (since there is not an output less than 0)
For output = 1: Total cost = £16

Average cost = TC/Q = £16/1 = £16
Marginal cost = TC of 1 unit – TC of 0 units
= £16 – 0 = £16

Average and marginal cost for outputs 2 and 3 are calculated in the same way.

Figure 8.1 shows the mathematical relationship between average and marginal cost as average cost varies.

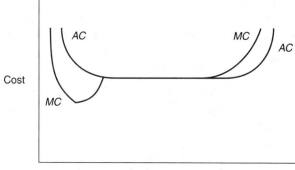

Figure 8.1 Relationship between average and marginal costs

The following points should be noted:

- If average cost is falling, marginal cost is less than average cost.
- If average cost is constant, marginal cost is equal to average cost.
- If average cost is rising, marginal cost is greater than average cost.
- But: *marginal cost can be rising, even when average cost is falling* (see Figure 8.1).

In most industries, empirical estimates suggest that cost functions tend to fall fairly quickly and then become flat, or decline very slowly. There have never been many instances where the long-run average cost curve rises. The explanation for this is simple. If a firm finds that the average cost curve for its establishment is rising, it will limit the size of its production unit, otherwise it would be uncompetitive. If it needs to expand production to meet demand, it will open up an extra establishment. This even likelier in the hospitality industry, where two different locations will improve the coverage of the market in most cases.

Note that a firm's short-run average cost curve can still be rising, even if has a falling long-run average cost curve. This is because a limited amount of one input in the short run prevents the firm from operating at its most efficient if it needs to expand output in the short term.

Demand and revenue terms

(Total) Revenue, TR
=   *Income from the supply of the commodity.*
=   *Price × Quantity (P × Q), when the same price is charged to all customers.*
Average Revenue, AR
=   *Total revenue/output.*
=   *Price × Quantity/quantity, when the same price is charged to all customers.*
=   *Price.*

Marginal Revenue, MR
= *Increase in total revenue as one more unit is sold.*
= *Revenue from n units – Revenue from (n-1) units.*

Table 8.2 illustrates the meaning of these terms:

Table 8.2 Total revenue, average revenue and marginal revenue

Q Quantity	P Price (£)	Total revenue (£)	Average rvenue (£)	Marginal revenue (£)
0	21	**0**	—	—
1	20	[20 × 1 =] **20**	[20/1 =] **20**	[20 – 0 =] **20**
2	19	[19 × 2 =] **38**	[38/2 =] **19**	[38 – 20 =] **18**
3	18	[18 × 3 =] **54**	[54/3 =] **18**	[54 – 38 =] **16**

We assume a firm knows or estimates how much it can sell at each price. So it can work out the revenue terms given in bold type:

For quantity sold = 0: Price will be £21 (or above)
Total revenue   =   P.Q   = £21 × 0 = 0
Average revenue is undefined, because 21/0 is undefined.
Marginal revenue is undefined, since there is no sale less than 0.

For quantity sold = 1, (maximum) price is £20
Total revenue   =   P.Q   = £20 × 1 =   £20
Average revenue =   TR/Q = £20/1   =   £20
Marginal revenue =   TR from 1 unit – TR from 0 units = £20 – 0 = £20
Similarly for other output levels.

Figure 8.2(a) shows the relationship between price (= average revenue) and marginal revenue for the price-taker or competitive firm. Figure 8.2(b) shows the relationship for the price-searcher or monopolistic or oligopolistic firm.

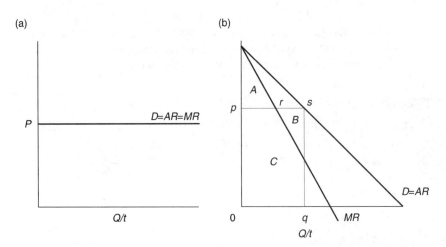

Figure 8.2 Demand and revenue curves

It should be noted that, when drawing Figure 8.2(b), use the fact that the slope of the marginal revenue curve is twice the slope of the demand curve, so that the *MR* curve cuts the *Q* axis halfway along from the *D*-curve. The reason why the slope of the marginal revenue curve is twice the slope of the demand curve is:

Total revenue = price × quantity = *op* × *oq*
  = area *C* + triangle *B*
but   Total revenue = sum of marginal revenues
  = area under the marginal revenue (*obvq*)
  = area *C* + triangle *A*

- triangle *A* = triangle *B*, and
- distance *pr* = distance *rs*
- drop in *MR* = 2 × drop in price

Conditions for profit maximization

There are two conditions for profit maximization. They are:

1. The firm should increase the level of output produced until:

   Marginal cost = Marginal revenue.

   This means that we increase output as long as the extra costs are less than the extra income received. However, this condition is also consistent with making minimum profit (or maximum loss), so we have to add a second condition, namely:
2. *marginal cost is rising faster than marginal revenue* (or falling more slowly).

   We use this condition to distinguish points of minimum and maximum profits.

Table 8.3 explains and illustrates these conditions.

Table 8.3 The marginal rules for profit maximization

Output Q	[AR =] Price (£)	Total revenue (£)	Marginal revenue (£)	Total cost (£)	Average cost (£)	Marginal cost (£)	Total profit	Marginal profit (£)
0	0	0	—	0	—	—	0	—
1	5	5	5	6	6	6	−1	−1
2	5	10	5	11	5.5	5	−1	0
3	5	15	5	15	5	4	0	1
4	5	20	5	18	4.5	3	2	2
5	5	25	5	22	4.4	4	3	1
6	5	30	5	27	4.5	5	3	0
7	5	35	5	33	4.7	6	2	−1

Table 8.3 gives data cost and revenue. This allows us to calculate the profit profile, given in bold type. For instance, for output = 1:

Total profit = Total revenue – Total cost = £5 – £6 = –£1 (that is a loss of £1).

Marginal profit = Increase in total profit as one more unit is produced
= Profit from 1 unit – Profit from 0 units
= –1 – £0 = –£1.

We can also calculate marginal profit from the equation:

Marginal profit = Marginal revenue – Marginal cost
= £5 – £6 = –£1.

We see that:

1. maximum profit occurs at outputs $Q = 5$ and $Q = 6$
2. minimum profit occurs at outputs $Q = 1$ and $Q = 2$.

The First Condition: Marginal cost = Marginal revenue.

There are two outputs where marginal cost equals marginal revenue, namely:

Q = 2, with a minimum profit of –£1, (maximum loss of £1),

and $Q = 6$, with a maximum profit (£2).

Note that output, $Q = 5$, also gives us maximum profit, because marginal cost = marginal revenue at $Q = 6$, which means there has been no change in profit.

We now verify that the second condition distinguishes points of maximum profit from points of minimum profit.

The Second Condition: at the output where Marginal cost = Marginal revenue, marginal cost should be rising faster than marginal revenue.

This means that if we increase output by one more unit, marginal cost becomes greater than marginal revenue (so marginal profit becomes negative).

If we increase output from $Q = 2$ to $Q = 3$, marginal cost becomes 4 and marginal revenue becomes 5. So, marginal cost is now below marginal revenue, which means that the second condition is not satisfied and we have a point of minimum profit.

If, however, we increase output from $Q = 6$ to $Q = 7$, marginal cost becomes 6 and marginal revenue stays at 5. Marginal cost is now greater than marginal revenue, which means that the second condition is satisfied and we have maximum profit. This is illustrated in Figure 8.3.

Area A represents the first stage of increasing losses because marginal cost is greater than marginal revenue. Area B represents the stage of increasing gains because marginal revenue is greater than marginal cost. Area C represents the second stage of increasing losses. The firm must pass through stage A to get to stage B, but does not have to go into stage C.

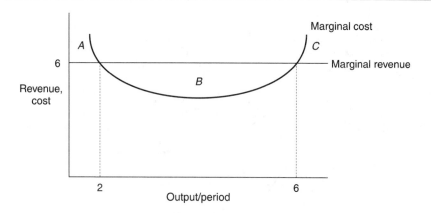

Figure 8.3 Illustration of marginal rules

In most cases, the structure of costs and demand usually means that the second condition is satisfied. So, we shall normally refer to the first condition only in subsequent analysis.

COMPARING MONOPOLY AND COMPETITION

We now examine the popular belief that monopolies charge higher prices than firms that are in competition with each other. We do this by comparing competition and monopoly on the same basis. So we make the following assumptions:

1. Demand is the same under competition and monopoly.
2. Costs are the same under competition and monopoly.
3. Firms are profit maximizers.

When the market is in equilibrium, firms produce where Marginal cost = Marginal revenue. However:

- Under monopoly: price is greater than marginal revenue,
    so price is greater than marginal cost.
- Under competition: price is the same as marginal revenue,
    so price equals marginal cost.
- Marginal costs are assumed to be the same,
    so price is higher under monopoly than under competition.

We illustrate this result in Figure 8.4.

To keep the diagram simple, we assume that long-run average cost is constant. Marginal cost is then equal to average cost.

Competitive firms supply according to their long-run marginal cost curve, so this is the supply curve for the competitive industry. Therefore the competitive output is Q_c and price is P_c, and the demand curve cuts the supply curve.

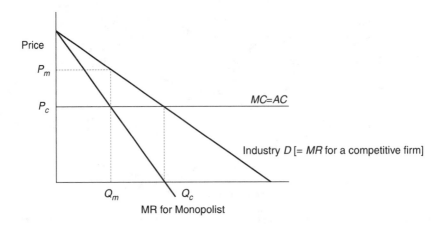

Figure 8.4 Comparing monopoly and competition

The monopolist's demand curve is the same as the industry demand curve and its marginal revenue curve is MR. So the monopolist supplies output Q_m at price P_m, where its marginal cost equals its marginal revenue. So monopoly output is less than the competitive output, and the monopoly price is higher than the competitive one.

DOMINANT FIRMS AND OLIGOPOLIES

Firms with large shares of market sales have market power and can exercise monopolistic or oligopolistic control over the market. This means that they can sell their products for higher prices than they would otherwise be able to. They may also be able to control the activities of small firms, who have little, if any, market power. If there are economies of scale or scope as well, the position of small firms is weakened in relation to their large rivals.

Smaller firms can deal with this situation in different ways:

- Where larger firms maintain a higher, oligopolistic price in *their main markets*, the small firms do not undercut it, even when they can do so. If they did, the large firms could cut their price and expand output using accumulated financial resources to sustain any losses incurred in a price war.
- Small firms avoid direct competition by concentrating on more remote or sparsely populated parts of the market. The large firms lose the advantage of economies of scale, because the scale of operations is too small or too seasonal.
- Small firms can redefine the market so that they convert a large uniform market into smaller differentiated segments by creating products aimed at those specific segments. This creates niches in the market, where the small firms can compete effectively on added value not low price. This

removes the advantages of economies of scale for large firms as they cannot get a big enough market.

Large firms may also tolerate small firms because they provide a useful source of risk-taking in trying out new ideas. If the small firm has a new idea but is unsuccessful, the large firm can analyse the failure to consider whether the idea can be made to pay. If the firm is successful, the large firm will become interested and start to compete or more usually buy the small firm from its shareholders. This is particularly the case where an entrepreneur has successfully developed and marketed an innovation, but subsequently requires capital to expand, or wishes to capitalize his future earnings. Although a high price may be paid for the small firm, it should be a lower risk investment.

Similarly, in oligopoly, one firm may establish itself as price leader if it can be relied upon to be more sensitive to changes in market demand or supply, or if it has sufficient capacity and financial resources to compete in a price war with any rival.

The industry may also contain a strategic group of firms, those that can operate on a national or international level. Other firms then operate only on a regional basis. The national firms will maintain their position through large scale promotional campaigns. The small firms, however, may have to rely on proximity to the local customer base, price shading (selling a little more cheaply) or consumer ignorance.

In order to protect the large profits that can be made, oligopolistic firms may form a *cartel*. This lays down by agreement prices and/or quality and/or quantity controls on the commodity. The cartel acts as a virtual monopoly, often with reduced output and excess capacity. Cartels, however, find it difficult to stay together. Any member of the cartel is usually better off if it can secretly or otherwise undercut cartel prices or increase output as long as the others do not perceive it or react to it.

Potential rivals

The higher profitability of oligopolistic or monopolistic markets sooner or later attracts new entrants into the market. The greater competition reduces both profit levels and also the certainty with which firms can make them. Existing firms can try to deter potential rivals from entering the industry by reducing the prospect of profit. Two methods of doing this are limit pricing and raising barriers to entry.

Limit pricing

In this situation, firms between them (through some form of tacit or explicit agreement) keep output below competitive industry production by an amount equal to the minimum efficient scale of production (see the comparison of monopoly and competition above). We can show this by extending Figure 8.4 as Figure 8.5 below.

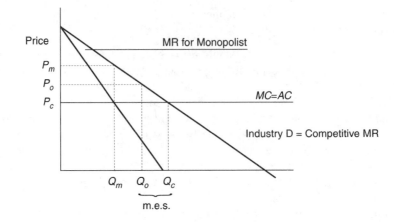

Figure 8.5 Limit pricing

For convenience, we assume the long-run average cost is constant $= C_c$, so that marginal cost equals average cost $= C_c$. As in Figure 8.4, the competitive supply curve is the same as the long-run marginal cost curve, C_c. So competitive output and price is given by quantity Q_c and price, P_c. Similarly, monopoly output and price are given by Q_m and P_m.

The colluding oligopolists, however, would keep output at Q_o. This is less than the competitive output by an amount equal to the minimum efficient scale. They charge the price P_o, which gives them some excess (oligopoly) profits. However, there is no incentive for new firms to enter the industry. Any new firm would have to produce at the minimum efficient scale to compete with existing firms. (It may even need to produce beyond that level to cope with the experience economies that existing firms enjoy). This would increase industry output to the competitive level Q_c and reduce price to P_c. Profitability would then fall to normal.

This strategy to keep new entrants out is more effective when the minimum efficient scale is large and so is more likely to happen the greater the internal economies of scale are. If there are no substantial economies of scale, the industry would quickly become competitive and existing firms would have to go for as much profit as possible, or else find some other way of keeping firms out.

Barriers to entry

Barriers to entry can be either natural or artificial. Internal economies of scale create the natural barrier of the minimum efficient scale. In this case, larger firms have an advantage over smaller firms and new entrants have to establish their position quickly in order to survive. Firms that have been in the business a long time may benefit from the experience curve effect, which leads to reductions in unit cost. Other natural barriers may exist. For instance, there may be a limited number of good operating sites from which an operator can serve customers.

An artificial barrier exists when, for example, firms practise product differentiation. Customer loyalty, or inertia, to existing products makes it more difficult for any new product line to be selected. This increases the risk in establishing any new product line and therefore the costs of entry. This reduces the potential return relative to the costs of entry and reduces the incentive to enter the industry. The costs of entry, incurred in planning and installing facilities or in establishing networks or market flows, are sunk costs and may be quite large. Established firms do not have the same uncertainty in establishing a market or expanding into new products. They will also benefit if production facilities are already geared to producing a basic product but can be easily (that is cheaply) adapted to produce a range of related but differentiated products. This approach can be supported by a high level of advertising. Natural barriers can be artificially increased by similar activities.

Where there are planning restrictions on development, local oligopolies can maintain their position through excess capacity. This then limits the claim by the new entrant to be providing for a need.

Raising artificial barriers does cost money and firms will see profits reduced. However, they will balance off short-term reductions in profit against increases in long-term profits.

MARKET STRUCTURE AND SOCIAL EFFICIENCY

Political aspects of market structure

The market is a politically determined system for *allocating resources* – deciding on what and how goods and services should be produced – and *distributing the output* – sharing out the income of society. The results should reflect the relative costs and benefits of the various activities involved to society. There is a widespread view that large firms do not benefit the consumer through lower prices and that monopoly power is bad for consumers. The political result is that most industrialized countries have legislation governing monopolies, oligopolies and mergers. Britain has the Monopolies and Mergers Commission and EU imposes its own regulations as well.

Social efficiency

The economic case for control of large firms is based on the concept of *social efficiency* or *welfare maximization*. The economic rules for welfare maximization for society are similar to those for profit maximization for a firm. However, we use the concept of *social value* or *social gain* instead of profit; and the concept of *social cost* instead of money cost. This means that we should increase the level of activity (or output) until

Marginal social cost = Marginal social value.

We define and measure social cost and social value according to the Western *liberal* (with a small 'l') or *individualistic* ethic that equates social value with value to the individual. This is in contrast to an *organic ethic* where society creates its own values to which the individual has to conform. These are extreme views and, in practice, liberal economists agree that the political system should have a social value system that takes account of the distribution of income. The state also has a legitimate interest in prohibiting certain activities such as drug-taking that have market value but no social value.

Under the liberal ethic, the marginal social value of the product is the price, because this is the value put on it by the buyer (the marginal consumer) who finds it just worthwhile paying this price. The marginal social cost is the marginal cost of production because this represents the alternative value of the resources used, what has to be given up. (This assumes there are no side-effects on people other than the producer and the buyer of the product.) Our condition for social efficiency is now: increase the level of activity (or output produced) until:

Price = Marginal cost.

Monopoly price is greater than marginal cost so the industry is under-producing and is socially inefficient. Competitive industry produces where price equals marginal cost and so is producing the correct output.

Notice that the argument against monopoly is not that price is higher than under competition. Higher profits for shareholders will be re-spent or invested. The argument is that it does not maximize social welfare because price is greater than marginal cost.

We may also criticize monopoly on distribution grounds because it increases the income of the owners who are usually well off at the expense of consumers, who are less well off.

However, monopoly would be acceptable if:

- There were considerable economies of scale. This could mean that the minimum efficient scale of output for the firm would be so large that only a small number of firms would be able to remain in the industry. The industry would still require regulation to ensure that profits were redistributed to the customer.
- Large firms were more innovative in reducing costs of production or increasing the value of products over time.
- Monopolies did not abuse their position.
- Entry into the industry were relatively easy so that the threat of potential competition is high.

GOVERNMENT CONTROL OF MONOPOLIES

Government control of monopolies is exercised in different ways according to the country concerned. In the UK, there is a mixture of statutory control and political discretion. A firm is classed as having monopoly power if it has 25% or more of industry output. The Director-General of the Office of Fair Trading may refer a group of such firms in a monopolistic industry to the Monopolies and Mergers Commission for investigation. The Monopolies and Mergers Commission will then produce a report with recommendations for the Secretary of State for Trade and Industry who then decides what controls to impose.

If two or more firms are involved in a merger or take-over and their combined assets are sufficiently large or their combined outputs would exceed 25% of industry output, the Secretary of State may refer their case to the Monopolies and Mergers Commission.

On the whole, UK policy has been rather lax towards monopolies with only a small proportion of proposed mergers and takeovers or existing large oligopolies being investigated. However, there are occasions when the lack of sensitivity of businesses to changes in the economic and political environment causes adverse reaction by the government. The most important recent case for the hospitality industry has been the investigation of breweries and their control over the licensed trade during 1990–92. Brewers had long been a target of suspicion and had previously been investigated on three occasions. The changed political climate of the 1980s saw a government committed to the increased use of market forces and a more vigorous anti-monopoly policy by the Office of Fair Trading. These led to an investigation by the Monopolies and Mergers Commission of the links between breweries and pubs. This uncovered a number of major concerns and led to the current government restrictions on brewery control over pubs. As a result, some brewing companies sold their breweries and switched to pub retailing, while smaller regional breweries expanded their market presence and other pub chains developed.

CASE STUDY: BREWERIES AND PUBS

The beer market matured towards the end of the nineteenth century, with further growth depending on population growth that was itself slowing down. The significant and unexhausted economies of scale in the production of beer led naturally to increasing concentration of ownership in the industry into fewer companies and of production facilities into fewer breweries, as happened in other manufacturing industries. This process continued during this century and, following a spate of mergers in the 1980s, the market was dominated by six large brewing companies, as shown in Table 8.4.

In addition, the nature of the product also means that there are considerable cost savings in distributing output to locally dense markets. The flow of funds to the large breweries is such that they have the advantage of establishing closely knit local distribution networks, usually through ownership of property. Hence the process of *vertical integration* between the manufacturer (the brewery) and the retailer (the public house) as the market matured and breweries acquired or built public houses.

Table 8.4 Brewers' shares of UK beer sales

	Percentage share of beer sales	
	1991	*1992*
Bass	22	22
Courage	20	18
Allied	14	
Carlsberg-Tetley		17
Whitbread	12	13
Scottish & Newcastle	11	12
Other UK Brewers	16	13
Imports	5	5
Total	100	100

Source: Key Note, *Breweries and the Beer Market*, 1992, 1993

According to the Monopolies and Mergers Commission, the return on capital invested for the large national brewers was twice as much as that for the smaller regional brewers in the mid-1980s, while local brewers had lower returns still.

Brewery control over pubs

Control of pubs can be split into three types:

1. *Free Houses*. Independently operated by their owners who are free to buy from where they want. Free houses may, however, be tied to a particular brewery through a loan tie. The brewery lends money to the pub at low rates of interest in return for their products being stocked.
2. *Tenanted Pubs*. These are owned by the brewery which has leased them out to tenants. Traditionally the tenant had to buy products from the brewery. They were tied to the brewery.
3. *Managed Pubs*. These are owned by the brewery and operated by managers of the company.

The control exercised by the breweries can be seen from the estimated distribution of pubs and bars in Table 8.5.

Table 8.5 Public houses and bars in the UK

	1985		1990		1994	
	Number	*%*	*Number*	*%*	*Number*	*%*
Managed houses	12,900	19	13,250	19	13,427	19
Non-managed houses	33,600	50	30,000	43	20,406	29
Total tied houses	46,500	69	43,250	62	33,833	48
Free houses/independents	20,850	31	26,750	38	36,091	52
Total	67,350	100	70,000	100	69,924	100

Source: Key Note, *Public Houses*, 1991, 1994

The actual influence exerted by breweries in general is understated in the table because brewery houses were on average considerably larger in terms of turnover. Key Note (*Public Houses*, 1991) estimated that tied houses accounted for 67% of drink sales in pubs and bars. The largest five breweries (Bass, Allied, Whitbread, Grand Metropolitan, Courage) controlled nearly 32,000 pubs, over two thirds of the tied estate and 45% of all outlets. Adding the rather smaller sixth largest (Scottish & Newcastle) gave the Big Six over 34,000 pubs or 49% of outlets. In fact, the control exercised was greater for two reasons. The first was that many free houses had tied loans. Secondly, the distribution of outlets held by each major brewer was not evenly spread over the country. As we would expect, brewery control was greatest in the core market areas of high population density and economic activity. Brewery-owned houses accounted for only 20% of pubs in Scotland but over 75% in the more densely populated and economically active areas of London, the Midlands, northwest England and Yorkshire. Local concentration was even greater with the major breweries having large shares of the market in particular areas, implying some tacit cartelization of the market. In particular, in half the licensing districts one brewer had 25% or more of on-licences, while in two-thirds of the districts two brewers had more than a third of on-licences.

It should be noted, however, particularly in the light of subsequent government action, that direct control of retail outlets by breweries had been declining for a number of years from about four-fifths in the 1960s. Since that period, the number of pubs had been increasing, but the breweries had been cutting their ownership. The likely interpretation of this, however, is that the breweries were concentrating on the larger, more profitable units in core locations. Where population movements made existing outlets more difficult to manage or obsolete, there would be little point in retaining them. Large organizations tend to cultivate centralised management that finds it difficult to adapt to local conditions. Relatively difficult outlets would not be worth the managerial effort required. However, the breweries continued to exercise some control over about a quarter of released houses through a tie being part of the condition of sale.

As a result of the Monopolies and Mergers Commission Report in 1989, government regulation (through the Beer Orders) required the major breweries to reduce their control over the industry. The most significant measure was the requirement that the breweries release from tie half of their estate of over 2,000 pubs by the end of 1992. The effect on the pub sector of the required speed of implementation was fairly predictable. The national brewers had to decide whether to continue in the retail business or brewing or both. Most decided to remain in both. Some, such as Courage and Grand Metropolitan did a 'pubs for breweries' swap, with Courage becoming a brewer.

The adjustment process, however, has been complicated by the changing pub, catering and leisure markets. In particular, the growth of pub restaurants has brought further changes as firms realign their core businesses, a process speeded up by the recession during this period. Some of the smaller brewers, such as Greenalls, moved out of brewing to concentrate on their restaurant and hotel business, but having a supply agreement with a major brewer. This process is likely to continue for some time, which means that a particular year-to-year comparison quickly becomes dated. However, some effect of the Beer Orders can be seen in Table 8.6.

Table 8.6 Public house ownership 1990–94

	1990		1994	
	Number	*%*	*Number*	*%*
National Brewers	31,000	44	15,862	23
Regional & other brewers	12,250	18	17,971	26
Total brewers	43,250	62	33,833	48
Independents	26,750	38	36,091	52
Total	70,000	100	69,924	100

Source: Key Note: Public Houses, 1991; 1994

The entry 'Independents' in Table 8.6 includes companies that are not brewery-owned and have no more than 50 units. The biggest gainers have been the regional independents. Some of these, however, have grown sufficiently large as to be able to exercise considerable market power in their own right. Whilst this may alter the balance of profit between pub operator and brewery, it is unlikely to benefit the customer or even the pub tenant.

Brewery development since 1994 has been to control the market by other means in order to maintain the profits of the brewing industry and its control over the retail market. The longer term trends can be seen in the further concentration of brewing interests. However, the new labour government prevented Bass acquiring Allied-Domecq's brewing interests, which would have given Bass greater control.

REVIEW EXERCISES

1. (a) Complete the following table:

output	price	total revenue	average revenue	marginal revenue	total cost	average cost	marginal cost	total profit	marginal profit
0						0			
1	6					8			
2	6					15			
3	6					21			
4	6					26			
5	6					30			
6	6					34			
7	6					39			
8	6					45			
9	6					52			
10	6					60			

   (b) Find the maximum and minimum profit.

   (c) Show that the function marginal cost = marginal revenue gives either maximum profit or minimum profit.

   (d) Show that marginal cost = marginal revenue *and* marginal cost rising above marginal revenue together give maximum profit.

2. Explain the economic reasons for considering monopoly power to be bad.

   (a) When may monopolies or oligopolies be acceptable?

   (b) Are there oligopolies in the hospitality industry and are they acceptable?

Business development and operations

Strategic product development and delivery

9

Key concepts

This chapter considers the production and delivery of services to improve the competitive position of the hospitality firm. We:

- derive an operational concept of services;
- analyse the effective planning of hospitality service production;
- analyse the improvement of service quality;
- analyse the conditions for efficient production and the use of labour.

Prerequisite: Chapter 8, especially the first three sections.

GOODS AND SERVICES

Nature of commodities

The distinction between goods and services exists in economics, management and marketing, implying that there are substantial differences in their production and marketing. Several attempts to define services as distinct from goods use some variation on the list of characteristics in Figure 9.1 (see for instance, Edgett and Parkinson, 1993). However, these distinctions do not always fit with reality, because we can find counter-examples.

The problem with these distinctions is that they do not help improve service production, marketing and delivery. So we use, instead, the following definitions of goods and services that is derived in part from the economist Peter Hill's definition (Hill, 1987):

A good is a commodity with only a small non-physical element, that is produced for consumers who decide the intensity, timing or manner in which the product is used.

A service is a commodity with large non-physical elements, that is produced with a pre-determined intensity, timing or manner of use.

1. Intangibility

Goods are tangible, services are intangible.
Example: Goods can be measured but services are difficult to measure precisely.
Counter-example: Fast food outlets rely on the timeliness of their product for people who do not have time to wait long for their meal. The timeliness of the meal can be measured in terms of the time to reach to the customer.

2. Perishability

Goods are storable, services are perishable.
Example: Many services fit this type. For instance, a hotel cannot store unused accommodation from one night to the next.
Counter-example: Pre-preparation is possible in some parts of food and accommodation services, particularly with modern technology.

3. Heterogeneity

Goods are homogenous, services are heterogeneous.
Example: Goods can be standardized so that one television is exactly the same as the next. However, one meal is not the same as the next because it is prepared for a different customer who requires a different service as regards time, place and possibly other components of the meal.
Counter-example: While the complete meal service has to be heterogeneous in at least one aspect, there is increasing standardization of most fast food services provided.

4. Inseparability or immediacy

The production of goods can be separated from their sale and consumption; but services are produced and consumed at the same time.
Counter-example: With modern production and storage technology, food services do not have to be produced and consumed at the same time.

Figure 9.1 Conventional distinctions between goods and services

These definitions identify the essentially different orientation of goods and service producers:

1. Consumers make further decisions regarding the use of goods, whereas services are already specified at the time they are bought (usually, to be consumed at the time of purchase). We should note here that producers can supply services to their specifications rather than to what the consumer actually wants.
2. A good does not change its nature according to when it is produced or according to the consumer buying it. A service, on the other hand, depends for its value on when it is produced and for whom it is produced. For instance, a restaurant meal must be produced at the right time for the right customer otherwise it will have no value.

We can note also:

3. There is usually no change to the consumer or her existing assets when she buys a good. However, buying a service usually changes the consumer

or her assets in some way. This reflects Hill's definition of a service as an activity affecting a person or her assets.

In practice, the line between goods and services is increasingly fuzzy as almost all goods have a service element and almost all services have a goods element, though in differing proportions. To deal with this, we adapt Kelvin Lancaster's *Goods Characteristics* approach to consumer demand (Lancaster, 1966), which treats each product as a bundle of characteristics. We identify various goods and services characteristics, so that any commodity becomes a mixture of *general goods characteristics* and *specific service characteristics* which together determine its value to the consumer.

General goods characteristics

These are the tangible, measurable aspects of the commodity that exist independently of the consumer. Their value depends on being:

- *Adaptable to consumer requirements.* For instance, a consumer adapts a ready meal from the supermarket, his or her own time and other resources (electricity and so on) to provide food services when he or she requires it. However, the meal itself does not change, until the customer alters it. The individuality of the product is not important, because the consumer adds that when he or she uses the product.
- *Precisely specified.* In order to adapt the product to his or her requirements, the consumer needs to know the performance capabilities of those characteristics that he or she values. The precise specification of these characteristics becomes more important the greater the variety of uses or the more expensive the product.
- *Reliable.* Every purchase carries a risk that the product will fail to conform to its specification in use. The risk of failure imposes a cost on the consumer that depends on the chances of failure and the costs incurred if failure occurs. As household or business activities become more complex, these costs of failure increase disproportionately. So reliability becomes increasingly important.

Specific service characteristics

These are the intangible, subjective aspects of a commodity. They exist only in relation to specific customers who value them differently according to their own special requirements. However, a firm has to assess the value to each consumer, because these are the features that give the business its competitive edge.

For instance, in a fast food unit, the standardized production of meals is similar to manufacturing cans of baked beans. The real, primary service characteristics are timing and location: the availability of a product when and where the consumer wants it or is prepared to accept it. In this way a food service operation is similar to a retailing unit that takes products from factories and provides them at convenient locations and times for consumers.

For a firm to establish or retain its competitive position it must identify the appropriate mix of goods and service characteristics and organize their efficient production and delivery. Efficient production, however, takes into account the structure of the costs as well as the composition of the product, and these are considered next.

COSTS OF PRODUCTION

The total costs of a particular product range consist of three components:

Initial or set-up costs

Initial or set-up costs are the costs of getting the production process ready and include:

- *transaction costs* incurred in buying the equipment;
- *installation costs* incurred in getting the production process working; and
- *switching costs* incurred in reallocating resources from another activity to this one.

Capital costs are only included if they relate to setting up production, such as survey costs, legal fees and installation costs. The firm must cover these costs by making enough profit from sales of the product after meeting all other costs.

Some of these costs are incurred whatever the production capacity planned and so they increase less than proportionately with the *capacity* of the plant. So average set-up costs fall as the capacity is increased. Longer production runs reduce average costs by spreading costs over a greater total output, so the firm can also reduce average costs by extending the period of operation.

Processing or operating costs

Processing or operating costs occur during the production operation and include:

- depreciation of plant and equipment as they wear out or become obsolete and the maintenance costs of the equipment used;
- the costs of materials and labour used;
- finance costs.

Average operating costs tend to be constant, but there may be some economies of scale at low rates of output.

End or shut-down costs

End or shut-down costs are the costs of clearing up net of any salvage costs. They behave in a similar way to set-up costs.

The combination of set-up, shut-down and processing costs means that the long-run average cost curve is downward sloping with average cost falling as the rate of output increases, as long as the total life of the operation remains the same. The curve will flatten out as higher rates of output are reached. This is shown in Figure 9.2.

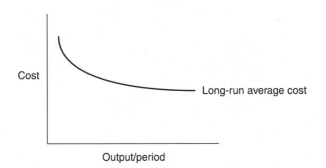

Figure 9.2 The variation of average cost with rate of output

This result applies to each product, though the actual cost curves for the firm also depend on other factors, such as its central administrative structure and procedures. It clearly implies that a service firm can reduce its costs considerably by using standardized procedures to increase the scale of output.

The hospitality firm can use the analyses of costs and product characteristics to structure its product range and production strategy. It can then use more specific information for more detailed production planning.

PLANNING THE PRODUCTION OF HOSPITALITY SERVICES

Structure of production

A product combines two sets of characteristics. The goods or general characteristics constitute the basic requirements of the good that are objectively measurable and can be duplicated. They are of relatively low value to the individual consumer because they are not specific to the individual. The emphasis should therefore be on methods to reduce costs. The specific service activities, however, are individualized characteristics that are specific to a particular individual. They are, therefore, relatively labour intensive and expensive to produce. The emphasis should be on increasing their value, or converting them to general characteristics if they do not cover cost. This leads to the following approaches to improve the efficiency of production:

Increase standardization of the product

This allows the firm to minimize long-run average cost by increasing the scale of production. However, different consumers have different, though similar, service requirements. This makes it difficult to standardize service characteristics. Production tends to be small scale and labour intensive, rather than large scale and standardized. To deal with these problems a firm can:

1. *Group customers with common service characteristics.* The firm identifies certain measurable standards which are sufficiently narrow to satisfy customers' requirements, but which are sufficiently broad to allow the firm to make savings. For instance, burgers can be produced in anticipation of customers rather than producing them when the order arrives. As long as the burger is not held for more than a few minutes, customers are unlikely to be able to tell the difference, yet the company can save itself considerable processing costs while still meeting the customer requirement for fast food delivered without waiting.
2. *Reduce the individuality of service characteristics.* This reduces switching costs into and out of its provision, lowers the labour intensity of the whole operation and reduces operating costs. The use of self-service can be very useful at certain points in the service process when:
   (a) the sub-activity is relatively uncomplicated: for instance, tea and coffee making facilities in hotel bedrooms;
   (b) the customer's time cost is relatively low: for instance, in partial self-service at breakfast or other meals. In this case the customer may actually prefer the flexibility of self-service.

Increase the standardization of production processes

Market demand may be too small to get all the benefits of large scale standardized production. However, the firm can still get many of the benefits through economies of scope by supplying products with similar production processes. For instance, grilling different meats is simpler than having different operations – grilling and frying the same meat, say beef. If necessary, the firm can simplify its processes by buying-in part-finished products so that on-site finishing is similar for each product.

EXAMPLE 9.1

McDonalds identified growth in demand for a fast food chicken alternative to beef. One way it responded was to introduce a chickenburger – the McChicken. Although this product requires its own separate processing, the processing is similar to that for existing burger production and so can be easily integrated into a unit's operations. The other method was through the chicken nugget –

dissimilar to the beefburger but retaining similar ease of handling. The firm reduces costs by standardizing the goods characteristics of the product or component. It only differentiates the product where the extra cost is less than the extra value to the consumer. This implies a long-run strategy of differentiation from a concentrated base. When we apply this concept to popular restaurants, we can see why processes are kept as similar as possible, as in burger, cheeseburger, and so on: one process, several products. Even when the market changes so that chicken has to be added to the menu, an astute company such as McDonalds sells it as a chickenburger. So even when the main ingredient changes, the process remains essentially the same. This cuts down on switching and other labour costs.

Supply a small number of standard product ranges with a high potential for individualization

This allows the firm to retain many of the cost advantages of standardization but exploit the market advantages of differentiated products. Ideally, standardization is based on similar materials but can be based on similar processes.

> *Standardization is a low profile, low visibility activity; individualization is a high profile, highly visible activity.*

The standardized goods characteristics are common to every customer and so do not convey the individuality of the service. They are best done using as much high technology as possible and do not need to be visible to the consumer.

The individualized service characteristics, however, are the ones that create extra value specifically for the customer. They are also labour intensive and costly to supply. The customer should realize fully how much a particular service has been geared to his or her requirements and circumstances. This is best done by making the service elements highly visible.

Increase pre-preparation of food (and other products where possible)

The variation in demand for perishable services means that some capacity is under-utilized, which increases the cost of each unit produced. A firm can reduce the impact of demand variations by reducing the perishability or increasing the storability of the product where this does not make any significant difference to the actual service provided. Improving technology increases the extent to which firms can do this on-site through, for instance, more *mise-en-place* or, increasingly, off-site with pre-packaged portions.

Increased centralization of production

This allows greater utilization of equipment, because the variation in demand at one central production unit is less than the variation in demand at the different outlets.

Increase co-operation between different operations at central locations

People are increasingly buying in groups, such as the family out shopping. The firm has to provide a composite product of individual products for a group of people. The individual products may require quite different production processes. These can be provided more efficiently through specialized one-process units that co-operate by providing standardized access and accommodation as, for instance, in food courts. Similarly, motels and restaurants share sites and increasingly leisure centres and restaurant chains do so also.

Standardization takes production further away from the consumer, while differentiation brings it nearer to the consumer. Table 9.1 summarizes the different aspects of hospitality services, where the general or goods characteristics favour one type of production and the service characteristics require another form of production.

Table 9.1 Structure of service production

Strategic feature	General 'goods'	Specific 'service' Characteristics
Market strategy	cost-based – small number of standard product ranges	value based – potential for easy differentiation
Key production feature	standardized by material ⟶ standardized by process ➤finishing large batch ⟶	small batch finishing
Factor intensity	capital intensive ⟶	labour intensive
Location of production	off-site, service distant ⟶ finished on-site	on-site, close to consumer
Visibility to consumer	invisible ⟶	highly visible
Time before delivery	not time specific, storable ⟶	immediate service, delivery as produced

Source: based on Cullen and Foxcroft, 1987

Production processes must match the composition of characteristics

The product characteristics must match the set required by the consumer to optimize value to the customer. Highly individualized characteristics are by nature relatively expensive to produce, because they are unstandardized. If the firm has identified them correctly, however, they attract a high consumer value. Standardized characteristics are low cost, but are also relatively lowly valued.

Customer orientation

The principles above also improve customer orientation of the product and improve the market sensitivity of the firm. Example 9.2 shows the different orientations between traditional and modern fast food catering methods.

EXAMPLE 9.2

Production is oriented along two dimensions: the customer dimension and the producer dimension. Figure 9.3 gives a model of a modern fast food operation. The horizontal line represents the customer dimension and this clearly dominates the vertical line, representing the producer dimension. The model emphasizes the importance of the workers at the interface. This is consistent with the importance of the service encounter concept in service management and the quality management philosophy that empowers the worker to take responsibility for delivering what the customer requires. In this process, behind-the-scenes workers are responsible for delivering to their own, internal customers.

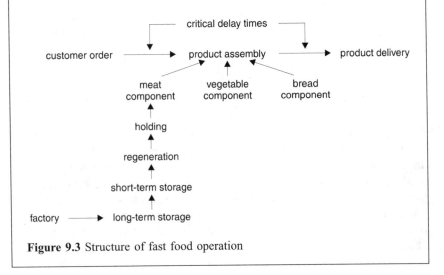

Figure 9.3 Structure of fast food operation

PRODUCTION PLANNING IN A CHANGING ENVIRONMENT

Production planning takes place in an environment of risk and uncertainty. Risk applies not just to the perception of the consumer but also to the choice of technology and this affects the balance between goods and service characteristics over time. Initially, a successful new product is produced with highly valued service characteristics, but using relatively unstandardized and relatively expensive methods (even if cheaper than other alternatives at the time).

The higher profits, however, lead to adjacent market positioning by rivals and a decline in the profitability of the chosen service characteristics. The firm can use its experience to maintain a cost advantage over its competitors for some time, but the rival products eventually becomes mass produced with low unit cost and low market value.

Economic change alters the pattern of consumption. Certain characteristics retain their value for consumers but existing commodities become less efficient in supplying those characteristics and so they decline in value. Existing methods of production also become out of date and relatively costly. The firm should discard the product, change the process or face increasing losses on the product. Table 9.2 describes these stages of a service product.

Table 9.2 Value cost and risk in hospitality services

Stage	Consumer perception	Consumer value	Technology	Goods–service mix	Risk	Profitability
1.	New	Highly differentiated characteristics	High cost unstandardized	Low–high	High	Increasing if successful
2.	Established	Differentiated with high customer value	Improved	High–high	Low	High to falling
3	Imitated	Falling differentiation	Low cost standardized	High–low	Rising	Falling to satisfactory
4.	Outdated	Changed consumer	Outdated	Low–low	High	Low

SERVICE QUALITY

Service quality has become an increasingly important instrument of competitive strategy as the service economy has developed. There is also an increasing awareness of the power of the consumer through both non-market activity and in the market itself. For instance, while breweries may have been seen to have extracted oligopolistic profits through their control of pubs, they have been all too aware that they have to provide for customer requirements as the level and direction of consumer leisure spending changes.

Economic development has increased the interaction of household activity with the formal production economy. This has raised the political and economic importance of quality. As households have increased their capital base, they have become less adaptable in their lifestyle and made their quality of life more dependent on the performance of goods and marketed services. The result is that consumers have switched from making a series of independent but related purchases to a series of integrated transactions. These integrated purchases make it difficult and relatively expensive for households and firms to change direction, as they need to guarantee the continuance of and improvement in an appropriate lifestyle, whether using a particular computer system or buying a timeshare in a tourist locality whose desirability may change significantly over time. Producers now find that their products are increasingly subordinate to particular consumer lifestyles. Consumers and producers are free to renegotiate their purchases and sales at least periodically. The hidden costs could, however, be excessively high. This reinforces the integration between producer and consumer. The question then arises as to the balance of power between the two sides.

Producers are fewer and so should have significant power. However, consumers react consistently in large groups, so that there becomes, effectively, only a few such consumer units. Where economies of scale or scope exist, firms have to hold a large share of the market. Firms must carve out their own niche and, as is the case with most markets, where total market size is growing more slowly than the potential competition, firms have to be seen to provide a more suitable product. For instance, in a protected and regulated oligopolistic market in the early 1980s, British Airways was losing money and suffered cutbacks. Yet within a few years, following an intensive service quality programme, the company was earning significant profits.

This makes the modern service economy a set of integrated production–consumption activities. The relation between consumer and producer is effectively an economic (not legal) relationship of *principal and agent*. This occurs when repeated individual market transactions are replaced by a contract whereby the agent undertakes delivery of some specified output over a period of time. Although there is no contract, the widespread information network and consistent patterns of behaviour mean that firms are increasingly working for the consumer, with the shareholders and/or managers acting as team monitor.

The principal must articulate his or her requirements, communicate them to the agent and ensure that the agent delivers the required output. So how can consumers control firms through the market and how far do they control product specification and performance through non-market processes, whether the product is sold for profit and or provided free or at controlled prices by public agencies?

New consumers and existing consumers to some extent can make use of new situations and recontract. Existing firms have an advantage of familiarity, but there still remain the problems of shirking and maintaining effort. Where, as is likely, the consumer can be seen to be risk-averse, the consumer needs to be well informed. Where infrequent expensive purchases effectively isolate the consumer or where the consumers may not be able to test the output (and hence the effort of firms) because of technical inability, legal control of quality will be required or implemented, as in the EU package holiday regulations. Conversely, where firms shoulder the market risks and where the consumer can directly assess the outcome, firms can be expected to reap considerable profit if they get it right.

Quality management begins when there are positive preventive as well as remedial measures taken to eliminate defects in the system. Pioneers in modern quality management, such as Juran, saw zero defects too costly to achieve, though the organization should implement some kind of improvement programmes. However, Crosby (1979) developed and expounded the concept of 'Zero Defects'. Quality is free – a dynamic view of the production process where heavy initial expenditure on prevention leads to subsequent marked falls in costs, by eliminating scrap, rework and other recovery procedures.

This approach seems more suitable for service industries and underlies much current writing. Services are provided at particular moments in time, so that the product must be right first time; not least because bad service is difficult to rectify, and bad news travels fast. However, this requires management commitment. As researchers have shown, management has in many cases to make more effort to understand what customers really want and put more resources into service quality.

CASE STUDY: SMALL HOTELS AND QUALITY SERVICE

The National Heritage Department has just published a report of a benchmark study of 70 small hotels (of less than 50 bedrooms). Thirty of the hotels were in London and 40 in the country. The report describes small hotels as long on charm, with attentive staff and efficient billing systems but short on clean bathrooms, good mattresses, staff training and simple managerial controls. Small hotels are strong on 'the personal touch they can provide', but consumers wanted 'reassurance that individuality does not mean unreliability'.

Customers consider general cleanliness a major factor in evaluating hotels, but dusty furniture and stained carpets were common in public areas. Bathroom fixtures and fittings were usually workable but often in poor condition; customers often cited loose tiles, worn carpets, dampness, poor maintenance and inadequate ventilation.

It also points out that popular hotels are not always managed on a business-like basis. Training is the weakest area: only 25% of the managers had been trained; 85% of the hotels had some informal training for staff, but only 20% had some formal training programme. Less than 50% had written procedures for staff, such as checklists for maids cleaning bedrooms and public areas.

The 10 hotels with the highest score for training also scored highly for service and their annual achieved revenue per room was 40% higher than average.

The 10 hotels with the highest score for service and business skills had an average revenue per room of £20,400 a year compared with the average revenue of £13,200.

The National Council of Hotel Associations, an umbrella organization for groups representing small hoteliers criticized the report. One member said that there were 40,000–50,000 small hotels, guesthouses and bed and breakfasts. The small sample studied for the National Heritage report made it 'difficult to take the findings seriously'. He also added that high rates of VAT and uniform business rates were reasons why small hoteliers sometimes could not afford the investment needed to meet standards.

Source: Roderick Oram, Hotels report identifies room for change, *Financial Times*, 19 March 1996, p. 11.

ANALYSIS

Standard statistics texts tell us that the size of the sample and the way it is selected is more important than the percentage of the group sampled. A properly selected sample of 70 can give a sufficiently reliable picture of the industry. So these results should be taken seriously. The study shows that more could be done to meet customer requirements; and that reliability of service is more important than the personal touch. Training improves service which in turn improves revenue. However, many hotels are perhaps underfunded, but where this is the case the outlook is not good, as customers become more service conscious in the long run.

CASE STUDY: BUILDING THE HENRYS TABLES BRAND

Greenalls Group acquired the Henrys Tables brand when it bought the Boddington Group in October 1995. It was a brand of pub-restaurants that had strong similarities with Greenalls' own nineteen-strong steakhouse chain, Hudsons:

- a similar theme;
- operating in northwest England;
- performing well.

The conclusion was that resources had to be concentrated into developing one or other of the brands to economize on purchasing, marketing and operations. Greenalls chose to develop Henrys Tables within its Premier House pub-restaurant division because

- existing customer-awareness level was high;
- only six of the Hudsons did not fit in with the new format;
- minimal refurbishment was required at the other outlets.

The integration has now led to over forty units with average weekly turnover per unit between £12,000 and £15,000, about half of it from food. More units are planned with expansion taking place in other parts of the country.

The customer base includes families with children; business lunches and small group celebratory meals, now accounting for 30–40% of trade. The aim for the units are:

- a mix of traditional surroundings with bright lights and modern menus;
- wide range of fast food including steaks, barbecued chicken, tacos, pasta, curries;
- edge of town location, not far from a motorway, to catch passing trade as well as local customers.

Some units have added bedrooms that support the groups budget four-star Premier Lodge concept.

Christopher Allen, Operations Director of Premier House made the following comments about the brand:

- they are pubs with restaurants inside – with equal importance for both – not one with the other attached;
- the menu is the same in each pub: 'branding becomes useful because the customer is reassured . . . you can target the market you want and they know what they are going to get';
- the main competitors are Beefeaters, Harvester and some independents: 'they're setting up virtually the same menus because they can get hold of very similar food, so it doesn't have to be a large company such as a Whitbread who is your competitor'.

In order to meet this competition, future development lies in developing the 'unique selling points' to differentiate the brand. Its strengths are:

1. looking after staff – so that they focus on the customers:
   (a) identifying role-models, or 'team leaders' at all grades in the units,
   (b) ongoing and on-site training,
   (c) avoiding scripted language and actions;
2. developing strength as a special occasions venue;
3. continuing menu development:
   (a) more vegetarian and pasta dishes from the current base of steak and other meat dishes,
   (b) encouraging ideas from managers that can be generalized across all units to take advantage of centralized distribution with lower prices that have raised profit levels by five percentage points on average.

Source: Gillian Drummond: Hooray Henry, *Caterer & Hotelkeeper*, 27 June 1996, pp. 62–64.

ANALYSIS

This case illustrates several points in the previous analysis of this chapter and Chapter 4:

- positioning for an appropriate stage of the changing pub-restaurant market;
- brand development to reduce consumer risks;
- standardization to support brand with economies of scale;
- the competitive process is driving the service element down because of similar products coming on to the market. This competition is technology driven by the standardization of products from food processors outside the industry.

New services elements have to be developed:

- menu development with increasing variety but still with accessible standardization across units;
- customer focus through staff selection and training – delivering customer care.

FURTHER READING

Clarke, Roger and McGuinness, Tony, eds., 1987, *The Economics of the Firm*, Oxford: Basil Blackwell, chapters 1–3.

REVIEW EXERCISE

1. Select a production and delivery process in a hotel or catering outlet: examine the process and determine whether the structure of production accords with the principles of service delivery.

10 Business operations

Key concepts

This chapter introduces those economic concepts that are relevant to the internal management of the organization. We:

- analyse the efficient combination of resources in production;
- analyse investment decisions;
- explain the economic role of firms and the position of management.

Prerequisite: Chapter 9.

EFFICIENT PRODUCTION

Techniques of production

When the firm has determined the strategic direction of its products, it can use certain rules to improve the efficiency of its production and use of resources. When a restaurant prepares a meal it uses a specific method of production that defines the activities at each stage of production and the quantities of various inputs used. In most cases, the restaurant can choose between different methods of production, such as using more pre-prepared items (for instance, pre-prepared carrots) or preparing them freshly on-site. These different methods may deliver physically different products, but are the same in economic terms, if customers do not notice any differences or regard them as unimportant. The firm can then choose the cheapest process. In this case, the restaurant balances the cost of labour and other resources used (or saved) against the extra cost of the ready prepared ingredients.

If restaurant labour becomes more expensive, or factory prepared commodities become cheaper, restaurants switch to using more factory prepared products to cut down on the now relatively more expensive labour. If restaurant workers become more productive, for instance by speeding up the rate of working, restaurants use more on-site preparation.

In effect, the firm chooses its method of production according to:

1. the relative costs of the different inputs used; and
2. the relative productivity of the different inputs in the processes used.

Productivity

We use the following terms in measuring productivity:

The average product of an input = total output produced divided by the number of units of the input.

The marginal product of an input = the increase in total output as one more unit of the input is used.

It should be noted, that in measuring productivity, it is assumed here that the quantities of the other inputs used in the process stay the same. Marginal and average products of one input vary with the quantities of the other inputs used.

Table 10.1 illustrates the average and marginal products in cleaning hotel bedrooms and shows how we calculate average and marginal cost of the labour used.

Table 10.1 Productivity and cost of labour

Labour input: hours worked	Total product of labour: rooms cleaned	Average product of labour (APL): rooms cleaned per hour	Marginal product of labour (MPL): rooms cleaned per extra hour	Average cost per room	Marginal cost per room
				(at £4 per hour wage costs)	
0	0	—	—	—	—
1	2	[2/1 =] **2**	[2 − 0 =] **2**	[4/2 =] **2**	[4/2 =] **2**
2	6	[6/2 =] **3**	[6 − 2 =] **4**	[4/3 =] **1.33**	[4/4 =] **1**
3	12	[12/3 =] **4**	[12 − 6 =] **6**	[4/4 =] **1**	[4/6 =] **0.67**
4	17	[17/4 =] **4.25**	[17 − 12 =] **5**	[4/4.25 =] **0.94**	[4/5 =] **0.8**
5	21	[21/5 =] **4.2**	[21 − 17 =] **4**	[4/4.2 =] **0.95**	[4/4 =] **1**

Table 10.1 illustrates the usual pattern of productivity. Productivity is low to begin with, because work has to be done in setting up the process (getting the room cleaner's trolley ready) or because of inadequate resources. Marginal productivity rises, but eventually falls as people become tired or as machines require maintenance or because there is insufficient equipment available. Marginal and average cost, by definition, vary inversely with marginal and average productivity.

Efficient production and the principle of equi-marginal returns

Marginal product measures the physical output of the extra unit of input. However, the value to the firm of the extra output depends on the extra revenue produced, or marginal revenue product:

The marginal revenue product of an input = marginal physical product × marginal revenue of the extra product.

The efficient firm uses inputs up to the point where its marginal cost equals its marginal return. We can then apply the rules for optimization, so we use more of the input until

marginal cost = marginal revenue product.

In practice life is not so simple. It is often difficult to measure the marginal revenue product, because we cannot separate out the contribution of one input from that of another input. (How would you determine the contribution of the room cleaner to sales?) However, we can use apply the principle of equi-marginal returns (Chapter 1) which state that the marginal pound (or penny) spent in any activity should give the same net return. This gives us three rules for checking that we are using resources correctly:

1. Using an input efficiently:

   The marginal return to any input relative to its cost must be the same wherever it is used.

   This means that an extra pound spent on kitchen staff should give the same return as an extra pound spent on housekeeping staff.

2. Selecting the right production process efficient combination of inputs

   The marginal return relative to cost must be the same for each input in the production process chosen.

   That means the last pound spent on labour should yield the same return as the last penny spent on equipment.

3. Producing the most profitable output mix

   The marginal return from spending on production should be the same for each product.

   If they are not the same, the firm can increase profits or reduce costs by reducing production where marginal revenue is low and expanding output where marginal revenue is high. This is important, of course, where the firm has only a limited amount of working capital. In all these cases, marginal return is measured in relation to the last pound spent.

USE OF LABOUR

Marginal revenue product and wages

As the previous section explained, firms optimize by employing labour up to the point where the marginal revenue product equals the marginal cost of employing the worker. The structure of the industry will therefore affect the level of employment and wages.

1. In a competitive firm, price equals marginal product, so that the marginal revenue product is the same as its market value. The firm employs the maximum amount of labour. Setting a minimum wage above the going rate would unbalance supply and demand and unemployment would increase in that industry.

2. For a monopolist or oligopolist, marginal revenue is less than price and so the value of an extra worker is less than the value of the extra work done.

In a competitive labour market, less hotel workers can always seek employment in other industries if hotel wages are too low. So the effect should be to reduce employment still further (there is less anyway because monopolistic industry produces less). However, where an industry is becoming more oligopolistic, existing workers may not be mobile enough to move elsewhere and get trapped into lower wages.

3. Monopsonistic firms often face a rising supply curve for labour. This means that the marginal cost of a worker is greater than the wage paid and so, setting marginal cost equal to marginal revenue product will mean fewer workers being employed at lower wages. Setting a minimum wage rate at the level competitive firms would pay would increase both earnings and employment.

Marginal product is often difficult or impossible to measure. For instance, we may be able to measure the output of a team of workers, but we have no logical basis for measuring the relative contribution of a person to a team. This leads to seemingly arbitrary differences in rates of pay to different grades of worker. Also, the product, such as room cleaning, may be only part of a complete product, namely, providing overnight accommodation.

INVESTMENT DECISIONS

A firm produces goods or services by using various inputs to the production process. Some of these inputs (such as labour, business services and semi-finished products) are bought in as the firm requires them. Other inputs (such as land, buildings, equipment) are owned or leased for substantial periods by the firm to use as and when required in the production process. These latter inputs are the *assets* or *economic capital* of the business and provide an essential flow of services to the firm over time.

Traditionally, the assets of the business have been seen as its *physical capital* stock consisting of land, buildings, plant and equipment, and vehicles; and its *financial capital* consisting of cash and investments elsewhere. However, management and labour skills also represent considerable capital resources because they have those specialized skills, attitudes and knowledge of company practices that enable the firm to survive and prosper in a competitive world. A firm can only hire labour for short periods, but it should take appropriate steps to maintain its assets. The value of particular skilled workers to the firm can be far greater than their weekly wage and they should be discarded with reluctance.

A firm builds its capital stock by investing. Some investment replaces worn out capital; the rest is net investment in new or updated capital.

Investment and the cost of funds

Once the firm has decided on its correct market and products appropriate to that market, it has to invest in the assets required to produce the planned services. An *investment project* is any activity requiring a significant quantity of resources and generates a series of costs and benefits over time, called an *income stream*. This stream of income may be operating surpluses from a product line or may be in the form of cost savings. In order to evaluate the project properly, the firm has to compare the costs and benefits of the project on the same basis. £1 today is not the same as £1 in a year's time. Money can be lent out at interest so that £1 invested today will return more than £1 in a year's time. Whether the firm uses its own money or borrows it to pay for the project, the money is tied up and cannot be used to finance some other activity. The market for money exists to ration out available funds through the rate of interest.

The rate of interest enables us to compare objectively projects with considerably different time-profiles of costs and revenues. We can use the rate of interest to *compound* a sum of money forward to its *future value* at a given point in the future. Conversely, we can *discount* a sum of money backwards to its *present value* at this point in time.

EXAMPLE 10.1

The rate of interest is 10% (or 0.1) per annum.
  If we invest £100 now it will grow as in Table 10.2.

Table 10.2 Compounding to future value

Year	Amount at beginning of year (£)	Interest for year (£) = rate of interest × amount	Amount at the end of the year (£)
1	100	100 × 0.1 = 10	100 + 10 = 110
2	110	110 × 0.1 = 11	110 + 11 = 121
3	121	121 × 0.1 = 12.1	121 + 12.1= 133.1

When the rate of interest is 10% per annum, £133.12 in 3 years' time is worth:

  £121 in two years' time,
  £110 in one year's time,
  £100 now.

We can derive the standard formula for compound interest if we use algebra instead of specific numerical values.

- We replace the sum of money, £100, by the general term A.
- We replace the rate of interest, 10% (or 0.1), by the general term i.

Table 10.2 can now be rewritten as Table 10.3.
  So we calculate the future value of a sum of money n years in the future by multiplying its value now by compound factor $(1+i)^n$.
  This means that we can find the present value now of any sum n years in the future by dividing by the amount $(1+i)^n$. This is the same as

Table 10.3 General formula for compound interest

Year	Amount at beginning of year	Interest for year = rate of interest × amount	Amount at the end of the year
1	A	$A \times i = A.i$	$A + A.i = A(1+i)$
2	$A(1 + i)$	$A(1 + i) \times i = A(1 + i).i$	$A(1 + i) + A(1 + i).i = A(1 + i)(1 + i) = A(1 + i)^2$
3	$A(1 + i)^2$	$A(1 + i)^2 + A(1 + i)^2 .i$	$A(1 + i)^2 + A(1 + i)^2 .i = A(1 + i)^2(1 + i) = A(1 + i)^3$
n	$A(1 + i)^{n-1}$		$A(1+i)^n$

multiplying it by the term $1/(1+i)^n$ (or $(1 + i)^{-n}$). This term is called the *discount factor*. Discounting converts a future sum of money into its present value using the appropriate discount factor.

EXAMPLE 10.2

A firm plans to buy some equipment for £5,000 in two years time. The current rate of interest is 5%. How much should it invest to be able to pay for the equipment?

We need to find the present value of £5,000 in two years' time.

$i = 5\% = 0.05; n = 2.$

So, the present value of £5,000 in two years' time

$$= £5,000 \times 1/(1+.05)^2 = £5,000 \times 1/(1.05)^2 = £4,535.15.$$

Hence the firm must invest £4,535.15 into a *sinking fund* for the new equipment.

Investment decision

We can discount all future sums of money received or paid on a project to their present values and sum them. If we subtract the initial outlay, we then have *net present value* of the project.

Net present value = Sum of all discounted future sums of money to be paid or received minus *the initial outlay.*

We can use the present value to decide whether the project, by itself, is worth undertaking. The decision rule is simple:

Accept the project if the present value of the project is greater than 0.

Reject the project if the net present value is less than or equal to 0.

If the present value equals zero we are neither better or worse off. However, since people are generally over-optimistic about outcomes, we take the more cautious line of keeping to a positive present value.

It is important to remember that increasing the rate of interest lowers the present value of an investment in two ways:

- it raises the cost of funds and so reduces the present value of returns in the future;
- it decreases the level of demand in the economy and so is likely to reduce the cash flow in the future.

Investment alternatives

We can also use the present value criterion when we have to select a project or set of projects from a range of alternatives. In such cases, however, we have to establish the options available before applying the present value criterion. The decision rule becomes to choose the project with the highest net present value.

EXAMPLE 10.3

A common problem in restaurants and hotels is whether to have the laundry done in-house or whether to have it done outside. There are a number of elements to the problem and they should be approached systematically:

1. *Identify all feasible options.* These include the use of paper napery in the restaurant as well as contracting out. Some options can be ruled out at this stage because they do not fit in with the style or ethos of the organization or the capital expenditure cannot be funded from any source.
2. *Determine the time horizon.* This is the period of time over which any investment is going to be considered. This should reflect the degree of structural work to buildings required and the life of the equipment (including replacements). For some operations, five years may be adequate, but for other operations the period may be ten or more years.
3. *Estimating the present value of costs of each alternative.* All future cash flows should be discounted at the rate of interest that reflects the cost of borrowing to the firm.
4. *The alternative with the lowest present value of cost provides the base from which decisions can be made.* Any alternative must then generate sufficient extra revenue (because of greater customer attraction) to offset the extra financial cost. These extra revenues are, however, usually more difficult to estimate.

Financial constraints

When there is no limit on the availability of funds, the decision can be made according to the above procedure. However, the firm has other investments to make as well. This usually means that funds are insufficient to do all the projects that would be profitable or save money. In this case, another £1 in cash can increase the present value of the firm's profit by more than £1. The firm has then to spend its money where marginal return is greatest. We illustrate the procedure with the following example:

EXAMPLE 10.4

The board of a hotel company has allocated £3.0m to invest in leisure facilities. Table 10.4 lists the bids from its various hotels for capital expenditure on leisure club projects.

Table 10.4 Investment with capital rationing

Project	Initial outlay	Net present value	Benefit–cost ratio
A	1.5	.60	0.400
B	1.2	.52	0.433
C	1.1	.40	0.364
D	0.9	.34	0.378
E	0.8	.29	0.363

We first decide whether the projects are divisible or indivisible.

A project is *divisible* if halving the initial spending halves the return (present value) on the project. This is not likely in most cases, but we may assume that this is nearly so if the individual projects are small relative to the amount of money available to invest.

The project is indivisible if halving the initial spending gives less than half the return on the project (cases of more than half the return are usually rare).

For indivisible projects:

1. list all possible combinations that can be done within the budget allowed;
2. choose the combination with the highest net present value.

Table 10.5 Feasible choices within budget constraint

Alternative	Initial outlay	Net present value
A + B	2.7	1.12
A + C	2.6	1.00
A + D	2.4	0.94
A + E	2.3	0.89
B + C	2.3	0.92
B + D + E	2.9	1.15
C + D + E	2.8	1.03

Table 10.5 lists the feasible choices for the firm. B+D+E is the project combination that yields the highest net present value. We should ignore the surplus funds that would not be spent on the projects as their net present value is zero. This is because there are no other projects to invest in. If there were, we would have to respecify our original problem to include those alternatives.

If the projects are divisible:

1. calculate the benefit–cost ratio = present value initial outlay;
2. choose the projects with the highest benefit–cost ratios until the budget is exhausted.

From Table 10.4, in this example, we would rank the projects B; A; D; C; E. so

we spend £1.2m on B – leaving us £1.8m; so
we spend £1.5m on A – leaving us £0.3m; so
we spend £0.3m on 1/3 of D.

The total net present value would then be 0.52 + 0.6 + (1/3). (0.34) = £1.23m.

Note that, in this case, an extra £1 in capital funds would increase the net present value of the projects by £0.378, the benefit–cost ratio for project D.

Students should note that in some economics texts you may find an alternative definition of the benefit–cost ratio, where the benefit–cost ratio is defined as *gross present value ÷ initial outlay*.

Gross present value   = sum of discounted future cash flows
                                > (greater than) 1 if the project is profitable.
Net present value   = Gross present value – initial outlay.
                                > 0 if the project is profitable.

In this case the benefit–cost ratio is always greater than the benefit–cost ratio used in the example above by 1 and is greater than 1 if the project is profitable. The definition used here is more usual in business.

Multi-period constraints

A more complicated situation occurs if the hotel company faces budget constraints in the first and in subsequent years, particularly if investments take more than a year to come on stream and start earning money. Where these constraints are important, project appraisal needs to use more complex mathematical programming techniques, which are beyond the scope of this book, but can be found in books on capital budgeting or investment appraisal.

Risk in investment

A major problem in investment appraisal is that the future is so uncertain. It is difficult to forecast the increased revenue or reduced costs resulting from an investment. One way of dealing with this is to use sensitivity analysis. This analyses the effect on the investment of possible changes in interest rates or other factors affecting demand and costs. By looking at a worst case, a best case and an expected case, the firm can get a broader picture of what might happen. In these situations, a firm may choose a project with a lower expected return if it gives a significantly better return in a worst case scenario. There are various methods for dealing with risk, but the usefulness of any method depends ultimately on whether possible losses from any investment can be sustained without the firm going bankrupt or being taken over.

Finally, people tend to be over-optimistic about investments and discount the things that can go wrong. Perhaps 50% or more of investments should not have been made because they do not yield sufficient returns.

ORGANIZING PRODUCTION: THE ECONOMIC ROLE OF FIRMS

In the market system of production, the economic role of market exchange is to organize the major stages of production of a good or service. Firms complement the operation of the market by organizing all the details of production effectively and efficiently. We can illustrate this with the example of burger production, the stages of which are identified in Table 10.6.

Table 10.6 Burger production organized through the market

Farmer	sells cow to	cattle merchant
Cattle merchant	sells cow to	abattoir
Abattoir	sells meat to	meat merchant
Meat merchant	sells meat to	meat processor
Meat processor	sells burgers	burger merchant
Burger merchant	sells burgers to	caterer
Caterer	sells cooked burger to	consumer

Most of these stages of production can be broken down into further sub-stages, giving a long line of activities. For instance, the caterer organizes the purchase, storage, unstorage, cooking, serving, disposal, cleaning and financial transactions. These could all be organized through specific market contracts between individual caterers and other workers. However, the caterer owns a catering firm to *internalize* these activities, by agreeing with the workers that the owner (or her manager) will decide the specific activity each day. This happens for two major reasons:

Transaction costs

Production requires the continued decision-making about what to produce, how and when to produce it. Each decision involves a transaction between two or more individuals or organizations where time and other resources are exchanged. These transactions incur *transactions costs*, including all the costs of gathering information, making decisions and all the contractual arrangements regarding the use of capital and labour resources. These costs are low when production is relatively uncomplicated, repetitive and uses generally available resources, because the markets for the goods and the inputs are predictable. Neither buyer nor seller has much to gain from haggling about prices and how the resources are to be used.

However, many production processes are complex and may require changes to plans at short notice. Hiring skilled workers by the day for specific tasks is expensive because transaction costs are increased and the skilled worker has to be compensated for the increased risks of variable levels of employment. The firm reduces these costs by a longer term contract of employment. Even where the contract nominally guarantees work on a weekly basis, the relationship is expected to last unless there are substantial problems in continuing it. The contract also removes some of the employment risks and gives more certainty to the chef.

In these cases, the contract is *incompletely specified*. For instance, the firm cannot specify in advance what precisely a chef should do on a particular day, how many meals he or she should prepare and of what type. Decisions have to be made in situations of *bounded rationality*, where people's ability to make rational decisions is limited by their ability to gather and process information. We cannot make contracts that specify what will happen in all contingencies, and so some discretionary power is handed over to the management of the firm in return for some risk reduction for the workers employed.

Asset specificity

Many resources including skills and special equipment have a high degree of *asset specificity*, where the value in any alternative use is a lot less. For instance, workers and employers may agree wages and conditions of employment in an open market. However, once an employee is taken on, he or she develops company specific-skills and knowledge that make him or her more valuable to the firm. At the same time, he or she may lose some of the flexibility that is attractive to other firms. There is now much less effective competition from alternative suppliers of labour or alternative buyers. In such situations, more often than not, the employee is at a disadvantage. On the other hand, when contract renewal takes place, the present holder has an advantage because of the special knowledge gained. This makes the effective market in the resource implicitly a long-term market, not one based on day-to-day transactions.

Similarly, service firms create competitive advantage for themselves through the formation of a service concept or through the service process. The higher profit from specific assets is the *economic rent* of those assets. The intangibility of the service concept or process makes it difficult for a firm to obtain an economic rent by leasing the assets to other operators in the market. (This factor is important in the geographic expansion of a firm outside its own region or country, discussed below in franchising and internationalization.)

Management

The employment contract allows the management to have control over an employee's time and abilities, within defined limits. This creates the problem of *opportunism*, or devious self-interested behaviour. One party to a contract may keep some information from the other party so as to gain an advantage. Managers have to choose the right person for the job. This raises the problem of *adverse selection*. An individual may hide some facts from a potential employer in order to improve his or her position. The employer has to use a selection system that will overcome this problem. By the same token, an employer may seek to hide the true value of an employee in order to get him or her more cheaply.

Once an employee has been hired, the employer has another problem: that of *moral hazard*. This occurs when the employee has some particular knowledge about a situation that the more remotely placed employer does not. The employee may then be opportunistic and not work completely in the interest of the employer. So the firm has to devise an appropriate management system to overcome this problem, although it is likely to be more effective if it can ensure that the employee has a positive incentive through some specific benefits contingent on the increased profits of the owner.

Management structure affects the performance of firms because they may exacerbate some of these problems as well as encouraging different types of behaviour that may or may not be consistent with the goals of the organization.

FURTHER READING

Clarke, Roger and McGuinness, Tony, eds., 1987, *The Economics of the Firm*, Oxford: Basil Blackwell, chapters 5–7.

Reekie, W.D., 1989, *Industrial Economics: A Critical Introduction to Corporate Enterprise in Europe and America*. Aldershot: Edward Elgar, chapters 8, 9.

11 Business Development

Key concepts

This chapter analyses the development of the hospitality firm in the context of national and international change in economic activity. In this chapter we:

- analyse the stages of development of the firm;
- analyse integration and mergers;
- analyse franchising;
- analyse internationalization.

Prerequisites: Chapters 7, 8 and 9.

RISKS AND FINANCIAL REQUIREMENTS OF A BUSINESS DURING DEVELOPMENT

There are many small businesses in all sectors of the hotel and catering industry. Some of these are not registered for VAT and so are not included in official data. Even so, there were more than 114,000 firms in the hotel and catering industry in 1992, a small long-term increase in the number of firms by 1,500 over the previous 15-year period. The VAT inclusive turnover of these firms was £32,495 million, giving an average turnover of £114,050. Many of these firms are small with a limited life expectancy and a high exit rate from the industry. We now look at the stages of development of these firms.

The development experience of many businesses conforms to the following model:

- start-up;
- expansion;
- maturity.

Getting started

The major problems for most businesses come in the start-up phase. The would-be entrepreneur risks a lot of resources: often between £100,000 and £300,000 in cash during the first two years of operation; plus the loss of alternative income from working elsewhere; and the loss of free time as he works a 12–14 hour day, seven days a week, during that period. Other investors and lenders such as banks also risk large parts of that money and require a good business plan on which to base that risk. Experience shows that too many firms go out of business within the first two years because their expectations about demand, costs and cash flow are shown to be mistaken. Some of these failures are genuine bad luck cases, but most failures could be predicted from the beginning. Banks, as major financiers, may pull back from financing many projects, but as the evidence of many bankruptcies and insolvencies show, they often back projects that should be seen as very risky, because they can average out losses over other projects. So it is up to the entrepreneur to make sure that the business meets the five basic requirements for survival in the economic environment:

1. *The product must be right for the market.* This means that the product's positioning, location and pricing are correct. The entrepreneur should base his or her enterprise on what the market will support. The fond daydreams, beloved of small hotel and catering businesses, such as 'people will always pay for good food, well served in good surroundings' (whatever they may be) should be avoided.

2. *The structure of production is appropriate.* The structure of production should satisfy the requirements of standardization with low cost differentiability, so that expenditures are minimized (as discussed in Chapter 10).

3. *The timing is correct.* The firm should avoid major financial commitments at high costs at the peak of economic activity, just before the economy goes into a downturn.

4. *The staff have the appropriate mix of skills and abilities.* Very often, the founders of a business have a significant trade background but lack sufficient financial and marketing skills. They are also unduly optimistic at all stages. This leads to serious problems, all of which can sink the business. The entrepreneur should ensure:
   (a) proper contingency planning;
   (b) strict cost control over the initial investment;
   (c) clear specification in the design of properties and the delivery of the product, to avoid waste;
   (d) Careful selection of builders with proper control over the progress of building work. Every week the project is delayed means a week's business lost and makes the cash flow less satisfactory. For substantial risks, the firm should ensure penalty clauses are included in the contract corresponding to the costs of delay.

5. *Management structure and style is appropriate.* The management structure in small firms is often informal with the owners getting closely involved with staff in the business. However, even new restaurants or hotels may require a significant number of staff. Good management structure and style are needed to ensure good cost control and service style. The major problems are:
   (a) the dilettantism of people with little knowledge who invest in a business without reckoning on the cost of failure;

(b) the limited perspective of experienced people who endanger the business by concentrating too much on their specialist area to the detriment of the general running of the business.

Planning the first year

A properly constructed *business plan* covers these basic requirements as well as specifying how the project is to be funded over the first five or more years. Essentially the business plan explains how the business will develop during the first five years and provides a net cash flow forecast for that period. Commercial lenders require a business plan to assess the chances of success and so whether to risk money on the venture. However, the large number of failures of new businesses during the first two years of trading suggests that commercial lenders are unable or unwilling to provide the necessary advice and control to minimize risks. Therefore it is important to check the business plan carefully and guard against over-optimism. This also goes for opening new branches of a company and major refurbishment.

There are two major problems in establishing successful operations:

1. Bringing the business on stream within the given time at the stated cost. Inadequate allocation of resources to planning, design and control over development mean time and cost overruns. Time overruns increase the deadloss of rent and other costs incurred. Overruns occur because architects, designers and builders are inadequately instructed. Builders, in particular, need to be tied down to specific time schedules with contractual penalties for delays in completion.
2. Establishing and maintaining the projected cash flow during the first year of operation. For instance, in the case of restaurants, the pattern of trade is for an initial steep surge during the initial two months or so of opening as the novelty factor diffuses through the local population, as illustrated in Figure 11.1.

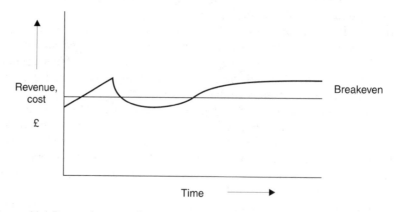

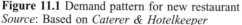

Figure 11.1 Demand pattern for new restaurant
Source: Based on *Caterer & Hotelkeeper*

As the novelty factor wears off, demand declines significantly during the year, as consumers fail to find sufficiently strong competitive factors in the product to counter their natural desire for variety of experience. In the majority of cases, turnover is below that projected. Costs are often kept down simply because the owners and their families provide, in effect, unpaid labour, often working twice the normal working week during the first two years of operation. Even so, costs are usually higher than expected. This reduces the net cash flow and increases the liquidity problems of firms.

Rising consumer standards and the increased burden of government control have also increased the investment required for any given customer base. This has increased the initial difficulties for the small business operator.

VERTICAL INTEGRATION

Production is a series of processes. Technically interlinked processes, such as the cooking of a meal and its service, are almost always carried out together by the same firm. Technically distinct processes such as the rearing of cattle and their processing into hamburgers, are more likely to be carried out by different firms. Technical distinctiveness can change with time. For instance, modern cook–freeze and cook–chill technology reduces 'cooking' on-site to reheating the meal that has already been cooked elsewhere. Even the traditional cooking process can be subdivided into a number of activities that can be carried out in different firms with the restaurant buying prepared products from outside. A firm is said to be *vertically integrated* when a sequence of two or more technically distinct activities are carried out in the same firm. The term should be used sensibly. For instance, we would not say that a restaurant that prepares its own gateaux instead of buying them in from a specialist supplier is a vertically integrated operation.

Backward or upstream integration occurs when a firm takes over a supplier: for instance, when a restaurant chain owns a food manufacturer from which it buys some of its food. Forward or downstream integration occurs when a firm takes over a customer or outlet: for instance, when a brewery owns a pub. There are also cases of quasi-integration where there are long-term supply relationships or joint product development.

Vertical integration occurs for the following reasons:

1. There is technological or market interdependence. Technological inter-dependence can be seen where a hotel owns a golf course or other leisure facility which caters for the modern activity-related holiday. Marketing interdependence also occurs frequently. For instance, modern technology such as cook–freeze and cook–chill enable the separation of production and service processes. However, such production facilities are often owned by contract caterers or welfare institutions because of the need to tailor the product closely to the market.

2. The market for the product is changing in such a way that market transactions become inappropriate. This is likely to be the case where:
   (a) production involves highly specific assets;
   (b) there is a high degree of uncertainty about future changes;
   (c) there are frequently recurring transactions.
3. There is an attempt to exploit monopolistic advantages. This is particularly useful where firms wish to keep potential entrants out of the market. The link-up with a customer or supplier exploits any cost advantages and forces any potential entrant on to a narrower market base.

MERGERS

Firms can expand their business by merger or acquisition as well as by organic growth. There are three considerations in such cases. From the shareholders' point of view, the question is whether such mergers are worthwhile. Mergers or acquisitions are one way of controlling managerial behaviour, allowing acquiring firms to utilize assets more profitably than the existing management. This encourages management to work more actively in the interests of the shareholders by increasing the value of the firm. This suggests that shareholders of the acquired company stand to gain, as is borne out by the evidence (Reekie, 1989). However, in their desire to acquire power and glory, many company boards make unwise decisions and often overbid for the other company because of over optimism about the future, particularly in the ability to use the increase in market power. Thus the acquiring firm often makes a less than satisfactory return on the investment activity.

EXAMPLE 11.3

The takeover of Thistle Hotels by Mount Charlotte in 1989 was too optimistic in view of the impending recession. This severely damaged the company's prospects and led to a significant drop in share value which led to the company itself being taken over.

Mature or declining industries tend to have more cases of relatively unprofitable firms whose value has fallen sufficiently to make a takeover attractive. Industries undergoing rapid technical or market changes will also throw up cases where entrepreneurial management can convince financial backers to support buy-outs and takeovers of other firms.

CASE STUDY: CREDIT RATING OF GRANADA AND FORTE DOWNGRADED

Granada Group, the TV and leisure company acquired control of the Forte hotel company in January 1996 for £3.9 billion pounds.

On 5 February, Moody's, the credit rating agency, cut the long-term ratings for £1.1 billion of the two companies' debts from Baa1 to Baa2, which rates them just two classes above speculative.

According to Moody's, the factors behind this were:

- Granada's financial profile was expected to weaken because of increased debt incurred in acquiring Forte;
- uncertainty regarding Granada's proposed sales of Forte's Exclusive and Meridien hotel chains for about £1.6 bn. to reduce its debt;
- Granada's long-term strategy could result in other debt-financed acquisitions.

Source: Antonia Sharpe, Granada And Forte Downgraded, *Financial Times*, 6 February 1996, p. 19.

ANALYSIS

Companies require a good credit rating in order to maintain fund raising ability. The lower credit rating increases the cost of raising further finance. It also increases the speed with which Granada has to sell off some assets, weakening their negotiating position. The increased cost of capital will reduce the returns to the company's shareholders. It may also bring some stringency into their operations which will increase pressure on management further down the line.

Conglomerate mergers

Conglomerate mergers occur when a firm diversifies into different lines of business. A firm may extend its operations into other products where there is either some marketing or production relationship. Alternatively, diversification may take place into unrelated products, so giving pure conglomerate activity.

A variety of reasons have been suggested for conglomerate activity. The important ones are:

1. *More profitable opportunities elsewhere*. This may occur where the existing markets are maturing and the returns on investment look higher in other markets which the firm could enter.
2. *Economies of scope*. In essence, however, this requires the diversifying firm to have a special expertise that is common to both activities, rather than in an area that is heavily product specific.
3. *Risk reduction*. If this occurs, debt capital is cheaper. Cheaper debt capital makes it easier to raise more capital in the form of debt and increase the return to shareholders. Diversified firms probably find it easier to enter new markets, because they have easier and cheaper access to finance.

CASE STUDY: VAUX TO SELL NURSING HOMES

The brewery company Vaux Group has had a long history of diversification. Starting with pubs, it had expanded into hotels including the successful Swallow hotel division. In 1988, it acquired Ladbroke's nursing homes and set up the St Andrews nursing homes, which it expanded through new construction. In this it was following a trend among some hotel groups to expand their hotel and catering expertise into the rapidly expanding residential homes market.

By 1996, the market had become more competitive, while government funding for residents was becoming increasingly tight. On 28 March, Vaux announced it was selling its nursing homes. 'this business needs to focus on a broader health care front and in the long term this may not fit comfortably with the rest of the group.'

Commented Mr Paul Saper of nursing consultants Laing and Buisson: 'They've picked the worst time to sell in the past 11 years'. *Source*: Roderick Oram, Vaux to sell nursing homes, *Financial Times*, 29 March 1996, p. 22.

ANALYSIS

Vaux follows other hotel groups, such as Stakis, which have moved into and out of nursing homes. The original attractions were:

- a rapidly growing market for residential care, particularly for the elderly as the population aged and was increasingly affluent;
- a relatively disorganized care industry that lacked hotel companies' relatively sophisticated management procedures.

However, a number of factors affected the relative profitability of the market:

- High and increasing costs would inevitably affect the government's willingness and ability to fund care at the same level. It would also limit individual ability to fund care privately. Therefore demand would not rise sufficiently to absorb the increasing cost of a relatively labour intensive activity.
- The relative ease of entry for the small firm would make it difficult to sustain competitive advantage. The marketing advantages of the brand would be fairly limited in a relatively dispersed market, because residents are not regular travellers nor would there be substantial communication between prospective purchasers. The main advantage would lie in cost management.
- The need to fund profitable investments in brewing, and defensive investment in pubs and hotels, which needed restructuring to meet changed market requirements.

> • The refocusing on special skills (or core competences, in the management jargon).

FRANCHISING: THE SOLUTION FOR A DISPERSED MARKET

A franchise exists when one firm, the franchisor, allows another firm, the franchisee, the right to supply the franchisor's brand exclusively within a defined territory for a specified period of time, usually five years or more. The territory could be railway stations, or motorway service areas, as Burger King have done with Compass and Granada respectively. The franchisee is usually prohibited from selling other products or services from the same outlet.

Franchises in the hospitality industry usually have the following characteristics:

1. Franchisees have to:
   (a) operate to specified service standards;
   (b) operate specified hours of business;
   (c) maintain standard prices.
2. Franchisees also:
   (a) pay a fixed initial royalty fee plus a percentage of turnover (total sales revenue);
   (b) make some specific investment for that product line;
   (c) may be tied to buying some material inputs from the franchisor;
   (d) may have to lease the premises from the franchisor;
   (e) have to use company approved design services.
3. The franchisor
   (a) provides advertising and marketing services;
   (b) provides training programmes, especially management training.
4. The franchisor monitors franchisees' performance and may terminate a franchise if the franchisee is under-performing.
5. The franchisee may only sell the business with the consent of the franchisor and must give first refusal to the franchisor.

Reasons for a franchise

A firm develops a distinctive format for its service product, including the design of the production and service systems and the specification of the product. The product format proves a success locally and gives a high return on investment. This encourages the firm to expand beyond its locality:

1. to develop a regional or national brand;
2. to forestall imitators who may destroy the firm's intellectual property and to head off rivals with alternative formats;
3. to gain important scale and experience economies (Chapter 7) that enable it to compete effectively on price once the product enters the maturity phase.

In order to expand, the hospitality firm has to open more units. It must then choose either:

1. *extensive* development of the market by opening branches in new population centres some distance away from the existing ones; or
2. *intensive* development of the market by opening more units in or close by its existing units.

Some activities, such as pubs and contract catering, favour intensive development because there are substantial production economies of scale in distribution and organization whilst marketing communication is less formal. Other activities such as fast food and hotels favour extensive development because their markets are more segmented and so have more limited potential for initial development locally.

Extensive development in the phases of early growth and of rapid expansion of the brand means that the units become relatively dispersed. This makes it more difficult for management to oversee the development of the market and ensure the quality of delivery of the new service. The firm needs to grow its own management organically to maintain the ethos of the product and protect its strategic development. Franchising allows the firm to recruit management that is already committed to the product through the initial royalty payments made. This allows the firm to concentrate on monitoring performance and develop the market for the brand generally.

Franchising may also have a secondary financial benefit for the franchisor. Internal finance, even from profitable firms, is usually insufficient to finance the large scale developments required to grow and stabilize the product in the market fast enough to forestall imitation and other competition. This can be a problem when the product comes to the explosive growth stage of product development and profitability is high.

External finance is expensive to raise. Lenders are usually less optimistic than the firm's managers and so debt financing is restricted. Franchisees effectively provide equity investment that does not dilute control of the franchisor firm. Of course, the franchisee will only purchase the franchise if he expects to make surplus profit or the investment risk is reduced. The amount the franchisee will pay depends on the amount of profit the franchisee expects to make. The method and amount of payment, however, depend on the structure of the franchise. However, the relationship is not all one way. In practice, franchisors have to sell their franchises and would-be franchisees can consider alternative franchises or may set up their own independent business.

The structure of the franchise

Once a franchise contract has been agreed, there are considerable costs of monitoring the contract to prevent opportunistic behaviour by both the franchisee and the franchisor. The franchisor is a *principal* and each franchisee is an *agent*. The franchisor is the owner of the intellectual property represented by the service format. Consequently, the franchisor establishes the payment system to extract the maximum profit from the product. The structure of the franchise usually seems weighted in favour of the franchisor, one of the reasons why they have to be registered with the Office of Fair Trading. However, there are often good reasons for this, as long as society allows the innovator, the franchisor, monopoly power represented by copyright in the service format.

The franchisor makes profits from the brand which is identified with a given level of service. He or she must therefore spend money on monitoring costs in order to protect him- or herself *and other franchisees* from any franchisee who may cheat by delivering a lower quality service. The structure of the franchise reflects an attempt to balance monitoring costs against non-conformance costs as well as improve joint profit sharing.

The franchisee usually has to make three types of payment:

1. an initial lump sum;
2. an annual royalty payment based on annual turnover;
3. investment in specific assets that have a low salvageable value or use in some alternative line of business.

We now analyse the economic factors in each of these.

Lump sum payment

The size of the lump sum depends on the net value of the franchise to the franchisee

The franchisees compete against each other for the right to rent the use of the brand to share in the monopoly profits it generates. The payments they make to the franchisor are then a form of rent. As they compete against each other the franchisees push up the price (or rents) of the franchise so that most of the expected future excess profits are handed over to the franchisor. In practice, franchisors allow their franchisees to retain some of the excess profits of the franchise. This generates queues of would-be franchisees and allows the franchisor to be more selective and reduces the risks of failure among franchisees.

The payments to the franchisor can be made through annual royalty payments or through their expected present value (Chapter 9.4) as a lump sum.

The lump sum payment reduces the risk of the franchisee cheating on the franchisor

The franchisee, however, has better knowledge of the local market, certainly once he or she has the contract. The franchisee could reduce his or her selling effort or lower quality. He or she would then lose some revenue, but this loss would be shared with the franchisor. However, the franchisee also keeps all the reduction in costs for him- or herself. The franchisee could end up better off by cheating on the franchisor (this form of cheating is called *chiselling* in the literature).

The franchisor reduces the risks of cheating by charging a lump sum to the franchisee. This reduces the benefits from cheating because more of any lost revenue is borne by the franchisee.

The lump sum must be small enough to prevent the franchisor cheating on the franchisee.

However, if all the potential profits of the franchise were paid up front to the franchisor, the franchisor would have an incentive not to deliver brand support to the franchisee. Therefore a reduced lump sum payment is a guarantee to the franchisee that loss of the local market would be unprofitable for the franchisor. The franchisor receives part of the profit after it has been made in the form of a royalty payment.

Royalty payment

The royalty payment is based on turnover to encourages franchisees to be efficient

The royalty payment transfers some of the economic rent (or surplus profits) of the brand from the franchisee to the franchisor on an ongoing basis. It is paid as a percentage of the franchisee's turnover, not profit. This means that the franchisee bears the cost of any inefficient operation and so acts as an incentive to better cost control and deters chiselling by local operators.

Established franchises have relatively high lump sum and relatively low royalty payments

The size of the royalty payment depends on the expected surplus of the franchise and the size of the lump sum payment. Where the franchise is well established, the returns from the franchise are more certain. The lump sum is higher and the royalty payment is lower. The franchisor of an established brand also has more to lose by cheating. This reduces the risk for the franchisee in paying out the lump sum.

The royalty payment is not all profit for the franchisor. Some of the revenue must be used to support the brand locally and nationally, since they are interdependent. Support for the brand comes through suitable marketing and support services, including monitoring.

Specific investments

Franchisees usually have to make some investment in specific equipment, signage and sometimes property sub-leases from the franchisor.

Specific investments reduce monitoring costs

Specific investments represent sunk costs to the franchisee, because their alternative use value or their salvage value is much less than their cost. The franchisor also has the right to terminate the franchise if the franchisee breaches the agreement, for instance, by failing to maintain quality standards or by selling non-standard products from the premises. In this case the franchisee would lose the sunk costs of these investments. These specific investments are a *hostage* for the franchisee's good behaviour. They allow the franchisor to reduce monitoring costs by making the penalty for non-compliance much higher than the benefits of cheating to the franchisee.

The franchisee agrees to the hostage, because the value to the franchisor is similarly small if the franchisor decides to terminate the agreement. The low value would not offset the costs of switching to direct management. Where this is not the case, the franchise agreement should contain a buy-back clause where the franchisor must pay for these investments at cost or market value, whichever is the greater.

INTERNATIONALIZATION

A company internationalizes its operations when it carries them at in two or more states. We do not include companies operating only in Scotland and England, as these two countries lie within the same state. However, we would continue to include companies operating in two or more countries of the EU as the political ties are still loose.

Internationalization is a natural progression for large firms that have a significant share of the domestic market, and represents the next step up after moving from regional to national coverage. A company may internationalize its operations for the following reasons:

1. The marginal gain from widening the market abroad is greater than continuing to deepen the market in particular localities or widening coverage over more localities in the home country.
2. The company wishes to anticipate or forestall competitive action by other firms in its market segment. The internationalization of all sectors of the UK hospitality industry has increased significantly since the 1980s. This has been a two-way process with UK firms expanding abroad and foreign firms investing in the UK.

Internationalization can take different forms. Licensing the product or process is one method used in manufacturing, where licensees have the right to use a product or process for a fee. However, this is difficult with hospitality services and there are effectively three different methods of expansion:

1. *The firm can supply the product through a management contract.* This is frequently used in the hotel sector. The firm does not invest in (does not have any equity in) the business, but receives a fee for its operations plus, usually, a percentage of the profit.
2. *The firm can franchise the operation.* Again, the firm does not have an equity stake in the particular franchise.
3. *The firm can take part or full ownership in an operation.* The firm has an equity stake in the business.

The firm chooses the best method for capturing the economic rent from the assets that is specific to the particular product.

CASE STUDY: MARRIOTT EXPANSION IN THE UK

The US hotels group Marriott International has doubled in size between 1989 and March 1996, when it managed or franchised just over 1,000 hotels with a total of almost 200,000 rooms world-wide.

In 1995, Scott's Hospitality of Canada was the major franchisee in the UK, operating 16 of the 18 Marriott hotels in the UK. Whitbread, one of the major UK brewery groups, had been trying for some years to reposition its hotels towards the upper end of the market, using its Lansbury Hotels brand, later renamed Country Club Hotels. Now it has bought the Marriott hotels from Scott's Hospitality for £183 million and has now started on a £50 million investment programme to convert some Country Club Hotels to Marriott franchises. It is aiming for 33 Marriott hotels in the UK and one in Hamburg, Germany.

Source: David Blackwell, Marriott Eyes UK Century, *Financial Times*, 13 March 1996.

FURTHER READING

Clarke, Roger and McGuinness, Tony, eds., 1987, *The Economics of the Firm*, Oxford: Basil Blackwell, chapters 6, 7.

Reekie, W.D., 1989, *Industrial Economics: A Critical Introduction to Corporate Enterprise in Europe and America*. Aldershot: Edward Elgar , chapters 6, 7, 11.

Pricing and product development | 12

Key concepts
This chapter applies the basic theory of profit maximization to problems in pricing appropriate to different types of market and at different stages of development. We:

- analyse pricing in relation to the stages of product development;
- analyse pricing methods used in the industry;
- explain the principles and application of differential pricing in various markets.

STRATEGIC DEVELOPMENT AND PRICING

New products

When a firm launches a successful product, it knows that competition eventually increases until all firms are selling similar low priced products in a saturated market (Chapter 8). The firm has to take account of this downward path of price over time in its pricing and product strategy. In particular it has to decide how it should price its new product initially. A low price makes it easier for people to experiment with the new product and encourages the diffusion process in the growth of the market. A high price, however, slows down the diffusion process and may stunt the growth of the total market. If entry for competitors is fairly easy or experience economies are substantial, the firm should follow a low *penetration pricing* policy to achieve a large share in a substantial market. This gives it a long-term cost advantage over its competitors.

On the other hand, there may be some significant barrier to entry, such as technical knowledge, copyright laws or other factor that prevents quick entry on a large scale. The firm could then maximize its profits by having a *skimming price* policy. It sets its price high initially and gradually lowers it only when competition forces it to do so. In practice, barriers to entry remain for a short time and then quickly disappear. Price declines slowly at first, then rapidly crumbles as new competition suddenly seems to flood in.

Brand development and pricing

Brand development often goes together with large firms. In the hotel sector in particular, well-identified brands reduce costs for travellers by reducing uncertainty among travellers as to what is available. This allows the branded firm to increase its average prices to some extent across the country. However, the full marketing advantages of a brand may require the firm to pay less attention to local differences in cost, for instance, of land and other inputs.

PRICING METHODS FOR HOSPITALITY SERVICES

Cost plus pricing

A common technique in pricing products is to use some form of cost plus pricing. This prices products according to the cost of some of the inputs used in production plus a mark-up to cover overheads (use of other inputs) and provide a profit. The mark-up varies according to the product. In catering, pricing has often been based on obtaining a gross profit (G.P.) margin of between 60% and 65% on food cost.

EXAMPLE 12.1

The food material for a meal costs £1. The restaurant requires a G.P. of 65%.

Then the food cost must be 35% (= 100% − 65%) of the price charged.

So: 35% price = (35/100) price = £1.
  So: Price = (100/35) × £1 = £2.86.

This method of setting prices is based on conventions regarding the long-run relationship between cost and price that would sustain a healthy profit. It can be consistent with profit maximization. However there are three major problems with such a method:

- Profit maximization may not always produce the same fixed relationship between the cost of food or other inputs and the price to be charged. For restaurants, meal prices should reflect the use of all inputs. Some parts of the meals may have a larger labour input than others and the G.P. should reflect this.
- Fluctuations in the economy or in the particular market may require a different price to be charged to maximize profit.
- The costs on which cost plus pricing is based may be difficult or impossible to calculate. Where two or more products use a particular input in common, such as equipment or labour, it is not possible to allocate the cost of the input accurately between the two products. If a restaurant has

two separate kitchens, one preparing meat dishes and another preparing fish dishes, we know that the cost of maintaining and using each kitchen must be charged to meat and fish dishes respectively. Usually, though, restaurants use the same kitchen for preparing meat and fish dishes, beacuse it saves on total kitchen costs. However, there is no sensible, rational way of saying how much of the saving should be used to reduce the apparent cost of fish dishes and how much to reduce the cost of meat dishes. All we know is that the *joint cost* of using the same kitchen for meat and fish is less than the total cost of a kitchen for fish dishes plus a kitchen for meat dishes. In practice, industry conventions try to get round this partly for psychological reasons and partly for control purposes. For instance, modern restaurant pricing acknowledges that the cost of labour cannot be allocated to any particular meal and prices are usually adjusted to the local situation. However, head office often sets gross profit targets for labour, food and other inputs. These internal controls may be useful if they are set across major areas of operation rather than single items, but should not be used as a basis for pricing.

Backward pricing

The alternative to cost-based pricing is market-based pricing, sometimes known as backward pricing. The price and quality targets are set according to the state of demand and the competition in the market. Cost targets such as food or labour cost percentages are then used as a means of improving efficiency. Again, though, care has to be taken by central management not to set unrealistic targets that might not be consistent with profit maximization in the market. The basic idea may be sound but:

- it must be used in conjunction with an analysis of product characteristics to determine the value of the product;
- cost targets must relate to the value of the characteristics to which they contribute. In this sense, pricing cannot be separated from the service production and delivery process.

DIFFERENTIAL PRICING FOR DEMAND MANAGEMENT

Table 12.1 illustrates the product decisions a firm has to make at different levels. Level 1 decisions are often decided on a long-term strategic basis,

Table 12.1 Product decision levels for a hotel

Decision	Level 1	Level 2
Product range	Types of hotel; location	Provision of facilities
Quality	General standard of fittings	Quality of meals
Price	Price range per night	Price of specific meal

while level 2 decisions are decided on a shorter term basis with much more sensitivity to the market at the time. Many of the pricing decisions, particularly second level ones, have different prices for different customers for apparently the same product. They can do this for three good commercial reasons, all associated with demand management:

1. cost differences;
2. price discrimination – charging according to willingness to pay;
3. load pricing – pricing according to variations in demand.

Cost differences

The cost of providing a service should be the same for each customer, but there may be hidden cost differences that make the real economic cost or *shadow price* different:

1. One of the inputs used may be strictly limited in supply at a particular time. The cost of using that input is greater than its financial cost, because of the *indirect cost* of the profit lost by not being able to use the input elsewhere.

   Management resources and skilled labour are frequently limited in supply over short to medium periods. In those cases their real value to the company is significantly greater than the price paid for them. Similarly, conference rooms in a hotel may be worth more than the average cost per room would indicate.
2. Conversely, if there is too much of a resource available, its opportunity cost is zero and so it should not be costed in the short term.
3. There may be differences in *risk*. Risk can mean:
   (a) the chances that a customer will not pay the bill; but this is controlled through proper credit control procedures;
   (b) the variability of demand over the day, week, month or year. These variations in demand cause periods of under-utilized capacity and slack in the labour force, which reduces profitability. The firm takes account of regular variations in its long-term planning and uses appropriate load pricing techniques (see below) to maximize profit.

   However, there are always some irregular variations from the standard, expected fluctuation. They average out over the period concerned, but are not predictable on a day-to-day basis. The firm cannot vary its use of capital and labour to cope fully with these unpredictable changes in demand and so it incurs extra costs. Regular and frequent customers, such as tour operators, who book blocks of rooms for a period and local businesses, who regularly use the facility, reduce the variability of demand and consequently costs. This means that hotels and restaurants can reduce prices to these customers.

PRICE DISCRIMINATION

Meaning of price discrimination

Price discrimination occurs when the ratio of price to marginal cost is different for different customers. It occurs when:

- a firm charges two customers different prices for the same product when the costs of supplying them are the same;
- a firm charges two customers the same price for the same product when the costs of supplying them are different.

The reason for price discrimination is simple: the firm can make more profit. When a firm charges the same price to all customers, there are some customers who are just willing to pay the price charged and some who would be willing to pay more. If the firm can increase its price to those who are willing to pay more, without raising the price to others, it can increase its revenue from the same output and so increase its profits.

Similarly, if a firm wants to expand its market it has to cut its price. This means that existing customers would pay less, unless the firm had some way of restricting the price cut to new customers.

Conditions for price discrimination

There are three conditions for price discrimination to be effective:

1. There are different, separately identified markets or market segments.
2. The markets have different elasticities of demand (Chapter 2).
3. It is practically impossible for consumers to resell the product to other consumers.

Rules for price discrimination

The rules for price discrimination are based on two simple rules:

The two markets are independent, so the firm maximizes profit when it maximizes profit in each market separately. This applies a standard rule in optimization and means that the firm should sell output in each market up to the point where marginal revenue equals marginal cost. However, price is related to marginal revenue by the following equation:

Marginal revenue = Price $\times$ $(1 - 1/e)$,
where e = Elasticity of demand (positive value).

This is a standard result in economics and means that for a given marginal revenue, the lower the elasticity of demand, the higher the price. So where the marginal cost is the same for each market, customers who are less sensitive to price pay a higher price.

The following example illustrates the effect on price in each market.

EXAMPLE 12.2 PRICE DISCRIMINATION TO MAXIMIZE PROFIT

The elasticity of demand in market 1, e_1 = 2; and
the elasticity of demand in market 1, e_2 = 3; and
marginal cost of supply to both markets = £15.

To maximize profit, marginal revenue	= marginal cost	= £15
So in market 1: marginal revenue	= Price $\times$ $(1 - 1/e_1)$ = $\frac{1}{2}$ price	
so: price	= 2 $\times$ £15	= £30
And in market 2: marginal revenue	= price $\times$ $(1 - 1/e_2)$ = $\frac{2}{3}$ price	
so: price	= 1.5 $\times$ £15	= £22.50

Applying price discrimination

There are some basic principles for successful price discrimination:

A firm should identify as many *separate markets* as it can without increasing administration costs beyond the expected gain. It should identify groups or segments with differing (price-) elasticities of demand. There are two basic factors affecting elasticity of demand:

1. *Income per head*. Low income groups have a more elastic demand for hospitality products. A rise in price has a bigger relative impact on their real disposable purchasing power and makes them more sensitive to price changes.

   When we look for low income groups we should be looking for income per head of the group, because marketed products are priced on a per item basis not on a per group basis. A party of four adults is likely to have a higher income per head than a family group of two adults and two children. This makes a meal for four relatively costlier for the family group. The family group is less likely to buy (that is, they will have a lower *rate* of purchase) and they react more to changes in the price of the meal.

2. *The characteristics of the product*. For instance, travel takes time. If time is a scarce resource, the buyer trades time for money. Time is relatively scarce for higher income groups, whereas money is relatively plentiful. If saving time is important, price becomes relatively less important and the group becomes less sensitive to price changes. Business executives travel long distances by plane or train, whereas the less well-off ordinary consumer will travel by train or bus. This pattern is reinforced if the business travel is an allowable expense against tax.

   Time, however, can also have different values according to the time of day. The business executive has to travel from Leeds to London early in the day because he has to do business in London during the day not in the evening. He is therefore prepared to pay a higher price to travel early, whereas the ordinary passenger, with less pressure on time, is not.

Secondly the firm should segregate customers into separate markets:

1. *By person*. Discrimination by person is usually practised in two different ways:
   (a) *By tagging*. For instance, students may be pre-marked with a student identity card to identify them as belonging to a group with a higher price elasticity of demand. The card also prevents the resale of the service, for example a travel ticket.
   (b) *By using a visible identifier*. For instance, a family with young children is likely to have a lower income per head than a similar group without children. Therefore, they will be more price-sensitive. The hotel, travel company or other service supplier effectively uses the children as a marker in identifying price-sensitive customers. They offer children reduced rates when accompanying parents. They can sometimes improve the effectiveness of their discrimination by offering reduced facilities or lower grade products. Families that are sufficiently well-off not to be bothered by the extra costs will pay the higher prices and take the full facilities if available, leaving the less well-off to take the reduced facilities at the much lower total price.

EXAMPLE 12.3

A family railcard. These are issued to named adults (tagging) who can get a significant reduction on standard and cheap return fares together with very small charges (currently £2) per child traveller. However, there are certain restrictions on these reductions. They are only available if:

1. the adult (parent) is accompanied by at least one child (identifier);
2. they travel after certain times (9.30) during the morning;
3. they do not travel out of London during the early evening period.

If the parent is travelling by him- or herself to a town, he or she is travelling on business or for some special occasion on a certain date. Either way, he or she has to be at that particular location. The traveller is location (and time) sensitive. He or she will be correspondingly less price sensitive.

However, if that same person is travelling to the same place (on a different occasion) with a child, in all likelihood it is a family activity: the child has to be with the adult. The journey will be a recreational one and will have to compete with other recreational products. The family group is (on average) less location or time sensitive, but will be more price sensitive. The accompanying child is a useful identifier of more price sensitive journeys.

Conditions (2) and (3) also make use of the reduced time-sensitivity and increased price sensitivity of the family group. During the excluded period, demand (peak period demand) is very heavy.

> Accommodating the family group would mean displacing less price sensitive (business) passengers. The opportunity cost would be the loss of the business passengers' fares.

2. *Geographically.* This is a special case of discrimination by person. It is based on the belief that people from one area are similar in behaviour, but behave very differently from people in another area. This is used with pre-booking of foreign customers, but can be difficult to practise with chance customers.
3. *By facility.* Discrimination by facility is widely practised. Two or more quality levels of the service are provided. The higher quality level obviously costs more to provide. However, it is also priced disproportionately higher so that buyers of the higher priced good are being discriminated against.

EXAMPLE 12.4

First class travel can be 50% dearer than standard accommodation on trains, even more so when cheap returns are available to standard class passengers. First class travellers are paying for comfort, but the increase in price is disproportionately higher.

EXAMPLE 12.5

A la carte items are disproportionately higher in price than table d'hôte menus.

LOAD PRICING

Load pricing refers to pricing according to the variations in the level of demand over a period such as a week or a year. There are well-defined patterns of variation in the level of demand for various commodities. For instance, seaside hotels have a very low demand in the winter months, very high demand in the summer. City centre hotels face a low demand at the weekend, whereas country hotels are likely to face a higher demand at the weekend. Restaurants and pubs face a low demand early in the evening.

In all of these examples, the establishments have fixed capacity. There can be some variation in the amount of labour used. However, it is difficult, if not impossible, to vary the amount of capital used, in that it still has to be paid for whether fully utilized or not. This applies not just to the bedroom availability in a hotel but also to the use of other areas of the hotel and its equipment, and similarly for a restaurant or other establishment. The firm must then vary its prices so that the quantity demanded matches the quantity available.

We use the following definitions:

- The *peak period*: this is the period of greatest demand.
- The *off-peak periods*: periods other than the peak periods. There can be several off-peak periods with different levels of demand.
- *Shoulder periods*: in describing tourist patterns, these are the months nearest the peak months, as their demand is still quite high.

Pricing rules

The appropriate pricing policy applies the principle that marginal cost is equal to marginal revenue, which is the standard optimization procedure. In this case, however, we identify the relevant costs in the following categories:

1. *Capital costs*. These include the cost of the building and associated costs in purchasing or commissioning the building plus any reconstruction work. These costs are averaged out over the expected life of the asset and include the costs of financing the building. The average cost per year is called the *annuitized capital cost*.

    Note that this may be greater or less than any mortgage payment the firm has to make because the firm borrows less than the cost of the building (which makes the annuitized capital cost greater) and pay the mortgage back over a shorter period than the life of the building (which makes the annuitized capital cost less).

2. *Operational costs* (or *running costs*). These are incurred in each period according to capacity used.

The actual pricing decision can be fairly complex at the planning stage, but we can illustrate the general principles of the policy using a simple case of two periods, peak and off-peak, of the same length of time. If there are more than two identifiable periods we have to calculate running costs for each period separately and adjust our calculations for the different length of the periods.

    There are two different situations:

1. the *firm peak* case;
2. the *shifting peak* case.

Firm peak case

This occurs when the level of demand is very high in the peak period compared with the off-peak period. A typical case is that of seaside hotels. Occupancy can be about 70% or more during the peak period and less than 30% in the off-peak period (taking into account the hotels that shut during the winter season).

    In this situation, demand is so low in the off-peak period that even charging only operating costs does not lead to the same level of occupancy or resource usage as in the peak period. The demand is so large in the peak period relative to the off-peak period, that there is surplus capacity in the slack period. In these cases, the *capacity is effectively a free good in the off-peak period* and the firm should not include any capacity costs in the off-peak price.

This means that all the capital costs have to be paid for by the peak period customers as well as the operational costs. Hence we apply our marginal principle to get the following rule:

For the peak period:
Marginal operating cost + Marginal capital cost = Marginal revenue in peak period.

For the off-peak period:
Marginal operating cost = Marginal revenue in the off-peak period

Usage or occupancy rates will still vary considerably between peak and off-peak periods. The peak period customers bear all the capital costs, and the firm charges off-peak customers according to running costs only.

Shifting peak case

The shifting peak case occurs where demand is still relatively high in the off-peak although lower than demand in the peak period. A typical case of the shifting peak is the demand for London or large city hotels, where occupancy rates do not vary greatly over the year. Applying firm peak pricing would lead to the off-peak period becoming more important. In this case we treat the various periods as being *joint users* of the same facility, each contributing towards the capital cost.

In the simplest case where the peak and the non-peak periods are of equal length, the two periods contribute equally to revenue. The condition for profit maximization is then:

Marginal operating cost in the peak (Summer) period
+ Marginal operating cost in the off-peak (Winter) period
+ Marginal capital cost
> = Marginal revenue for the peak (Summer) period
> + Marginal revenue for the off-peak (Winter) period.

If the two periods are of different lengths or if there are more than two periods, the formula has to be adjusted according. This makes it rather complex. However the principle remains the same. The capital costs are shared out according to demand, and prices are closer together. If the firm has its long-term pricing right, there should be only very small differences (theoretically none) in occupancy levels between peak and off-peak periods.

Short-term situations

Most firms are often in a short-term situation, where they have to deal with unexpected changes in demand or in costs of supply. However, the size of the establishment is fixed, so the hotel must set its prices so that demand equals the available supply. In this case, price must always cover operating costs, but that may be all it does when demand is very low. However, the long-term view of pricing is helpful, even in these cases, as the same pattern of occupancy and cost sharing should prevail.

APPLICATION OF DIFFERENTIAL PRICING

We now look at some cases of differential pricing, where we apply the simple test:

1. If there are different prices at the same time, there is a case of price discrimination or cost differences.
2. If there are different prices at different times, there is a case of load pricing or cost differences.

EXAMPLE 12.6 LOWER WEEKEND PRICE IN CITY CENTRE HOTEL

This is an example of load pricing. City centre hotels have a large business trade from Monday to Thursday night. From Friday to Sunday night there is a much reduced trade.

EXAMPLE 12.7 WEEKEND BREAK PACKAGES

This is a case of load pricing when comparing weekend prices against midweek prices. However, the reduced price for staying two or three nights instead of one is an instance of price discrimination against the traveller who stays one night only. Someone who stays for one night only is less price sensitive than the weekend breaker. The one-nighter has to be in that area at that time, because of something on the same day or on the following day. He is certainly very time sensitive. He is also sensitive to location, unless neighbouring towns are easily accessible. Consequently he is less price sensitive.

The weekend breaker, however, is far more price sensitive and far less time and location sensitive. This is because:

- A weekend break is usually a second, third or fourth holiday. It is not seen as needing a high proportion of the household budget. Consequently it has to compete more strongly with other consumer products.
- The weekend breaker spends some resources searching for alternative locations and packages.

EXAMPLE 12.8 REDUCED PRICE FOR CHILDREN'S MEALS

This is an example of price discrimination in favour of family groups, using children as identifiers of price sensitive groups and using differences in the facilities offered to reinforce the selection.

EXAMPLE 12.9 REDUCED PRICE ACCOMMODATION FOR CHILDREN

This is an example of price discrimination by person. The children are used to identify price sensitive groups (with lower income per head).

EXAMPLE 12.10 HAPPY HOURS

This is an example of load pricing. Demand is low in the early evening so that the cost of using space and even the minimal amount of labour is very low. As long as the costs of the beverages are covered the pub is not losing out. Of course it is possible that the pub is using the beer as a loss-leader, losing money on it in the early evening to try to keep the customers later on. However, customers can stack drinks up to beat the time limit on low prices. Use of a loss-leader in this way would be ineffective against those customers who are on a drinking circuit, or who otherwise plan to spend the rest of the night elsewhere.

HOTEL OCCUPANCY AND CAPACITY UTILIZATION

One of the indicators of efficiency in production and investment planning is the extent to which productive capacity is being utilized. Capacity can be measured in physical terms either as the number of bedrooms or as the number of bedspaces that can be occupied. Efficiency can then be measured by the percentage occupancy of bedrooms or bedspaces. There are, however, some points to bear in mind.

- Capacity utilization is not necessarily a measure of profitability, particularly over the short-term economic cycle. As the general level of demand falls in a recession, firms have to decide how far they should cut prices in order to fill vacancies.
- Another problem is the mix of customer and the room rates they are paying. This will be particularly important for hotel companies as opposed to small independent hotels. Small independent hotels need only worry immediately about liquidity and return on investment. Companies, however, must look to the share price which reflects the relative profitability of the organization.
- Long-run cost competitiveness requires least cost production. In this sense, economic capacity becomes the highest occupancy rate for which cost per guest is lowest. Such evidence as there is suggests that this is probably quite high. It will not mean 100% occupancy, because there are always maintenance problems to deal with, which require some slack at some time. A major problem, however, is the difficulty of maintaining a stable occupancy level throughout a period such as a week.

- Occupancy rates are only part of the story. Larger hotels are cheaper per guest to run (at high occupancy levels) than are smaller hotels. Thus, if the same average occupancy level is maintained, but the average hotel size is increasing, this could still be counted as more efficient production. As discussed in Chapter 4, the effects of growth have been to even out the loading on hotels, with greater utilization in the off-peak periods.

PRICING IN SPECIAL SITUATIONS

A firm should plan its operations so that its pricing structure at least covers all its costs in the long run and makes a normal return on capital (which is the cost of capital invested in the business).

However, where the market experiences an unexpected change in demand or costs of supply, the firm has to adapt to a new situation where long-term pricing would be inappropriate. In these situations, the only relevant costs are variable costs, usually materials, labour, wear and tear on machinery, energy and bought-in services. Pricing should then be based on these variable costs.

It is better to continue in production as long as variable costs are covered, even if all fixed costs are not. The fixed costs have been incurred because of past decisions and they have to be paid whatever happens. Any surplus on variable costs represents a contribution to covering fixed costs and improves the firm's cash flow. For instance, when a business becomes insolvent, it may be taken into receivership. The receivers administer the company for the creditors. However, they usually try to keep the company trading as long as wages, materials and other running costs are covered, because the surplus pays off some of the debts and establishes a market value for the business.

It can, however, be problematic in deciding just how much of these costs are truly variable in any particular situation. For instance, not all labour could be dispensed with if there were no work during the next week. What is important, none the less, is that only these variable costs are relevant (these are approximately equivalent to the accountant's marginal costs).

We should also remember that cutting prices to increase occupancy is only one way of improving the finances of the business. Price cuts must only be made when demand is sufficiently elastic so that enough extra revenue is generated to at least cover the running costs of any extra production. The firm needs to make sure that the price cuts are marketed otherwise they will be ineffective. An increased emphasis on cost cutting or on marketing may be better. Firms should be doing this anyway, but improving marketing or production efficiency requires management time. Management time is usually scarce when trade is busy, partly because management do not see the need to invest in more management resources. When business is slack, management value the investigations more highly and also cost time lower. This often explains the reluctance on the part of hoteliers and restaurateurs to price according to variable costs during recessions.

However, since recessions occur anyway, a firm should take into account the likely pattern of the recession. This would allow the firm to gauge the appropriate movement in prices over the cycle, taking into account the fact that costs would also vary.

FURTHER READING

Rogers, L., 1990, *Pricing for Profit*, Oxford: Basil Blackwell, chapters 3, 9, 11, 12.

Epilogue

Maintaining and developing your economic skills | 13

Key concepts

Developing and applying any skill requires a significant investment in time and effort. If we can develop different skills together, we use economies of scope to reduce the cost and benefit from synergy to increase our returns. Our approach throughout is to use the simple principles of economics as an analytical framework within which we can use complementary social, technical and management knowledge to improve the process of hospitality management. In this chapter we develop the techniques to improve your investment still further. We

- show how to analyse situations within an economic framework;
- show how to read trade literature to improve your economic skills.

AN ANALYTICAL FRAMEWORK

We analyse people's behaviour by simplifying their complex set of feelings and motives. We make certain assumptions about behaviour and then derive their logical implications to explain a situation. We can make our theory more generally applicable, the more we concentrate on a few simple common features of behaviour. However, as our theory becomes more general, it also becomes more abstract and less descriptive of any one situation. So we need to use our experience and common sense when applying our theory to a particular situation and interpreting the results. Table 13.1 illustrates this process of analysis as we move from the real world into the abstract world and back again.

One way of making our analysis more effective is to use the 3–5 rule. This means we see the problem from:

- at least three aspects – otherwise we may be too simplistic in our approach; and
- no more than five – otherwise we end up with a list that gets descriptive rather than analytical and becomes too much for our field of vision.

Table 13.1 Problem analysis

Stage of analysis	Procedure	Relationship to real world
Structure	Simplify: identify main features. Make assumptions about motives	Convert real world into analytical
Analysis	Apply logic to reach conclusions	Analytical world
Application	Convert results into their real life equivalents	Convert analytical world into real world
Evaluation	Take account of special features appropriate to the situation	Real world

If there are more than five points we need to consider, we can usually keep no more than five main points by making some of the points subdivisions of a particular aspect.

When we apply this rule to a particular firm, we can identify the following factors the firm must consider:

1. Long-term structural change affecting markets for products
    (a) related to general economic change;
    (b) technological change;
    (c) lifestyle changes;
    (d) long-term political climate.
2. Fluctuations in the economy
    (a) macroeconomic changes;
    (b) macroeconomic policy;
    (c) events in foreign countries.
3. Market structure and strategy
    (a) scale and scope economies;
    (b) market power;
    (c) pricing strategies.
4. Service production and delivery
    (a) specifying customer requirements;
    (b) structuring production;
    (c) service quality;
    (d) demand management.
5. Business development and management
    (a) initial development;
    (b) expansion programmes;
    (c) business structure (franchising, agencies);
    (d) national and international development;
    (e) internal management structures and procedures.

You can develop your own version, but keep it down to a few categories to filter and extract what is useful from the mass of available information.

PLANNING READING

We can use this approach as a way of identifying, organizing and assimilating useful information to broaden, update and enhance our economic understanding of the industry. The financial press has information and commentary about the economy in general and changes in the industry. There are also publications such as the Treasury's *Economic Briefing* and the short broadsheets published by banks, such as Lloyd's, that also provide some more specific information on various topics. However, the trade press, such as the weekly *Caterer & Hotelkeeper*, also contains a wealth of material we can use. To do this we skim through the journal looking for material we can reshape within the economic framework in the previous section to provide cases that

- illustrate or *confirm* existing economic theories of economic behaviour;
- *extend* existing economic theories to (for you) new situations;
- *challenge* existing economic ideas because they are not what economics would have you expect. These are exciting because they make you think more deeply about the situation. Analysing these awkward cases may develop new ideas (very useful for projects). If there are enough awkward situations, you may even begin to develop or discover some new area of economics.

READING THE INDUSTRY LITERATURE: A CASE STUDY

We use here the 5 September 1996 issue of *Caterer & Hotelkeeper* to illustrate the process of blending economic analysis with the news and features in the magazine. We searched the news section and features to identify significant items, particularly for an understanding of trends, We ignored product and equipment advertisements – although they often indicate trends for the efficient running of businesses – and job adverts – although they reflect the job market.

Here we summarize the snippets and articles of significance that relate to those topics previously considered (you may like to compare the summary with the original):

Sutcliffe to Feed Granada Staff (The News Section pp. 7–12)

Granada-owned Sutcliffe Catering

1. wins staff feeding contracts at four Forte hotels acquired by Granada:
   (a) replaces Gardner Merchant's at two Forte Crest hotels at Gatwick and Heathrow, London and at Cumberland Hotel without formal tender processes;
   (b) replaced Summit at Le Meridien Piccadilly in London. Summit had previously supplied a vending service for staff, which Sutcliffe's is replacing with an electronic card-based system.

    i) Staff feeding (free according to entitlement) is a non-core activity – so it should be cost-effective to contract it out from a large unit supplying different classes of product;

    ii) different strategies: for the new system at Le Meridien, competitive bidding needed to ensure cost control; this follows standard rules that require internal pricing to be competitive to maximize the benefit to the organization. Replacing Gardner Merchant pursues longer term strategies (GM part of major group Sodexho). It may also improve the density of Sutcliffe's contracts, particularly near airports (business management).

    iii) ? is there going to be too cosy a relationship?

2. Sutcliffe is introducing their own brands – three of them
    (a) illustrates growing importance of brands across all areas of catering;
    (b) illustrates the growing expectations of staff about standards of treatment and quality of food – eating out as part of total food consumption planning (trends).

Compass in the US (p. 7)

1. Buys Service America for £77m – 7, 000+ contracts; 13,000 staff
    (a) relate to internationalization trends and structure of industry – the growth of the large firms (note regular snippets on this in the journal).

CCG scoops its first contract in retail sector (p. 8)

1. CCG taken over by Granada (!) in February
    (a) look at the range of contracts
    (b) where does it fit into Granada contract catering divisions – overlaps? Specialist areas?

GM brand hits the high street (p. 8)

1. Opens Strollers (GM concept) in London Piccadilly
2. *We want ... experience from the high street ... that we can reflect back into our core business* – Peter Hazzard, food services director
    (a) staff feeding must be competitive with alternative meal sources (eating trends);
    (b) testing against the market.

Best Western in Credit Card Deal (p. 10)

1. Ties up deal with Company Barclaycard – 10% discount for using Barclaycards in return for promotional advertising
    (a) target key business spenders with leisure spin-offs, consistent with market image
    (b) differential pricing

2. Recruiting drive – earmarked properties
   (a) competitive pressures from large chains – as a consortium, need to strengthen brand by clearly identifying with specific types of properties (although they remain individual).

Shake-up at Muswell's (p. 10)

1. Regent Inns buy Crossgates Holdings, owners of the café-bar chain Muswell's plus eleven snooker and sports bars.
   (a) Regent chain growing through acquisition of suitably placed existing chain
2. Muswell's to be remodelled along lines of Spoofers bar, Croydon
   (a) restaurant element becoming standardization of design – economies in marketing and production
3. Restaurant element to be downgraded relative to bar, reducing kitchen size
   (a) important decision contrary to trend → interesting question to be answered – are there special conditions for this – is this the opening of a gap in the market as firms move towards a more standardized market.

Texaco woos fast food retailers (p. 12)

1. Texaco now has three Burger King and seven Pizza Hut takeaway franchises at service stations; several more planned over the next eighteen months. Other brands may also be franchised or land leased to them; some free-standing chains restaurants may be added.
   (a) convenience element of fast food – location for travellers and locals;
   (b) ease of entry into franchise business threatens other smaller firms;
   (c) large market power of petrol retailers who control location should shift distribution of profit towards retailer.

Industry grapples with new directive on working hours (p. 14)

1. News analysis section dealing with a tough political and economic current issue on working conditions
   (a) several points raised – but how will people behave ? – material for discussion.

London five-star market thrives (p. 16)

1. Market buoyant; prices expected to continue rising; shortage of supply developing because of lack of new hotel accommodation
   (a) reflecting increasing activity in the economy;
   (b) cyclical nature of investment – hotels were not being built in great numbers during the depression and immediately afterwards.

Eating out spending fights off summertime slump (p. 16)

1. Monthly variations in eating out reflect increasing confidence in the economy.

Letters (p. 26)

A quick skim through the letters will turn up some well aired questions. However, there is probably at least one a week that provides useful information or insights, the one this week is on leisure clubs. Comments to note include reasons considered to contribute to the success of the firm's leisure club and the secondary benefits in use of hotel facilities.

Business In Ireland: Rough crossing (p. 66)

One of the occasional features, this one deals with the problems of investing outside the UK:

1. similarities in selling new idea in a city contrasted with the institutional differences.

Bare necessities (p. 71)

Feature on Accor's Formule 1 standardized budget accommodation in Britain

1. Units opened: 2 in 1991 (64 rooms each); 1 in 1992 (80 rooms); 1 in 1996 (80 rooms)
   (a) this is slow for a budget accommodation group, compared with other groups in the UK;
   (b) ? is this because the firm's operations (312 units in 8 countries since 1984) are world-wide, but mainly based in France, so that Britain is low priority?
   (c) ? or is the brand not well adjusted to the UK market?
2. Location near motorways/trunk roads close to large towns.
   (a) accessibility.
3. Fast-food or mid-spend restaurants to be nearby; continental breakfast only is served.
   (a) essential function of hotel with convenience breakfast only.
4. Factory built, limited, standardized, high tech facilities, low staff requirements with live-in couple to manage
   (a) increased capital intensity to reduce use of increasing relatively expensive labour.
5. Self-cleaning toilet and shower shared between five rooms, maximum of three persons per room; washbasin in room (1 double, 1 single bunk bed).
   (a) cost cutting, probably works because two thirds of users are males on business (and so are travelling alone);
   (b) may account for relatively limited success compared with British travellers who may have got used to the more expensive but en-suite and more family friendly Travelodge units.

6. Occupancy 50% – 60% in UK compared with 75% world-wide.
   (a) ? suggests problem just noted.
   (b) ? could be slow for idea to take off? Problems of brand awareness?

The short analysis highlights some economic questions or illustrative examples. If you can get hold of the back copy you may read other aspects into the problem because there is not just one right way of analysing a situation. Even more interesting, of course, is to get the benefit of hindsight by seeing how the situation has developed two or three years into the future, given that many hospitality firms do not see out their fifth birthday.

Bibliography

This bibliography contains references and other source materials used in the text. Some reading may require advanced mathematical and statistical understanding exceeding undergraduate hospitality studies.

Annual Abstract of Statistics, annually, London: Central Statistical Office.

Archer, B. 1982, 'The value of multipliers and their policy implications' *Tourism Management*, Vol.3(4), pp. 236–41

Becker, Gary, 1965, 'A theory of the allocation of time', *The Economic Journal*, Vol. 30(100).

Becker, G.S., Lands, E.M. and Michael, R.T., 1977, 'An economic analysis of marital instability', *Journal of Political Economy*, Vol. 85(4), pp. 1099–1139.

Begg, D., Fischer, S. and Dornbush, R., 1994, *Economics* (4th edn) London: McGraw-Hill.

British National Tourism Survey.

Browning , M., Bourgignon, F., Chiappori, P.-A., and Lechene, V., 1994, 'Income and outcomes: A structural model of intrahousehold allocation', *Journal of Political Economy*, Vol. 102(6), 1067–96.

Butler, R.W., 1980, 'The concept of the tourist area cycle of evolution: Implications for management of resources', *Canadian Geographer*, Vol. 24, pp. 5–12.

Clarke, Roger and McGuinness, Tony, eds., 1987, *The Economics of the Firm*, Oxford: Basil Blackwell.

Crosby, Philip B., 1979, *Quality is Free: The Art of Making Quality Certain*, New York: New American Library.

Cullen, P.F., 1985, 'Economic aspects of hotel and catering industry changes', *International Journal of Hospitality Management*, Vol. 4(4), pp. 165–71.

Cullen, P.F., 1994, 'Time tastes and technology: the economic evolution of eating out', *British Food Journal*, vol. 96(10), pp. 4–9.

Cullen, P.F. and Foxcroft, E.G., 1987, 'Economic features of efficient catering service production', *Service Industries Journal*, Vol. 7(2), pp. 340–52.

Davies, David, 1992, *The Art of Managing Finance* (2nd edn.). London: McGraw-Hill.

Edgett, S. and Parkinson, S., 1993, 'Marketing for service industries a review', *Service Industries Journal*, Vol. 13(3), pp.19–39.

Elfring, Tom, 1989, The main features and underlying causes of the shift to services, *Service Industries Journal*, Vol. 9(3).

Euromonitor, 1984, *The Catering Report*, (2nd edn.) London: Euromonitor Publications.

Fletcher, J.E. and Archer, B.H., 1991, 'The development and application of multiplier analysis', in Cooper, C.P. (ed), *Progress in Tourism, Recreation and Hospitality Management*, Vol. 3 London: Belhaven Press.

Frisbee, W.R, and Madeira, K., 1986, 'Restaurant meals – convenience goods or luxuries?' *Service Industries Journal*, Vol. 6(2), pp. 370–92.

Gilbert, David and Guerrier, Yvonne, 1997, 'UK hospitality managers past and present', *Service Industries Journal*, Vol. 17(1), pp. 115–32.

Griffiths, A. and Wall, S. (eds.), 1995, *Applied Economics: An Introductory Course* (6th edn.). London: Longman.

Gronau, R., 1977, 'Leisure, home production and work: the theory of time revisited', *Journal of Political Economy*, Vol. 85(4).

Hill, Peter, 1987, 'The service sector: current state of knowledge and research frontiers, in Grubel, Herbert G. (ed.), *Conceptual Issues in Service Sector Research: A Symposium*, Vancouver, BC: Fraser Institute.

Hotel Occupancy Survey, London: English Tourist Board.

Hughes, H.L., 1994, 'Tourism multiplier studies: a more judicious approach', *Tourism Management*, Vol 15(60), pp. 403–406.

Key Note, 1991, *Public Houses*, 8th edn., Hampton: Key Note Publications.

Key Note, 1992, *Breweries and the Beer Market: A Market Sector Overview*, 7th edn.. Hampton: Key Note Publications

Key Note, 1993, *Breweries and the Beer Market: A Market Sector Overview*, 8th edn. Hampton: Key Note Publications

Key Note, 1993, *Business Travel*, 5th edn. Hampton: Key Note Publications.

Key Note, 1994, *Drinking Habits*, 7th edn. Hampton: Key Note Publications.

Key Note, 1995, *Catering Market*, 8th edn. Hampton: Key Note Publications.

Key Note, 1995, *Public Houses*, 11th edn. Hampton: Key Note Publications.

Key Note, 1996, *Breweries and the Beer Market: 1996 Market Report* (ed. Simon Howitt), 15th edn. Hampton: Key Note Publications.

Key Note, 1996, *Contract Catering: 1996 Market Report, 9th edn* [ed. Zoe Ratcliff]. Hampton: Key Note Publications.

Key Note, 1996, *Fast Food and Home Delivery Services*, 13th edn. Hampton: Key Note Publications.

Key Note, 1996, *Restaurants*, 11th edn.. Hampton: KeyNote Publications.

Lancaster, K.J., 1966, 'Change and innovation in the technology of consumption, *American Economic Review*, Vol. 76, Supplement.

Parkin, M. and King, D., 1995, *Economics* (2nd edn.). Wokingham: Addison-Wesley.

Payne, M. and Payne, B., 1993, *Eating Out in the UK: Market Structure, Consumer Attitudes and Prospects for the 1990s*. London: Economist Intelligence Unit: EIU Special Report No. 2169.

Reekie, W.D., 1989, *Industrial Economics: A Critical Introduction to Corporate Enterprise in Europe and America*. Aldershot: Edward Elgar.

Reekie, W.D. and Crook, J.N., 1989, *Managerial Economics* (3rd edn.) Deddington: Phillip Allan.

Riley, M., 1994, 'Marketing eating out: The influence of social culture and innovation', *British Food Journal*, Vol. 96(10), pp.15–18.

Social Trends, annually. London: Office of National Statistics.

Stigler, G.J., 1958, 'The economics of scale', *Journal of Law and Economics*, Vol. 1, pp. 54–71

Tourism Intelligence Quarterly, London: British Tourist Authority

Wanhill, S.R.C., 1988, 'Tourism multipliers under capacity constraints', *Service Industries Journal*, Vol. 8(2), pp. 136–42.

Winston, G.C., 1982, *The Timing of Economic Activities*, Cambridge: Cambridge University Press.

Wood, R.C., 1994, 'Dining out on sociological neglect', *British Food Journal*, Vol. 96(10), pp. 10–14.

Wood, R.C., 1995, *The Sociology of Food*. Edinburgh: Edinburgh University Press.

SOURCE ARTICLES FOR CASE STUDIES

Caterer & Hotelkeeper
  22 December 1988, pp. 24–25: 'Trading places, review of hotels '88'.
  22 August 1990, p. 11: 'Hotel sector building boom'.
  20 September 1990, pp. 27, 29: 'High hopes for economic recovery'.
  20 December 1990, pp. 25–26: 'The way we were'.
  10 January 1991, p. 25: 'Receiverships up 220% as recession bites'.
  23 May 1991, p. 28: 'Industry thinks its way out of recession'.
  18 July 1991, p. 14: 'UK trends'.
  10 October 1991, p. 16: 'Barometer notes realistic attitudes'.
  19 December 1991, pp. 24–29: 'A year of living dangerously'.
  18 December 1992, pp. 28–31:1992: 'Goodbye to all that'.
  24 March 1994, p. 23: 'Recovery on course as room occupancy rises'.
  27 April 1995, 'Sea changes' (D. Goymour).
  18 May 1995, pp. 56–59: 'The tide is turning' (B. Gledhil).
  27 June 1996 pp. 62–64: 'Hooray Henry' (Gillian Drummond).

Food Service Management [published with *Caterer & Hotelkeeper*]
  July 1995, pp. 1415: 'Orchard's bitter fruit' (Jane Baker).

Financial Times
  1 February 1996, p.26: 'UK company news: Vaux to sell five Swallow Hotels' (Scheherazade Daneshkhu).

6 February 1996, p.19: 'Granada and Forte downgraded' (Antonia Sharpe).

19 March 1996, p.11. 'Hotels report identifies room for change' (Roderick Oram).

13 March 1996, 'Marriott eyes UK century' (David Blackwell).

29 March 1996, p. 22: 'Vaux to sell nursing homes' (Roderick Oram).

Index